▼▼▼▼▼▼▼▼▼▼▼▼▼▼▼▼▼▼▼▼▼▼▼▼▼▼▼▼▼▼▼▼▼▼▼▼

Toward Faculty
Renewal

*Advances in Faculty, Instructional,
and Organizational Development*

▲▲▲▲▲▲▲▲▲▲▲▲▲▲▲▲▲▲▲▲▲▲▲▲▲▲▲▲▲▲▲▲▲▲▲▲▲▲

Jerry G. Gaff

TOWARD
FACULTY
RENEWAL

Jossey-Bass Publishers
San Francisco • Washington • London • 1975

The Jossey-Bass Series
in Higher Education

▼▼▼▼▼▼▼▼▼▼▼▼▼▼▼▼▼▼▼▼▼▼▼▼▼▼▼▼▼▼▼▼▼▼▼▼▼▼

Preface

▲▲▲▲▲▲▲▲▲▲▲▲▲▲▲▲▲▲▲▲▲▲▲▲▲▲▲▲▲▲▲▲▲▲▲▲▲▲

How can teaching be improved? What can an institution do to facilitate the development of its faculty? Until recently, these questions were like the weather: everyone talked about them, but nobody did much about them. All that is changing now. New concepts of faculty and instructional development are being advanced, and new programs are being created to aid faculty members in their teaching.

Some of these programs are full of promise, while others seem trivial or inconsequential. Some rest on a careful and thoughtful rationale; others appear to lack explicit justification and direction. The purpose of *Toward Faculty Renewal* is to provide a comprehensive analysis of these various new efforts to improve instruction. Its specific goals are three: (1) to identify current college and university programs to improve the quality of teaching and learning; (2) to describe the range and variety of these programs, particularly the more promising ones, and to examine their organization, politics, financing, staff, and impact; and (3) to place the programs in the context of current trends in higher education,

ix

research on teaching and learning, and the experiences of individuals associated with different kinds of programs.

The intended outcomes are guidance for policy makers—faculty leaders, administrators, trustees—at institutions considering such endeavors and guidelines for the improvement of existing programs. By drawing on the experience of those who have pioneered in the establishment of in-service programs for the improvement of instruction, designers of new programs may have a good view of the options available to them as well as the advantages and limitations of each alternative.

The original impetus for this study came from Laura Bornholdt, then of the Danforth Foundation. Under her leadership the Foundation awarded small grants to six institutions to establish "centers for the improvement of undergraduate teaching." In the spring of 1973 representatives from those campuses as well as other interested persons met in St. Louis to explore the whole issue of improving undergraduate teaching. The diversity of ideas, approaches, and structures which were discussed and the community of interests, assumptions, and strategies which transcended these differences merited serious study, and I thus prepared a research proposal to examine this new phenomenon. Bornholdt was then in the process of moving to a different foundation, but she discussed the idea with Richard Johnson of the Exxon Education Foundation. He expressed interest in it, and in the fall of 1973 the study was funded by Exxon. *Toward Faculty Renewal* is the final report of that study.

The book is divided into two parts. The first analyzes three different approaches to instructional improvement, and the second examines in detail the operation of all three approaches. The first part should prove useful to anyone concerned about faculty renewal and instructional improvement—faculty member, administrator, trustee. The second will be of particular use to faculty and staff who specialize in instructional-improvement programs and who need specific information about program operations and problems.

The five chapters in Part One address the following questions:

What are the new concepts and approaches to instructional improvement? (Chapter One)

What is faculty development, and how do different schools assist the growth of faculty members? What is known about the course of human development during adulthood and the principles of change in adults? (Chapter Two)

What is the instructional-development process, and how can it be used to improve courses and curricula? How can schools help faculty members design effective learning experiences for students and adopt innovative methods of instruction? (Chapter Three)

What is organizational development, and how does it differ from faculty and instructional development? What strategies are colleges and universities employing to encourage institutional renewal through the improvement of teaching? (Chapter Four)

To what extent are faculty, instructional, and organizational development complementary approaches? What does a mature or comprehensive instructional-improvement program look like? (Chapter Five)

Part Two of this volume emphasizes the implementation of programs to improve the quality of teaching and learning:

How do different colleges and universities organize and structure instructional-improvement programs? What are the advantages of a separate center charged with the responsibility for improving instruction? (Chapter Six)

What are the politics of efforts to improve teaching and learning? What strategies have been devised to secure faculty participation and administrative and institutional support? (Chapter Seven)

How are campus-based programs financed? What ways have different institutions found to support these new activities during difficult times? (Chapter Eight)

Who staffs instructional-improvement programs? What are their professional backgrounds, and what personal qualities should they have in order to consult effectively with their colleagues on teaching and learning matters? (Chapter Nine)

How much and what kind of impact do these programs have on faculty, students, and institutions? How can their impact be enhanced? (Chapter Ten)

Chapter Eleven recapitulates the current status of the movement and specifies the changes that are still needed if present efforts are to realize their full potential for improving academic life.

Toward Faculty Renewal differs from other books in the area. In one sense it is a natural follow-up to *Faculty Development in a Time of Retrenchment* (1974), by the Group for Human Development in Higher Education, which has been widely distributed through the auspices of *Change Magazine.* That booklet raised consciousness about the need for faculty development and contained useful suggestions about starting points. The present book describes what is actually being done by many colleges and universities, draws on the experiences of those persons who have pioneered in this new field, and provides an overview about issues to consider in creating different kinds of programs.

A Handbook for Faculty Development (1975) was prepared by William Bergquist, Steven Phillips, and Gary Quehl to aid people who are already involved in faculty development work. It focuses on various aspects of teaching and includes handouts, exercises, and instruments for use in faculty workshops and other programs. In contrast, *Toward Faculty Renewal* is designed for anyone who wants to understand the scope of this new movement by learning what various institutions are doing to aid the development of their faculty and how they implement their programs.

Teachers for Tomorrow by Terry O'Banion (1973) argued that the task for the future is to improve the effectiveness of the existing faculty through in-service programs rather than to train new faculty through preservice programs. But while that report focused on community colleges, the attempt here is to range far beyond community colleges and to provide considerably more analysis of existing campus-based programs.

Toward Faculty Renewal also differs from the publication by Lawrence Alexander and Stephen Yelon, *Instructional Development Agencies in Higher Education* (1972). Their useful booklet presents descriptions of a number of the larger and better known instructional-development centers around the country. In contrast to their fairly concise case descriptions written by persons in the different centers, the present book provides a comparative perspective, includes more analysis, contains a more unified perspective, and examines more kinds of programs.

And unlike many other publications which are essentially reports of empirical research on different aspects of teaching and learning, *Toward Faculty Renewal* is an attempt to present the state of the art: to point out important comparisons and contrasts, identify key issues, and highlight some of the significant early results of these efforts. In short, this book is one man's attempt to make sense of what is going on and to determine what its significance may be for the future of higher education.

Although little reliable information regarding instructional improvement or faculty development has been assembled in one place, a veritable "movement" has evolved within the last few years. Some consider this to be simply the latest of the fads which occasionally sweep higher education. But I see it as a long-overdue attempt to reverse the neglect of teaching which has characterized academia and also as an attempt to resolve a fundamental and enduring issue: how to develop the professional and personal talents of faculty members, particularly as they pertain to their most central professional activity, providing effective instruction to students. If *Toward Faculty Renewal* contributes to the understanding and advancement of that end, I shall be gratified.

The substance of the book stems from many sources that deserve acknowledgement:

First, staff members of 73 of the 107 state boards and agencies that oversee community colleges, four-year colleges, or universities, who alerted me to teaching improvement programs and centers with which they were familiar. Officers of federal agencies and private foundations that have funded faculty-development and instructional-improvement projects told me about other programs, as did officials of several national higher education associations, directors of several instructional development centers, and doctoral students working on dissertations in this area—in particular, Roberts Braden of Virginia Polytechnic Institute and James Holsclaw of Azusa Pacific College.

Second, the directors of the approximately two hundred programs discovered by this method and listed at the end of this volume supplied much valuable information about their programs, including progress reports and evaluative studies. Fifty-five of these directors also completed a questionnaire about the operation of their programs.

Third, the directors of programs at nine institutions of diverse type, geographical location, organizational structure, and approach to the improvement of instruction allowed me to examine their work in person: Gabriel M. Della-Piana of the University of Utah, R. Irwin Goodman of Brigham Young University, John Harris of Florida State University, James A. Kulik of the University of Michigan, Parker E. Lichtenstein of the University of Redlands, B. Claude Mathis of Northwestern University, John F. Noonan of Virginia Commonwealth University, David Outcalt of the University of California, Santa Barbara, and Carol Zion of Miami-Dade Community College–North.

Fourth, my colleagues on two other projects gave me added perspective. At the University of California, Berkeley, Robert C. Wilson, Evelyn R. Dienst, Lynn Wood, and James L. Bavry, with whom I worked on *College Professors and Their Impact on Students* (1975), kept me aware of the importance of research on faculty members, student-faculty relationships, and the changes experienced by students during their college careers. At the California State University and Colleges, where I organized the Center for Professional Development in 1974, my associates in Los Angeles and on the individual campuses helped test ways to initiate programs and bring staff members from the campuses together to learn from each other.

Besides these many colleagues, who have helped with this research by gladly and freely sharing their experiences and views, the assistance of several other people deserves acknowledgment: Frederick deWitt Bolman and Richard Johnson of the Exxon Education Foundation for their intellectual and financial support; Laura Bornholdt of the Lilly Endowment for her early encouragement and advice; and Mary Searight and James Enochs for permitting me to undertake this project by reducing my earlier commitments at California State College, Sonoma. Special thanks are due to Haywood Vaughan, a researcher in the Department of Nursing at Sonoma, for helping me design procedures for finding out about these new endeavors; to Mary Condon, a secretary at Sonoma, for helping gather information from many colleges and universities; and to Ann Bednarczyk for typing the manuscript. Kay Hartshorn Cutter, a doctoral student at the University of California,

Berkeley, and research assistant at the Wright Institute, gave valuable assistance in the preparation of Chapter Two, as did Barry Phegan, also a doctoral student at Berkeley and consultant to various groups, in the preparation of Chapter Four. John F. Noonan, director of the Center for Improving Teaching Effectiveness at Virginia Commonwealth University, gave the manuscript a careful critical reading and saved me from several potential mistakes of omission and commission. JB Hefferlin, director of special projects at Jossey-Bass, gave valuable professional advice, editorial assistance, and personal encouragement at several crucial points in this project. And Sally, my wife, helped me think through and solve numerous problems I encountered, protected my time to write the manuscript amid other pressing family concerns, and gave personal support and encouragement in untold ways.

Washington, D.C.   JERRY G. GAFF
October 1975

Contents

TWO: IMPLEMENTING THE PROGRAMS

▼▼

Toward Faculty
Renewal

*Advances in Faculty, Instructional,
and Organizational Development*

▲▲

Chapter 1

▼▼

New Concepts for Improving Teaching and Learning

▲▲

Recently a highly acclaimed and innovative university that was created during the expansive days of the 1960s calculated that 63 percent of its faculty members are not scheduled to retire until after the year 2000. How can it keep that now largely middle-aged faculty educationally alive and growing during the next two to three decades?

Elsewhere a long-established university has become virtually "tenured in," with over 90 percent of its faculty members now holding tenure. How can it help this aging faculty appeal to young students or devise new educational programs to meet emerging needs?

It is becoming apparent that in the years ahead colleges and universities will have to rely on their current faculty members to

1

provide fresh perspectives, infuse new ideas, and give leadership to innovative programs if they are to maintain vigorous educational climates. Faced with the prospects of reduced student enrollments and declining faculty positions, many of them are unable to add young faculty to the staff. This young blood has always been an important stimulus to institutional renewal; but now some substitute for it will have to be devised.

Faculty members themselves find the going tough. Faced with the tightest job market in decades, they find it difficult to get jobs, to change jobs, or even to obtain tenure in their own institutions. Instructors discover that they must present more and better evidence of their teaching effectiveness to secure positions, tenure, or promotions. But how can they become more effective teachers? As job opportunities decline, faculty members increasingly will be confined to one institution, and they will look to that school to provide the enriching experiences they need to grow professionally. But what can faculty members expect their schools to do to cultivate their professional growth, assist them to find challenges in their work, particularly their teaching, and help them derive satisfaction from this central professional activity?

Changes in clientele, educational settings, and instructional methods require many faculty members to alter their usual teaching practices and adopt new relationships with students. New student groups such as ethnic minorities, first-generation college students, and adults require teachers with special sensitivities and techniques suited to them. New structures such as external degree programs, cluster colleges, and living-learning centers provide new environments and impose new demands on learning and teaching. Traditional lecture and seminar methods are supplemented by such techniques as independent study, self-paced learning, mediated instruction, and field-studies projects. Interdisciplinary programs and courses which focus on intellectual themes or social problems are found more frequently; these approaches require faculty members to range beyond their familiar specializations in conventional academic disciplines and to collaborate with colleagues in other fields. How may faculty members acquire the new ideas, techniques, and skills required in their teaching? And how may faculty members who do not use these innovative approaches understand and accept

their more innovative faculty colleagues as well as refine and improve their own more traditional methods?

In order to meet these new needs many colleges and universities are setting up programs to facilitate the development of faculty
and improve instruction. In the process of fashioning these programs,
new concepts of instructional improvement are being devised, new
organizations established to apply the concepts, and new approaches
to the improvement of instruction attempted.

First consider the changing concepts. New pressures on colleges and universities cause many faculty members and administrators
to reexamine traditional concepts of professional development.
Academic folklore holds that "a teacher is born, not made" and that
"teaching is an art, not a science," implying that little can be
done to facilitate the instructional improvement of professors. This
folk wisdom is given expression in the standard prescription to
"hire good people and get out of their way." Such negative injunc-
tions are interwoven with the tradition of academic freedom, and
faculty have come to feel that "a professor's classroom is his castle,"
that it is somehow unprofessional for a faculty member to criticize,
interfere with, intrude upon, or even observe another instructor in
his classroom. These proscriptions make it difficult for instructors to
learn from their colleagues and to improve their teaching competencies. In their more candid moments, most faculty members
readily confess that they learned to teach by being thrown into the
classroom and either swimming or sinking; almost all will testify to
doing considerable thrashing about before discovering how to swim.
And even yet some go under. Given the new realities of higher education, this "do nothing" approach is not sufficient. Whatever its
merits may have been, the call to hire good people and get out of
their way becomes a hollow slogan when student enrollments dip,
faculty positions are trimmed, and the very survival of some institutions is threatened.

But traditional concepts of instructional improvement do
have active components too. Who has not heard the plaint that
instruction would be improved if only the teaching load were reduced, classes were smaller, more assistants were available, and the
faculty job were made easier? The fact is that the working conditions
of college professors have been improved ever since World War II

(Jencks and Riesman, 1968), and the financial crunch today makes it unlikely that further improvements will occur. More important, better is not to be equated with easier, and none of these beliefs enjoys much support from leaders in higher education. Also, faculty typically long for bright and highly motivated students and hold that the quality of education would be improved if admissions requirements were higher or if grading were more rigorous. However valuable this view may have seemed in the past, it is not very useful today, when many institutions have an open door policy which draws adults, ethnic minorities, lower ability students, and a variety of other new students in substantial numbers.

The most active professional-development programs of the past have been those which helped professors to upgrade and update their knowledge of the academic specializations. Sabbatical leaves, travel to meetings of professional associations, and research support have been typical mechanisms to achieve this purpose. It has been an article of faith among academics that just as training to conduct research in one's academic discipline—certified by a doctoral degree— prepares one to teach, the acquisition of additional knowledge and the conduct of research improves teaching. While the need for instructors to know what they are talking about can not be disputed, we have learned over the last several years, when research was well supported, that professors' scholarly competence does not necessarily translate into teaching effectiveness. It is a necessary but not a sufficient condition.

As these traditional conceptions have been called into question, new concepts of professional development for faculty have emerged. Because the primary professional activity of most faculty members centers around their teaching role, the improvement of instruction is a central part of this concept. The basic assumptions are that the instructional behavior of faculty members is a learned complex of knowledge, attitudes, values, motivations, skills, and sensitivities, and that faculty members may learn to improve these instructional competencies. The focus is directly on the improvement of instruction, and the aim is to help faculty develop in the several aspects of their instructional roles. Efforts are now being made to assist faculty members to reconsider their traditional conceptions about teaching and learning, expand their instructional repertoire, sharpen their sensitivities and skills in working with students and colleagues, and work effectively with new techniques, new programs, and new students. In short, attempts are being made to help faculty members develop greater competence and a greater sense of efficacy as teachers.

The new concept of faculty development for instructional improvement may be better understood by an examination of the conceptual framework that underlies the work of new programs in this area. A close reading of the documents produced by these programs reveals a distinctive configuration of interrelated assumptions and propositions. Although no individual program necessarily incorporates all these propositions, and many fail to make their basic assumptions explicit, the following is a list of the most important components of the conceptual framework that characterizes the new approach to professional development.

1. Faculty members are the most important educational resource of a college or university, and just as material resources must be given special care and attention to retain or enhance their value, so must the talents, interests, and skills of faculty be systematically cultivated.

2. Teaching is the primary, though by no means the only, professional activity of most faculty members. A major reason why professors choose to work in a college or university is their commitment to teaching, and most faculty members are interested in excelling in this activity.

3. Scholarship and research—another major professional activity of many faculty members—need not be antithetical to effective teaching. Ways can and should be found by which research enriches and complements teaching.

4. Teaching is much neglected by academic tradition. In most schools this neglect is not due to the lack of interest in teaching among individual faculty members. Rather, the neglect can be traced to factors pervading the general academic culture, such as the lack of preparation for teaching roles during graduate education, the relative absence of in-service education which is found in other professions, and the paucity of academic policies (for example, promotion, salary increase, tenure) which provide incentives and support for effective teaching.

5. Although there is little systematic evidence about how good the quality of teaching and learning actually are in most institutions, there is a general feeling, shared by many within and outside academia, that it can be improved.

6. Improving teaching requires working with administrators and students—perhaps even members of the larger community—as well as with faculty members. All of these groups have a legitimate interest in and responsibility for making the instructional program work well.

7. Just as faculty members receive little preparation for their instructional roles, administrators have little training for the leadership, policy formulation, administrative, and managerial roles of their work. Department chairpeople, deans, vice presidents, and presidents—no less than faculty members—need to develop and, furthermore, they need to encourage and support the growth of the individuals in their charge.

8. Teaching is a complex set of attitudes, knowledge, skills, motivations, and values. The improvement of teaching and learning requires an awareness of the complexities involved in faculty, students, and institutions and hence the avoidance of simplistic solutions.

9. Effective teaching involves helping students to attain desired learning objectives. Faculty members can be assisted to specify learning objectives for students, choose learning experiences designed to achieve those outcomes, and evaluate their attainment. These procedures can make instruction more systematic, thereby increasing the probability that desired competencies are attained.

10. There is no single model of effective teaching or learning; proposals advanced as panaceas with a doctrinaire approach are suspect and to be avoided.

11. There is great diversity among students. Their various learning styles, which are based on differences in ability, interest, educational background, future aspirations, and personality orientations, call for different kinds of learning experiences.

12. Faculty members, too, are a diverse lot. They vary on such key factors as age, field of specialization, teaching experience, and educational philosophy. Because diversity is one of the greatest strengths of any faculty, every effort should be made to assist individual faculty members in ways consistent with their diverse values,

needs, and personal styles and with student needs and institutional goals.

13. An individual's professional work is intimately connected with his personal life; the quality of his work may be affected for good or ill by events in his family, his health, and his personal habits. An instructional-improvement program may require efforts to promote the personal growth of individuals as well as their professional development.

14. Intrinsic interest rather than extrinsic demand is what leads individuals to seek improvement. Lasting change can best be brought about by stimulating, supporting, and reinforcing positive efforts of faculty members. When external motivation is used by instructional-improvement programs, the carrot—not the stick—is the most common form of incentive.

15. The willing involvement of faculty members and others in the various programs typically is seen as a necessity if enduring improvement is to be obtained.

16. Every institution contains many persons with expertise and experience which may be included in instructional-improvement programs. Faculty members with the ability to assist their colleagues are generally willing, often eager, to do so. These people may be utilized to develop a rich pool of talent at an institution which may be used by individuals with various needs.

17. Teaching and learning are individual but not solitary activities; they occur within a social context. The climate of the institution, the relationships between faculty, administrators, and students, and the policies and practices of the school affect the character of teaching and learning. The improvement of instruction requires attention to these social and institutional factors as well as to individuals.

These items represent a radical new view of teaching and of how its quality may be enhanced. This conceptual framework, containing assumptions that have no empirical aspects as well as propositions that may be tested scientifically, provides the intellectual substratum on which new approaches to the professional development of faculty rest.

Special organizations are being established at many colleges and universities to implement these new concepts of instructional improvement. (An extensive list of instructional-improvement programs and centers may be found in the List of Programs and Centers, following Chapter Eleven.) Centers, offices, divisions, programs, and projects that provide services variously referred to as Faculty Development, Teaching Improvement, Instructional Development, Learning Resources, Professional Development, or Educational Development have been created to assume responsibility for facilitating the improvement of instruction. These organizations have been established in all kinds of institutions—public and private universities, state colleges, liberal arts colleges, community colleges, professional schools, consortia, state systems, and educational associations. They are found in all regions of the country, probably in every state, and are growing in number, size, and significance. Furthermore, such programs are gaining increasing support among the faculty. As one director of an instructional resource center reflects, "It would have been heresy a few years ago to suggest to the faculty that they could be helped to teach better. But now that suggestion is accepted more readily."

Although most of these programs rest on a common set of assumptions and have the same general goal of improving instruction, many of them involve disparate types of enterprise. Among their variety of activities, three different—albeit related—approaches can be distinguished. Each approach tends to focus attention on different areas, strive after different goals, draw from different intellectual traditions, and involve different kinds of activities. These different approaches may be called *faculty development, instructional development,* and *organizational development;* the essential characteristics of each are summarized in Table 1. Eact of these different approaches will be discussed in detail in the next three chapters.

Faculty development focuses on faculty members and seeks to promote their individual growth and development. Because the instructional role is a major part of the faculty members' professional lives, most programs help them to explore their attitudes about teaching and learning, acquire more knowledge about educational matters, develop additional skills, enhance their sensitivities, improve their relationships with students and colleagues, and consider the teaching role in relation to other professional responsibilities. The intellectual underpinnings for faculty development are

Table 1. ALTERNATIVE CONCEPTIONS OF INSTRUCTIONAL IMPROVEMENT

	Faculty Development	Instructional Development	Organizational Development
Focus:	Faculty members	Courses or curricula	Organization
Purpose:	Promote faculty growth; help faculty members acquire knowledge, skills, sensitivities, and techniques related to teaching and learning.	Improve student learning; prepare learning materials; redesign courses; make instruction systematic.	Create effective environment for teaching and learning; improve interpersonal relationships; enhance team functioning; create policies that support effective teaching and learning.
Intellectual base:	Clinical, developmental, and social psychology; psychiatry; socialization.	Education, instructional media and technology, learning theory, systems theory.	Organizational theory, organizational change; group processes.
Typical activities:	Seminars, workshops, teaching evaluation.	Projects to produce new learning materials or redesign courses; workshops on writing objectives, evaluating students.	Workshops for group leaders or team members, action research with work groups, task forces to revise organizational policies.

in clinical, developmental, and social psychology, psychiatry, and the sociology of work and socialization. Seminars, workshops, and retreats are common mechanisms for faculty members to work on aspects of their professional or personal development.

Instructional development focuses on courses or curricula, and it seeks to improve the conditions and materials that promote student learning. Helping faculty members to specify learning objectives for students, design learning experiences to achieve those objectives, and evaluate student achievement are the basic elements of the instructional-development process. Projects in which faculty members draw on the expertise of instructional design, media, and evaluation specialists to develop learning materials, redesign courses, and make instructional programs more systematic are common in instructional-development programs. This approach derives from intellectual roots in education, instructional media and technology, learning theory, and systems theory.

Organizational development focuses on the institution as a whole or on some subunit, such as a division or department, and seeks to create a more effective environment within which teaching and learning can occur. Workshops for leaders to learn how to better lead, administer, or manage their units, training for teams, and procedures for the observation of departmental groups are typical activities as are techniques for group members to define common goals, implement policies, and evaluate results. This approach draws intellectual sustenance from knowledge about organizational theory, organizational change, and group processes.

These three approaches are conceptually distinct, but the reader should not overestimate the extent of conceptual purity found in operational programs. Most programs are governed as much by pragmatic need and opportunity as by intellectual prescriptions or guidelines. Also, each approach is shaped and modified by individuals and institutions; as we will see in the coming chapters there are several variations in the application of these three major approaches. Furthermore, these approaches are not mutually exclusive; many campus programs have elements of faculty, instructional, and organizational development. Since faculty members are responsible in large part for governing their institutions, designing and implementing curricula and courses, and developing professional competence, these various programs correspond to various aspects of the faculty role. Nonetheless, the distinctions are useful for understanding the wide range of activities that are carried on in the name of instructional improvement.

Although these new efforts are directed toward the improvement of college and university instruction, they may involve activities and have consequences that extend well beyond that specific focus. Faculty members' hopes, dreams, beliefs, and relationships may facilitate or impede their professional work, and their personal lives in turn are enriched or impoverished by their jobs. Programs designed to produce a change in professional practice may involve the personal as well as the professional growth of faculty.

Instructional improvement, when considered in this way, is a very powerful concept indeed. Because it is based on several propositions that are alternatives to conventional academic folklore concerning teaching, and because it has led to the establishment of new organizations with new programs that seek to effect significant change in faculty members, in courses and curricula, and in the structure and function of academic organizations, the idea of professional development for instructional improvement is one of the most powerful—even revolutionary—concepts to emerge in higher education in recent years.

In an ideal world a special instructional-improvement program perhaps would not be necessary—the work it does would be done by the various members of the academic community as a regular part of their jobs. However, the Group for Human Development in Higher Education (1974) points out the realities of the situation on most campuses.

> In theory, professors could individually arrange for students, friends, widely admired teachers, or consultants on pedagogy to evaluate their work in detail and discuss their reactions. Some of this is already happening, but not to any great extent. In theory, too, groups of professors and students could simply get together in order to share and deepen their knowledge about learning as an activity. Some of this happens too, but few structures exist to intensify and draw others into these

conversations. Departments could, and some do, offer
training to their own graduate students about the very
demanding job of being a college teacher, apart from
the disciplinary knowledge that must be mastered. But
even where an effort is made, we know of few departments in which programs on pedagogy call forth the same
intensity and sophistication as ordinary course work. As
a result, few institutions benefit from a rich pedagogical
culture that would support the improvement of teaching.

This conclusion is supported by a national survey of four-
year colleges and universities conducted by Many, Ellis, and Abrams
(1969). Although they found that 503 of the approximately one
thousand schools in the sample reported the existence of a formal in-
service program for faculty, the majority of these programs were
relatively unstructured, casually implemented, rarely the responsibility of one designated person, and even less frequently supported
by an item in the instructional budget of the institution. Moreover,
the primary purpose of the programs was to improve subject matter
competence; sabbatical leaves, guest lectures, support for attendance
at national and regional professional meetings, and leaves of absence
were among the most common practices. Little direct work in the
improvement of instruction was found.

An earlier survey by Miller and Wilson (1963) of over
two hundred small colleges in the South reports similar findings.
The most commonly reported development activities for new
faculty were "giving new faculty members information about the
total institution, its aims, policies, and regulations" (the familiar
orientation session), "having socal activities for introducing new
members" (the president's tea), "helping the new faculty member
to become sympathetic with and concerned about the aims and
purposes of the college" (distributing a copy of the catalogue and, if
available, the faculty handbook), and "assuring faculty members of
freedom of thought, action, and expression." The most common
practices were financial assistance for attendance at professional
meetings, conferences in some departments to consider teaching
problems, periodic faculty study of the college, and the preparation
of a faculty handbook. In general, these activities were rather dis-

connected, related more to basic employment practices than to the holistic development of faculty members, and emphasized subject-matter competence of faculty rather than development in their instructional roles. The authors concluded that "few persons involved in this study tended to think of faculty development as involving a range of *interrelated* development activities."

A special campuswide program can assume responsibility for a systematic, comprehensive, and integrated approach to the development of faculty members and administrators aimed at the improvement of instruction. But until very recently few institutions have had such programs.

It is time to take a careful look at these programs—not to evaluate them, because it is too early for that, but rather to understand what they are up to and to learn about their potential for renewing the lives and work of individuals and the functioning of educational organizations.

Chapter 2

▼▼

Faculty Development

▲▲

Faculty development, although not a new term, assumed a new sense of importance during the early 1970s; the phrase gained currency with the publication of *Faculty Development in a Time of Retrenchment* by *Change Magazine*. It may be defined as enhancing the talents, expanding the interests, improving the competence, and otherwise facilitating the professional and personal growth of faculty members, particularly in their roles as instructors. With the decrease in faculty mobility, it appears that faculty members will remain at one institution for a longer period of time, they will look to that institution to provide the opportunities and support for their own professional and personal development, and current faculty will have to play a key role in maintaining institutional vitality. For these reasons several campus administrators, leaders of educational associations, statewide planners, and foundation officials have championed programs to facilitate the growth and development of faculty.

Despite some understandable concern about who wants them to develop and why, many faculty members have responded posi-

tively to the advocacy of faculty development by campus administrators and educational statesmen. Faculty seem to have taken
seriously the intense criticism of irrelevant courses, uninspired teaching, and impersonal relationships with students which reached a
crescendo during the 1960s but which continues today, albeit with
diminished intensity. After bearing the brunt of recent attacks by
students, citizens, and politicians, and today facing declining college
enrollments, witnessing new patterns of student interests, and ex-
periencing a tight job market, many faculty members are responding
favorably to efforts to aid self-development in their instructional
roles. Another not unimportant motivation of faculty grows out of
their vague feeling that academia has not yielded them what it once
promised, resulting in a hunger for personal renewal. Celia Morris
(1973–1974, p. 13) describes their situation in these terms:

> Many were drawn to the academic world because
> it seemed to them a better place than most in America
> to nourish the intellectual life, in some cases to live with
> a love and respect for things that may well have no
> practical utility. Willing to forgo the more dazzling re-
> wards of a culture of unprecedented affluence, they
> looked to college and university campuses for intellectual
> companionship, cultural richness, perhaps a more genial
> spirit than the one that seemed to dominate corporate
> America. And they wanted to transmit those values to
> their students. Perhaps naive, such hopes were not igno-
> ble, but more often than not, they have been disap-
> pointed. . . . The angry competitiveness academics
> spotted so readily outside was often more virulent within
> the academy. The disciplines, entrenched both as guilds
> and as units of administrative power, had drastically
> narrowed the scope of professionally acceptable knowl-
> edge, so that success frequently came to depend on mas-
> tering a tiny area others were too sensible to care about.
> Or it could mean devising elaborate measurements to
> prove what people of ordinary intelligence already knew,
> or could if they bothered. And instead of being blessedly
> free from the brutal scarring of mainstream America,
> their emotional life shrank to fit a very narrow space.

If the current concern for faculty development were simply a response to current pressures on the profession, however serious, it would be reasonable to regard it as just another passing fad, of which higher education seems to have more than its share. However, the movement is an attempt to remedy a fundamental and long-standing deficiency in the preparation of college professors. Ohmer Milton and E. Joseph Shoben, Jr. (1968, p. xvii) have stated the problem succinctly: "College teaching is probably the only profession in the world for which no specific training is required. The profession of scholarship is rich in prerequisites for entry, but not that of instruction." Not only have the vast majority of college professors had no formal preparation for their instructional roles during their graduate training, but many are deeply suspicious of efforts to teach them how to be better teachers and deprecate persons having such intentions with "educationist" stereotypes. Considering the way many schools of education have sought to prepare teachers for elementary and secondary schools, faculty members may well be justified in their suspicions. However, the fact of the matter is that our colleges and universities are now staffed by faculty who, in general, have never studied the history of their profession, are unfamiliar with the topography of the educational landscape, are unaware of the professional literature in higher education, and have never been expected to formulate systematically their own philosophies of education or their views about teaching and learning. In-service training programs, based largely on college campuses, are attempting to remedy this state of affairs, improve a range of faculty competencies, and thereby increase faculty accomplishments and their concomitant satisfactions with their teaching.

The concept of faculty development may be better understood if its principles are made explicit. Although the concept is still in its formative stage and subject to varying interpretations, the following are major propositions distilled from the writings of several leading spokespersons, such as John F. Noonan (1972; 1974), Nevitt Sanford (1971), and John M. Bevan (1974).

1. Instruction is the primary role of most faculty members, but instructional quality is affected by their performance in other roles, such as research, committee work, and community involve-

ment. Faculty members can and should be encouraged to grow in each of these areas.

2. Teaching makes demands on the whole personality of the instructor. Although changing teaching styles and procedures does not require a reorientation of an individual's personality, programs that seek to improve instruction will have more impact if they emphasize a wide range of attitudes, values, skills, and sensitivities concerning teaching and learning than if they focus on a narrow concern—for instance, on classroom techniques.

3. When offered opportunities to improve their performance, substantial numbers of faculty will accept the offer. Although all persons, including faculty, resist change, they also are motivated toward growth and improvement.

4. When environmental conditions are supportive and nonthreatening, an individual's native growth tendencies are elicited. A person who is defensive and threatened will not reveal his true feelings and cannot take the risks necessary for change, because his energy must go into maintaining and supporting his own position.

5. For significant and lasting change in a teacher to occur, his emotions and affections must be engaged as well as his ideas and cognition.

6. Change in an individual requires a challenge to his habit patterns, one strong enough to stimulate new forms of behavior but not so strong as to overwhelm him. In childhood there are many such challenges, but in adulthood this may require a change in social roles or relationships that tend to protect people from growth.

7. Faculty members will change when: (a) they have knowledge about alternative ways of behaving, such as information about alternative teaching-learning practices; (b) they have the belief that change is desirable; (c) they believe that they can change in the desired ways; (d) they receive nonthreatening feedback about their own behavior; (e) they are praised, recognized, and rewarded for effectiveness and for improvement. For faculty, this means the reward structure must recognize their development efforts or they will not long strive for improvement.

8. All faculty members, regardless of age, experience, or effectiveness, can develop in many ways. Faculty development is not a remedial concept for poor teachers or underachievers.

9. Each faculty contains many persons with expertise that can be used in a faculty-development program. These persons should be identified and encouraged to share their perspectives and expertise with their colleagues.

10. Faculty development is not just an individual matter. A college or university is a rich repository of human talents, and if each faculty member develops himself to the fullest and shares his expertise with his colleagues, the entire community can benefit.

11. Because faculty are part of social groups, it is often important to work with whole departments, colleges, or other units in order to improve the climate for teaching. This often means working with administrators as well as faculty and may involve altering institutional policies or procedures.

12. Not every faculty member needs to be involved in any one program for it to be successful. Any faculty contains many different kinds of persons, each of whom is concerned with his own situation. Every program will appeal to some, and no program will appeal to all. A program may operate most effectively if it starts with those few persons with most interest and only later involves those who initially were less enthusiastic.

How Adults Develop

"College professors develop as individuals in much the same way that other people do," says Sanford (1971, p. 6). "Their development is progressive and marked by distinguishable stages which are loosely related to chronological age." But how do adults, including college professors, develop? Surprisingly little is known about this matter. Psychologists and sociologists, following Wordsworth's dictum that the child is the father of the man, have long studied child development and, more recently, changes experienced by the elderly. The assumption seems to have been that youngsters grow and develop during childhood and adolescence, but as soon as they reach adulthood, development ceases for all intents and purposes until old age, when physical and mental decline set in. The resulting state of affairs is succinctly summarized by Bernice L. Neugarten (1968, p. 138): "there is no integrated theory that encompasses total life span." More metaphorically she observes: "as psychologists seated under the same circus tent, some of us who are child psychologists remain seated too close to the entrance and are missing much of the action that is going on in the main ring. Others of us who are gerontologists remain seated too close to the exit. Both groups are missing a view of the whole show."

Even lacking a comprehensive theory, much research has been conducted on the course of human development, most of which indicates the pervasive influence of the early years. Benjamin Bloom (1964) summarizes the findings of the major longitudinal studies in which the same individuals have been studied repeatedly as they passed through several stages of their lives. He examines a wide range of human characteristics, including physical attributes such as height, weight, and strength, mental ability as revealed by intelligence tests and academic achievement, and psychological characteristics such as general interests, basic attitudes, and personality orientations. He concludes that all of the human characteristics he has examined become set at a very early age and become increasingly stable as individuals grow older. Bloom demonstrates the importance of the early years by calculating the "age of half-development" of selected characteristics, defined as the time at which one-half of the development at ages eighteen to twenty—only the beginning of adulthood—is taken as the criterion. For instance, the age at which one-half of the development of height occurs is two and one-half years; general intelligence, four years; aggressiveness in males, three years; dependence in females, four years; intellectuality, four years; general school achievement, grade three. More specifically, "in terms of intelligence measured at age seventeen, about 50 percent of the development takes place between conception and age four, about 30 percent between ages four and eight, and about 20 percent between ages eight and seventeen" (p. 88). Furthermore, stability rather than change is the rule for the remainder of life.

The early environment plays a crucial role in shaping these characteristics for three reasons. First is their very rapid growth during the early years; the early environment may shape them during the period of most rapid growth. Second, much of human development is sequential, and the developments of early years form a base for subsequent behavior throughout life. Third, learning theory holds that it is easier to learn something new than to eradicate earlier learned behaviors and replace them with others. The implications of this research for faculty development are that change in many basic human characteristics becomes more difficult as people grow older, that a given amount of change will require more effort and more powerful environments as a trait becomes stabilized, and that if change can be produced at all, it will be at a greater personal cost to the individual.

At first glance one may consider this work to foreclose possibilities for faculty development. But fortunately it is often possible to produce change in adults without altering basic personalities or deep-seated human characteristics. Change strategies for older individuals, whether they be psychotherapy or social action programs, may be designed to help the person understand and accept his distinctive qualities, feel better about himself, and find more effective ways to express them. Clearly, this leaves considerable room for helping faculty members find more effective ways of teaching during their adult years; youth has no monopoly on effective teaching or on the ability to change toward that end.

Although these findings are useful, Neugarten (1968, p. 138) correctly observes that "longitudinal studies thus far have a child-centered or what might be called a 'childomorphic' orientation. The variables selected for study have been those particularly salient in childhood; or else those measured retrospectively from the data gathered when the subjects were children. In either instance, the investigator is confined to data and to concepts which may be only of secondary relevance when he attempts to explain the varieties or sequences in adult behavior."

Orville G. Brim, Jr., in a long essay entitled "Socialization After Childhood" (Brim and Wheeler, 1966), points out several important differences between adult and childhood socialization, differences that have relevance for faculty development. (1) "In general, . . . socialization after childhood deals primarily with overt behavior and makes little attempt to influence motivation of a fundamental kind or to influence basic values" (p. 27). This implies that although faculty members may have their values and personalities fairly well set, they may be able to learn new behaviors, additional skills, and new techniques of teaching. (2) "The content acquired in adult socialization is not so much new material as it is the aggregation and synthesis of elements from a storehouse of already-learned responses with perhaps the addition of several fragments that are newly learned when necessary to fill out the required social acts" (p. 28). Faculty developers should realize that professors have a rich storehouse of experience with learning and teaching—their own as well as that which they have observed in their students and colleagues. Additional information about the needs of students, various learning styles, or innovative instructional methods can be useful, but it will be most helpful if it makes connections with this previous experience, leads to a new synthesis of understanding, and culminates in new, and hopefully more fruitful, approaches with students. (3) Whereas early socialization emphasizes idealistic views of society, in later socialization a person "learns to take his part in society according to the realistic expectations of others, rather than attempting conformity to idealistic norms" (p. 29). Neophyte faculty, no less than other young professionals, tend to believe the rhetoric of their profession and develop idealistic views such as the notion that there is a community of scholars or that academics pursue the life of the mind and have no taste for campus politics. While idealism has a definite place in faculty-development programs, Brim reminds us of the importance of helping professors to meet the realistic demands and expectations found in a college or university. Alternatively, institutional demands and expectations, which are perhaps embodied in the reward structure, for instance, may be changed to be more in keeping with the realistic achievements of faculty. (4) Resolving conflicts between competing legitimate and desirable commitments becomes a greater part of the socialization of adults partly because, unlike children, they are no longer shielded from the realities of conflict in life and "in later life there are more roles and more complexity within roles, so that a much greater possibility exists of role conflict" (p. 30). Professors generally are expected to teach, remain active in scholarship, participate in the governance and life of the institution, and contribute to the larger community, each of which could become a full-time job. The instructional role itself is complex, requiring the determination of priorities among such diverse activities as preparing class sessions, grading papers, advising and counseling students, and reading in

one's subject and related areas. And, frequently, instructional strategies are contradictory; for instance, reinforcing and encouraging
mediocre efforts to draw students out versus setting and enforcing
high standards to challenge students to higher levels of achievement.
Attention to these conflicts facing the professor and various ways of
coping with them might well be incorporated in faculty-development
programs. (5) Although children are taught general values and
prescriptions, "the content of later-life socialization tends to be role
specific, rather than general in nature" (p. 32). This implies that
the improvement of instruction will be more likely to occur when the
specific activities of the teacher and students in particular courses
and specific classrooms (or wherever instruction occurs) is emphasized. Learning that is general or abstract and experiences that occur
in settings apart from where instruction naturally occurs (such as
workshops or retreats) may not translate into specific instructional
improvement unless careful follow-up efforts are made. These
differences point to many kinds of changes, and strategies to bring
them about, that can reasonably be expected from adults who participate in faculty development or other change-oriented programs.

Other scholars are turning their attention to the middle
years of life and are trying to chart the progress of adult development. In particular, Roger Gould (1972) and Daniel J. Levinson
and his colleagues from Yale University (1974) have been doing
some of the most creative work, having obtained evidence that
adults, like children and adolescents, develop through several distinguishable stages. Although Levinson and his colleagues studied a
small group of forty men and Gould examined a large group of
524 men and women, each independently derived distinct stages of
adult development that are remarkably similar. For simplicity
Levinson's terminology will be used.

The first stage, *Leaving the Family,* typically takes about
three to five years and usually occurs between the ages of eighteen
and twenty-two. During this time the young adult seeks to become
independent of his family but usually avoids cutting all ties; he often
feels like he is half in the family and half out. Several social institutions such as college and the military facilitate the freeing of the
young man or woman from home; going away to college or to the

army provides an opportunity to grow independent without reject
ing the family.

The next stage is *Getting into the Adult World,* and it runs
its course between ages twenty-two and twenty-nine, approximately.
This stage involves exploration and provisional commitment to adult
roles, relationships, and responsibilities. Individuals generally live
out their fantasies of what the adult world is like without seriously
questioning their values or ultimate direction. Particularly important
at this stage, according to Levinson, is the "Dream," a vision of one's
personal future that for the men in his sample was often articulated
in an occupational context. The Dream provides direction and
meaning for the individual, and crises in later stages often center on
the realization, betrayal, or compromise of the Dream.

A period of transition extends from around twenty-eight to
thirty-two; about this time a person begins to ask, "What is this life
all about now that I am doing what I am supposed to do?" At this
stage a person either reaffirms his provisional commitments or de-
cides they are not really for him and makes a major shift in occupa-
tion and life structure.

Following transition comes *Settling Down,* which begins
during the early thirties. Two primary aspects of this stage are
"order" and "making it"; it becomes very important to move on-
ward and upward toward the realization of the Dream, usually
according some inner time schedule, and there tends to be a
change in tone toward a quiet desperation and an increasing awareness of a time squeeze.

Levinson identifies the culmination of the Settling Down
period as the stage of *Becoming One's Own Man,* which happens
between thirty-five and thirty-nine. No matter what he has accomplished to date, a person comes to feel that he has not been his own
man, that he is constrained on all sides. He seeks to escape from the
control of those with authority over him, to overcome dependency
on others, and to avoid those who seek to influence him.

The *Mid-Life Transition* lasts from around thirty-nine to
forty-three and is a boundary region between two periods of greater
stability. A person wants to be affirmed, and often he will fix on
some key event which becomes particularly symbolic—a promotion

or recognition—and may take several years to unfold; Levinson says that men around forty frequently live in a state of suspended animation.

At about age forty-three to forty-five a new life structure, *Restabilization and Flowering,* begins to take shape and provide for living throughout the remainder of the decade. Gould says that during this phase a person tends to become resigned to finite time and accept his personality as pretty well set.

Although Levinson and Gould have not carried their work into the fifties, the research of Neugarten and her associates (1964) can help to fill this gap. They found that when an individual approaches the later years there is increased preoccupation with the inner self and decreased emotional investment in other persons and objects, as he slowly "disengages" himself from his social system. Measurable changes in intrapsychic processes appear in the forties and fifties, at a time when biological changes are occurring but when measurable changes in the competence and range of social interaction have not yet appeared. However, even though there is shrinkage in psychological life space, other investigations have shown that factors such as work status, health, financial resources, and marital status are more decisive than chronological age in influencing the degree of adjustment in persons fifty and over.

The implications for faculty and administrators of Levinson's theories have been speculated on by Hodgkinson (1974a). In Provisional Adulthood he sees both doing a lot of career testing, while the dreams for faculty of this period are to become a famous scholar, writer, or influential advisor or to wield power and influence (administrator). During the Settling Down period the concerns for academics include obtaining a desirable faculty position, figuring out the "real" requirements for tenure, and obtaining recognition for one's own intellectual contributions. He envisions the Mid-Life Transition as coping with the loss of illusion and scaling down the dream to fit within the realities of the actual job; by now it is apparent to most that they never will be a full professor at Harvard or a key advisor to presidents, and they become reconciled to seek excellence in their own work. The stage of Restabilization and Flowering involves increased loyalty to the institution, new confidence, and a definition of productivity based on internal goals rather than external criteria.

It is apparent from even this cursory synopsis that academics who are at different points in their life and their careers will look for different things in a faculty-development program. Younger faculty may seek information about what academic life in general and teaching in particular are all about, and, judging from the findings about the importance of the early environment in human development, their basic instructional styles and values may be formed for the remainder of their careers. Older professors may desire specific information or particular skills that will allow them to modify their instructional styles somewhat in an attempt to achieve better results. Or they may seek personal or professional renewal, contemporary challenges, or new experiences that can bring fresh perspectives and approaches to life and work that may have become routine. And, of course, each may benefit from learning about persons who are at different stages of their careers and lives through sharing their views, perspectives, and experiences with colleagues—opportunities that unfortunately are often missing in the normal course of academic life.

Other scholars are seeking to discover factors that facilitate change and development in adults. For a symposium in honor of his aging mentor, Henry Murray, Sanford (1973) prepared a paper, "Notes Toward a General Theory of Personality Development—at Eighty or Any Old Age," in which he listed several principles of adult change that, as the title implies, apply at any age or stage of development. These too seem applicable to faculty development programs. (1) "Change in behavior depends upon the presence of an appropriate and effective challenge, one that is sufficient to upset equilibrium but not so extreme as to induce regression, that is to say, not too severe in an objective sense and not beyond the limits of the individual's adaptive capacities" (p. 16). For faculty the depressed market for professors, the prevalence of student evaluation of teaching, and the increased importance attached to teaching effectiveness in the advancement procedures may provide such a challenge. Of course, if a person is confronted with an immediate threat such as a loss of job, this may be so debilitating that he will be unable to realize the potential he possesses. (2) "In childhood and adolescence there are usually challenges in abundance, but for adults the presentation of an effective challenge will ordinarily require a change in the person's general situation—in the social roles, relationships, responsibilities, and reward systems that structure the life and which are, in effect, external barriers to development" (p. 16). Participation in a new curriculum, adoption of a team-teaching or interdisciplinary approach, or teaching different kinds of students, such as adults, may alter a professor's situation sufficiently to constitute an inducement for change. It is for this reason that some persons see faculty and course or curriculum development occurring hand in hand. (3) "Personality development requires the knowledge, or at least the implicit assumption, that one can develop" (p. 18). Unless faculty members believe they can change, they will be unlikely to make the effort, and any change, especially a major one, requires considerable expenditure of energy. (4) "Steps can be taken to prevent the projection onto new situations of psychological contents of the past, to overcome resistance to the assimilation of knowledge and to consideration of alternative ways of behaving, and to connect new stimuli with inner needs and potentialities" (p. 21). Nothing is more natural than to encounter the new in terms of the old, to try old strategies so long as they work. However useful it may be to use past experience as a guide to coping with new situations, such psychological devices may undermine efforts to adopt innovative instructional approaches; competency-based programs, for example, may be transformed into course-based programs by faculty members who do not fully shed their old views. For an instructional change to be complete and to become embedded in the teacher, he must work through the new approaches, form a new synthesis of familiar and unfamiliar elements, and connect the resulting configurations to several elements of his personality. (5) "Personality development in adults requires self-examination aimed at self-insight" (p. 23). Attempts to produce change by behavioristic or mechanistic means are likely to be neither effective nor long lasting unless they are understood, accepted, and integrated within the person. No "cookbook" approach that lists recipes of classroom do's and don't's is likely to produce much significant change. (6) "People develop together" (pp. 24–25). As much as an individual may want to change and develop, it will be difficult for him to do much unless he has the support and encouragement of his associates. It is this proposition that serves as the basis of Sanford's oft-repeated assertion that faculty development and student development must occur together, that faculty develop most fully when they are sensitive to the developmental needs of students and further their growth.

Programs

Given this modest albeit growing knowledge about adult development and principles of faculty development, what are people actually doing to promote the growth of faculty? While some scholars seek to construct a useful theory of adulthood and others conduct research on changes during the adult years, many other academics are busy establishing and maintaining programs of faculty development. Pressing needs cannot be put off until scholarship paves the way for them to be met; on the contrary, implementing operational programs and acquiring additional knowledge about the persons served are related enterprises that may be carried out in tandem, although in reality they tend to proceed independently of each other. The remaining portion of this chapter will discuss kinds of faculty-development programs and the activities that are part and parcel of each.

At the outset it would be helpful to examine in some detail a single program to note what is involved in such an enterprise. One particularly noteworthy early program is that devised for members of the College Center of the Finger Lakes. Gary H. Quehl (1974), then the Executive Director of the five-school consortium, wrote that "the consortium was reorganized at the end of the 1970–1971 academic year, and faculty development came to be a leading priority for the 'new' CCFL. I searched in vain across the country for new faculty development models. In the absence of adequate demonstration projects, we decided to plan an experimental faculty workshop that gave high priority to 'affect' in the teaching-learning process." He contracted with the National Training Laboratory, which had held workshops for executives and professionals for several years, to stage a pilot four-day workshop for faculty in 1972; it yielded mixed results, and was not the success for which he had hoped. During the course of the next year, Quehl encountered William Bergquist and John Noonan, two young men whom he thought had promising ideas about ways to combine affective and cognitive approaches to faculty development. They, along with Nevitt Sanford and William Barber, put on the next and pivotal workshop.

A subsequent brochure (College Center of the Finger Lakes, 1974) indicates the rationale behind the plan. "A major shortcoming of this growing faculty development movement is that the programs created in its name tend to focus on the faculty member as teacher (instructional development) while ignoring other faculty roles that are critical to effective instruction: as persons (personal development) and as organization members (organizational development). Because a college or university is a complex, dynamic social system, the development of faculty requires a comprehensive program that assists them in all three roles."

Prior to the workshop a two-hour interview with each participant about his own assumptions, attitudes, and beliefs about teaching and learning was conducted. This interview allowed each participant to take stock of himself as a teacher, to start thinking about how he could benefit from the workshop, and to confront personal questions about his own strengths and weaknesses. During the week-long workshop the mornings were devoted to personal development, the afternoons to instructional development, and the evenings to organizational development. Personal development was encouraged by means of several small groups of individuals from different schools on the assumptions that they might feel freer to reveal their feelings to strangers than to colleagues and that they would be less likely to be distracted by institutional matters. Each group was led by a consultant, and the conversation focused on the content of the personal interviews. "The primary purpose of these discussion sessions [is] to explore with peers, and expand upon, the information which has been generated by the two hour interviews. . . . The primary role of the group consultant . . . [is] not to give advice, to explore the personal problems of the participants, or to determine the specific direction of the group's discussion. Rather the consultant is to assist each participant in fully clarifying his own attitudes and values, with specific reference to instruction" (Quehl, 1973, p. 7).

The afternoon sessions had a more cognitive emphasis, with the focus on several basic concepts of instruction. Led by the workshop staff, the participants considered curriculum design, procedures to diagnose the dynamics of a classroom, feedback concerning teaching behavior, student evaluation, instructional technology, and teaching styles. The evening sessions focused on organizational aspects of campus life. In these sessions participants met as campus teams and sought to identify problems at their institutions with reference to instruction, devise alternative solutions to the problems, and draw up a plan to implement some kind of change. Follow-up workshops for participants and consultations with the members of the administration of each campus were also included in the overall design to help translate the activities of the workshop into changes at the home campus.

This program is described in some detail because it contains the vision, breadth, and comprehensiveness that make it a model of instructional-improvement programs. Further, this particular program was a catalyst to the thinking of several individuals who were to become leaders in this new movement, provided them with a proving ground for testing their ideas, and confirmed their value with a favorable evaluation. This approach to faculty development has been diffused widely through the writing, speaking, and consulting of each of the major figures in this early workshop.

There is great variability among faculty-development programs, which reflects the diversity among institutions, faculty interests, available resources, and staff expertise. But perhaps more than anything else, the variations among programs are determined by differential analyses—or at least implicit assumptions—of what would make faculty better teachers. There are, in other words, genuine differences of opinion concerning what is wrong with instruction and what can and should be done to help faculty improve it. Some persons assume that faculty are too narrow and limited in their knowledge and experience; they seek to help faculty extend the range of their knowledge and awareness to other academic disciplines and the community. Others hold that faculty are not knowledgeable about higher education in general, or teaching and learning in particular, and seek to promote such learning. Still other persons assert that instruction would be improved if faculty possessed more skills for teaching students; some programs emphasize skill development. Some critics argue that cognitive knowledge or additional skills will produce little change in faculty unless they also experience affective growth, which receives emphasis in certain programs. Some believe that faculty need to become more aware of their own teaching behavior, and there are several efforts to give them useful feedback. And still others assert that the concern ought not to be with teachers and teaching at all but with students and learning; several programs seek to sensitize faculty to the learning styles of different kinds of students. The range of activities carried on under the rubric of faculty development will be discussed below in terms of the major kinds of changes they seek to foster in faculty members.

Extending the range of knowledge to include other disciplines and the community. A persistent criticism of professors is that they have specialized in such a small portion of an academic discipline that they have little of relevance to say to their colleagues in other fields of specialization or to the wider community. Some schools seek to assist their faculty to broaden the scope of their work by encouraging them to learn about other academic disciplines and to gain practical experience in the community.

Macalester College in Minnesota, with the assistance of a grant from the Fund for the Improvement of Postsecondary Education, has launched a program to expand the range of faculty competencies, partly to improve the quality of instruction and partly to provide greater staff flexibility for the difficult times ahead. Their Auditor-Consultant Program brings two faculty members from related disciplines together in an unusual teacher-consultant relationship which has been described by Charles R. Green and Walter D. Mink (1973, p. 3). "As a major part of his consultantship, the consultant would attend (audit) the course of his colleague, suggest ways in which the content and methods of his own discipline could apply to the course, and serve as a tutor to his colleague in some important trends in that discipline. For his part, the second faculty member would serve as a tutor to his consultant-auditor in the trends in his own discipline." In a personal conversation Green reported that the amount of interdisciplinary conversations and cross-fertilization of the academic disciplines seems to have increased, as have the number of proposals to introduce interdisciplinary courses and programs.

Complementing this program is a Faculty Community Internship Program which attempts to broaden the experience of several faculty members outside the institution. A few faculty members are assigned on a part-time basis to businesses, public agencies, and other organizations in the community. Professor interns are not expected to be consultants to the organizations but rather participants, observers, and inquirers in their community assignments. The internship lasts for a year, and during the second semester the intern is expected to incorporate some aspects of his experiences into his teaching. Assignments are sought in organizations that hold interest to students, so that faculty will have greater sensitivity to social issues, community problems, and career alternatives that will be expressed in their teaching and advising activities. Faculty members in these two special programs participate in a weekly seminar during which they discuss and clarify their experiences.

The Center for Teaching and Learning at Stanford University places a heavy emphasis on interdisciplinary education. Directed by David Halliburton, a senior faculty member of the interdisciplinary program Literature and Modern Thought, the center sponsors a series of workshops on interdisciplinary teaching for faculty members at Stanford and other institutions in the region. The early workshops were primarily content oriented and concerned intellectual issues and themes that cut across disciplines with some discussion of pedagogical issues involved in this special kind of teaching.

Gaining knowledge about higher education in general and teaching-learning in particular. Some individuals assert that faculty have little knowledge about education and that they would benefit from becoming acquainted with the professional literature and diverse practices of higher education. Mechanisms created to provide that knowledge include inviting lecturers to analyze contemporary educational issues, holding formal and informal discussions among interested groups of faculty, having campus conferences on effective teaching, acquiring books, articles, and reports on educational topics, publishing a newsletter, incorporating substantive educational discussions in faculty meetings, and providing opportunities for individual consultations with interested faculty.

Several schools have established faculty seminar programs. At Cleveland State University an informal conversation among a few faculty members led to an open meeting attended by about thirty faculty members to discuss common concerns about teaching large introductory courses. The outgrowth of that meeting was the delineation of several additional topics that served as foci for future conversations, including teaching in small groups, refining lecture techniques, using and interpreting the university's instructor evaluation form, using simulations and games in teaching, using audiovisual materials, defining instructional objectives, and employing computers. In order to institutionalize this process and to extend the range of activities to improve teaching, a Center for Effective Teaching was established. First, Lance Buhl, and later, Ferris Anthony directed the center to provide expertise, information about alternative approaches at other schools, and administrative leadership for activities concerning matters of teaching. Similar discussion groups have been set up elsewhere following more extensive surveys of faculty interests or in response to expressed interest of departments or other organized groups of faculty for such dialogue.

Sometimes the discussion groups have considerable continuity and seek to benefit others than the core group. At California State University, Northridge, an Institute for the Advancement of Teaching and Learning was established for the purpose of fostering dialogue about these matters. Sixteen faculty members, nominated by their departments and chosen by the president upon the advice of an ad hoc group, have a quarter-time assignment in the institute. The fellows set aside one half day per week for a continuing discussion of topics of interest to them and of relevance to education in the University. The reading, thinking, writing, and conversing that the fellows do is intended primarily to benefit themselves, but the fruits of their work are made available to the entire faculty through a university conference toward the end of the year. Nearby, the University of California, Santa Barbara, has held similar annual campus conferences on effective university instruction, drawing heavily upon faculty members from the institution, publishing the papers, and distributing them to all faculty.

There is a rapidly proliferating literature about higher education and about innovative instructional techniques, and some schools have systematically collected books, journals, articles, and reports for use by the faculty. The collection need not be extensive nor expensive to be of value; a fine library of published material as well as fugitive documents that represent current thought about higher education can be assembled for a modest expenditure. Perhaps more important than collecting materials is making them available and useful to the faculty. Some schools do this by putting them in places frequented by the faculty, such as a faculty lounge or club; others provide small collections in departmental offices. Still others provide their faculty with complimentary copies of one of several educational journals of their choice, such as *Chronicle of Higher Education* or *Change Magazine,* on the theory that they will be more likely to read educational materials that they choose and that come directly to them.

Many of the new instructional-improvement centers publish newsletters containing information about current publications, summaries or syntheses of selected topics, articles about teaching-learning issues written by faculty members, and information about their own campus programs. Although these newsletters typically are written for the faculty of that institution, they frequently are available to outsiders free or at very low cost. Some of these newsletters are listed in the Bibliography. The newsletter *Memo to the Faculty,* of the Center for Research on Learning and Teaching at the University of Michigan, is an excellent case in point. Published since shortly after this center was established in 1962, it contains substantive discussions of such topics as improving the conditions of learning, the evaluation of teaching, and assisting the apprentice teacher, each of which is written by outstanding authorities at the university. Approximately twenty thousand copies of the *Memo* are printed for distribution all over the world. Ironically, there is some suspicion that this excellent publication may be more warmly received by persons outside the University of Michigan than inside.

Finding time to pursue faculty-development activities, however valuable they may be, is a difficult problem. Some institutions have decided that it is possible to incorporate such activities into the regular departmental meetings. Periodic meetings in which the regular business is set aside in favor of substantive discussions about improving the quality of instruction in a department or about key issues affecting their programs is one way of making time for these activities. Some people are surprised to learn that the school or department can continue to function when occasional business meetings are suspended in favor of discussions of more substantive educational matters.

Developing instructional skills. Some critics say that although faculty may well benefit from additional knowledge, whether about other disciplines, community life, or instructional matters, additional knowledge does not mean they will necessarily become any more effective teachers. Knowing what to do and doing it are two different things. What is needed, so goes the argument, is training in the development of specific instructional skills. Again, there are many different approaches to this end.

Most faculty members are aware that traditional instructional methods have been criticized and that there are a number of alternative procedures available, but few have had any firsthand experience with them. Still, they have a genuine interest in developing skills in innovative methods of instruction. Workshops which include basic information about the concept, an opportunity to obtain some experience with aspects of these new methods, guidelines about putting them into practice, and awareness of problems to avoid have been held at many institutions. Such workshops typically go beyond seminars in that participants get some hands-on experience as well as the basic ideas; there is more emphasis on doing and less on talking about doing in this kind of program.

While some programs emphasize the use of innovative procedures, others speak to the need to improve traditional lecturing and seminar teaching techniques. In some sessions faculty members share tips about ways to prepare and conduct classes or compare notes about evaluation and grading procedures. Other times experts participate in workshops designed to teach specific skills such as listening or questioning. The instructional program marketed by the Xerox Corporation, "Effective Listening," has served as the basis of workshops conducted by Frank Collea for about seventy-five faculty members at California State University, Fullerton; two thousand students subsequently went through the training. Proponents, like advocates of speed-reading courses, claim that a short training session can increase listening effectiveness dramatically.

Becoming sensitive to the interpersonal dynamics of a classroom is another set of skills taught by faculty developers. Kiyo Morimoto of the Bureau of Study Counsel at Harvard University, at the request of graduate teaching assistants, has observed their teaching and taperecorded section meetings, seminars, tutorial sessions, and office-hour conversations. About two hundred of these recordings, as well as the accompanying transcripts, have been gathered into a Library of Teaching Styles. These documents, edited to preserve anonymity, now are used in workshops for teaching fellows. Segments of various tapes are played, and participants attend to the interaction of teacher and students, offer interpretations of what is occurring, suggest alternative strategies, and make predictions of what follows certain critical points, for example, after a teacher corrects a student or asks a particular kind of question. According to Morimoto's (1972) account of an evaluation by participants, they reported overwhelmingly positive responses to the experience; many of them reported that it helped them to consider and try new approaches, become aware that teaching is a two-way communication process rather than a simple transfer of information, hear more in each student's comment, and discover some of their own assumptions about teaching and how they affect their interactions with students.

A different approach has been used in the Mentorship Program of Eckerd College originally coordinated by Robert Hatala, which sought to help faculty become more sensitive to student needs, attitudes, and personal growth. A group of twenty mentors, about one-third of the entire faculty, participated in two-hour luncheon seminars for the spring semester and took part in a two-week, full-time workshop during the summer. The purposes were to give all faculty members who volunteered to teach in a new freshman program which required them to serve as mentors to the freshmen a better picture of the character and resources of the college from the student point of view, to offer them additional tools for discovering student attitudes, deficiencies, and concerns, and to expose them to different approaches to teaching and learning. In the seminars and workshop the faculty sought particularly to learn how to teach values, facilitate students' discovery of meaning, and use counseling procedures. The participants, after completing the program, reported acquiring skills mostly in two specific areas, classroom teaching techniques and practical approaches to informal counseling or private conversations with students. They also evidenced an easing of anxiety concerning deeper involvement with students and were more eager to work with students in personal and social as well as academic areas. Although it is perhaps not entirely attributable to the consequence of this program, the previously high drop-out rate at the college was significantly reduced among the first class of freshman students who benefited from the skills of these mentors.

Encouraging affective development. Some critics argue that the increase of cognitive knowledge or the acquisition of additional classroom techniques—by themselves—are not promising methods for the improvement of teaching. Marvin Ack (1973, pp. 6–7) observes that traditional teaching styles among college faculty have remained unchanged for years and hypothesizes the reason:

> The psychological resistances to change were totally ignored. Teaching methods were discussed as though they were exclusively a cognitive function. To over-simplify, all one had to do was tell somebody 'the truth or give them the word' and their behavior would change. My position, on the other hand, is that teaching —like all significant behavior—is a reflection of intimate aspects of the personality. Change in teaching style demands a concomitant change in personality organization. Not only is teaching style more a product of personality organization than of cognitive beliefs, but the methods used provide drive gratification or reinforcement which are hard to approximate in other social situations and thereby fix the style.

Further, Ack advises faculty that "you can appropriate someone else's style or recommendations successfully only if it is in accord with your own beliefs about people and affords you emotional satisfaction equal to that which you are currently deriving from your present teaching methods." According to this position, change and improvement in teaching will occur only if faculty undergo personal and affective change as well as changes in cognition and skill.

Ack, serving as a consultant from the Meninger Clinic to the Kansas City Regional Council for Higher Education, held a series of workshops for faculty of several schools in the consortium at a noncampus site. The primary activity of the workshop consisted of what he called a "task-oriented sensitivity program." Although it differed significantly from a therapy session or T-group in that it focused on the task of teaching, participants were expected to think about and articulate their personal assumptions, values, and beliefs about teaching, grading, testing, and how people learn. In the workshop they looked at the bases and origins of these views, for the purpose of becoming more aware of themselves as teachers, including both positive and negative aspects, a condition that can stimulate growth and change as a teacher.

One technique that is used to facilitate the exploration of values, assumptions, and beliefs is the depth interview. This technique has been used by scholars at the Wright Institute for both research and action purposes. Sanford (1971, p. 18) has commented on their experience with this procedure.

> Almost without exception those we have interviewed said they enjoyed the experience and derived benefit from it. It is our firm conviction that they do indeed benefit . . . : they are given a chance to reflect on important matters that have been little in their attention, they do a certain amount of personal stock-taking, they discover—often with considerable relief—that it is possible to talk about troublesome and revealing aspects of their experiences with students; in short, a process leading to increasing self-awareness is set in motion.

The individual interviews of teachers may be analyzed by the staff, and the collective results used in discussions among small groups of faculty, thereby expanding the personally relevant two-person private conversation to a larger and more public forum. In such discussions faculty often discover that it is all right to share views and concerns about teaching with colleagues, that others have similar doubts or concerns, and that one can learn from the experiences of one's colleagues.

Simulations and games are still other devices to expose the affective side of teaching. Various games are available that cast faculty into different roles from which they are familiar and cause them to see the world from new perspectives. For example, Edventure is a game in which players choose among several post-secondary institutions and thereby learn about market factors affecting the competitive position of a school. In the counter-game, developed by Eileen Kuhns and S. V. Martorana, people must not only take a position different from one they would normally occupy but develop arguments to support their assigned positions. Thus, they begin to feel what it is like to hold a position contrary to one's own views. The debriefing session following a game gives each person an opportunity to express his feelings and reactions to aspects of the game; this is a significant component in the process of clarifying the experience and enhancing the learning.

Getting feedback about one's own teaching behavior. Some persons believe that the best way to induce change in faculty is to give them useful information about how their students or colleagues perceive their teaching. Several devices have been utilized to provide faculty with a mirror with which to obtain external perspectives on their teaching.

Student ratings are by far the most widely used feedback device. Their popularity derives largely from the apparent simplicity of the approach. It is relatively easy to write a few items thought to be indicative of effective teaching, simple to administer and score rating forms, economical to administer, and nonthreatening, particularly if faculty are given the choice of whether to use the forms, as is usual. However, the simplicity is deceptive; a good deal of intellectual, technical, and administrative work is required to mount a good student evaluation program. Because of the widespread interest in instituting a program of student evaluation of teaching, several fine rating forms are now available.

One difficulty with this approach is that student ratings frequently are used for two quite different purposes: to give information to individual faculty members which may foster their self-improvement, and to provide information to the institution to aid decisions about promotion, salary, and tenure. Glasman, Killart, and Gmelch (1974) have argued that each purpose is best served by a different kind of instrument. Self-improvement rating forms should be diagnostic, have items that are quite specific and detailed, and emphasize the improvement in a single instructor over time. Forms for administrative decision-making should be more judgmental, contain general and summary items, and emphasize the comparative effectiveness of all faculty at the time a decision is required. Because many instruments seek to serve both purposes simultaneously, they may provide information that has limited utility for each.

One of the most useful approaches to the use of student ratings has been adopted by Kansas State University. Their program is based on a sophisticated conception of effective teaching, grows out of a sustained program of research, and is directly related to follow-up improvement activities. Over a period of years Donald Hoyt developed a refined student rating scale based upon extensive research. Unlike many other instruments, it is based on the assumption that there are different styles of effective teaching, depending on the goals of the teacher, the nature of the course, and the characteristics of the students. In addition, effective teaching is defined by what students learn rather than by what teachers do.

Hoyt developed a questionnaire on which students in various classes were asked to rate their progress on eight different learning objectives, describe the instructor's behavior, and describe various aspects of the course; a copy of the rating scale is found in Table 2. A separate form was used to collect instructor ratings of the importance of each of the eight objectives. Hoyt (1973, pp. 156–157) describes the results of the initial research in this way:

> In the end a few items were found to be characteristic of effective teaching regardless of the objectives being sought or the size of the class. A few others were predictive of progress ratings in small classes but were unrelated to progress in large classes; the reverse was also true. And a few items didn't differentiate among progress groups on any criterion. But for the most part,

Table 2. STUDENT REACTIONS TO INSTRUCTION AND COURSES

PART I. Describe the teaching procedures used by your instructor by using the following code: 1 = hardly ever, 2 = occasionally, 3 = sometimes, 4 = frequently, 5 = almost always.

The instructor:

1. Seemed to have a well-developed plan for each class session.
2. Promoted teacher-student discussion (as opposed to mere responses to questions).
3. Explained course material clearly, and explanations were to the point.
4. Seemed to lack energy.
5. Answered student questions as completely as reasonable.
6. Adjusted his pace to the needs of the class.
7. Wasted class time.
8. Encouraged students to express themselves freely and openly.
9. Was incoherent and/or vague in what he was saying.
10. Seemed enthusiastic about the subject matter.
11. Changed his approach to meet new situations.
12. Seemed unprepared for class.
13. Received student comments without asking for them.
14. Spoke with expressiveness and variety in tone of voice.
15. Demonstrated the importance and significance of his subject matter.
16. Made presentations which were dry and dull.
17. Monopolized class discussions.
18. Made it clear how each topic fit into the course.
19. Encouraged student comments even when they turned out to be incorrect or irrelevant.
20. Presented examples of what he wanted by way of homework, papers, etc.
21. Presented material in a humorous way.
22. Lectured in a low monotone.
23. Explained the reasons for his criticisms of students' academic performance.
24. Attempted to induce silent students to participate.
25. Summarized material in a manner which aided retention.
26. Stimulated students to intellectual effort beyond that required by most courses.
27. Lectured in a rambling fashion.
28. Understood student comments and questions even when these were not clearly expressed.
29. Stated clearly the objectives of the course.
30. Failed to differentiate between significant and nonsignificant material.
31. Introduced stimulating ideas about the subject.

Table 2. (Continued)

32. Repeated material to the point of monotony.
33. Related course material to real life situations.
34. Found ways to help students answer their own questions.
35. Told the class when they had done a particularly good job.
36. Made good use of teaching aids (chalkboard, projectors, models, etc.).

PART II. Describe the course in terms of other courses you have taken at this college or university. Use the following code: 1 = much less than most courses, 2 = less than most, 3 = about average, 4 = more than most, 5 = much more than most.

The course:

37. Amount of reading.
38. Amount of work in other (nonreading) assignments.
39. Difficulty of subject matter.
40. Degree to which the physical condition of the classroom facilitated learning.
41. Degree to which reading materials (including text) seemed up-to-date.
42. Degree to which too many topics were covered.
43. Degree to which assigned readings were clear and understandable.
44. Degree to which the course material was valuable to me.
45. Degree to which the course hung together (various topics and class activities were related to each other).
46. Degree to which examinations gave balanced coverage to major topics.
47. Degree to which examination questions were unclear.
48. Degree to which examinations stressed unnecessary memorization.
49. Degree to which examination questions were unreasonably detailed (picky).

PART III. Compare the progress you have made in this course with that made in other courses you have taken at this college or university, using the following code: 1 = lowest 10% of courses I have taken here, 2 = next 20%, 3 = middle 40%, 4 = next 20%, 5 = upper 10%.

Your progress:

50. Gaining factual knowledge (terminology, classifications, methods, trends).
51. Learning fundamental principles, generalizations, or theories.
52. Learning to apply course material to improve rational thinking, problem-solving, and decision-making.

Table 2. (Continued)

53. Developing specific skills, competencies, and points of view needed by professionals in the field most closely related to this course.
54. Learning how professionals in this field go about the process of gaining new knowledge.
55. Developing creative capacities.
56. Developing a sense of personal responsibility (self-reliance, self-discipline).
57. Gaining a broader understanding and appreciation of intellectual-cultural activity (music, science, literature, etc.).
58. Developing skill in expressing myself orally or in writing.
59. Discovering the implications of the course material for understanding myself (interests, talents, values, etc.).

PART IV.   Describe your personal attitudes and behavior in this course, using the following code: 1 = definitely false, 2 = more false than true, 3 = in between, 4 = more true than false, 5 = definitely true.

Self-rating:

60. I worked harder on this course than on most courses I have taken.
61. I had a strong desire to take this course.
62. I skipped this class more than three times (not counting absences due to illness).
63. I took an active part in class discussions and related activities.
64. To date, I have completed all required assignments in this class.
65. I would like to take another class from this instructor.
66. As a result of taking this course, I have more positive feelings toward this field of study.
67. I have reason to believe I will make an A or a B in this course.

If your instructor has extra questions, answer them in the space designated. Your comments on how the instructor might improve this course or his teaching are invited.

Copyright 1972 by Donald P. Hoyt and Richard E. Owens.

... the particular teaching behaviors which were related to student progress were different for each objective and for large and small classes. Rather than one model of teaching effectiveness, we had discovered sixteen.

These lists of items that were descriptive of the different types of effective teaching have become the focal point of the university's instructional-improvement program. All participating faculty receive a report of their ratings along with comparison of average scores of others with similar objectives in similar fields and with similar-sized classes. Although some faculty may make some changes as a result of these reports, some are unable to interpret the reports or determine what to do to improve; for these persons group interpretative sessions are held. Typically faculty members have mediocre or poor ratings on one or more items associated with successful achievement of objectives they have set for their students. Although some faculty may forget the entire matter, some may resolve to do better, and others may attend a special seminar conducted by Richard E. Owens, the Director of Educational Improvement and Innovation, and still others may seek an individual appointment to plan and embark upon improvement activities. The important point is that unlike most similar programs, evaluation feeds directly into a follow-up program of improvement.

One of the most effective ways for a professor to see himself the way others see him is by means of the videotape machine. Classroom episodes may be put on tape and the nature of the interaction later analyzed in detail by the class, with a group of colleagues, or in a confidential consultation with a faculty-development staff member. Because the first time a person sees himself on tape may be rather traumatic, a professor usually is encouraged initially to view the tape by himself so that a later discussion about the proceedings may be more productive. The use of videotapes offers strong support for the old saying that "one picture is worth a thousand words," at least where gaining feedback about one's teaching is concerned.

Most programs designed to give faculty members feedback about their teaching focus on the person receiving it, but it is obvious that the kind of information and the way it is given are critical. John Noonan, at Virginia Commonwealth University, has established a Teaching Laboratory where faculty members may go to obtain descriptive—not evaluative—feedback from a group of specially trained observers. The rationale is that descriptive feedback about a teacher's behavior is less threatening and more useful than judgments of his behavior. Scholars who have studied group processes are very aware of how difficult it is for a person to observe the dynamics of any group; untrained observers, however well intentioned, often miss much of the action. A few students and faculty at Virginia Commonwealth have been given special training in teaching observation, communications, descriptive feedback, and helping relationships. This small cadre has been available to consult with faculty by observing their teaching behavior in the laboratory or, by mutual agreement, in an actual classroom setting.

Learning rather than teaching. Some analysts assert that the problem is not to improve the teaching of faculty members but the learning of students. If faculty were more sensitive to the learning styles, aspirations, personalities, and needs of different kinds of students and employed curricular and teaching strategies responsive to them, instruction would be improved. Some institutions support research into the learning needs of students who vary on such factors as intellectual ability, social background, learning style, and personality orientation. Others examine students' educational experiences as a part of an evaluation of their entire instructional endeavor. And still others support seminars and workshops for faculty to learn how to individualize instruction and insert the student variable into the instructional-development process.

Ohmer Milton, Director of the Learning Research Center at the University of Tennessee, operates essentially a "one man shop" that is concerned primarily with instructional research and its use for the improvement of instruction. A recognized authority on teaching and learning in higher education, Milton (1972) has published extensively about factors that affect, and do not affect, the teaching-learning process and the outcomes of college for students. He puts this expertise to use on the campus by administering a small-grant fund designed to encourage faculty to experiment with new approaches to undergraduate instruction, staging an orientation meeting for new faculty on learning, assisting faculty to design educational research projects, and promoting dissertations dealing with teaching-learning issues. The major purpose of this program is to stimulate experimentation with teaching-learning arrangements that may be sounder than those based on tradition, hunch, or dogma. A major emphasis is on stimulating careful evaluative research about the consequences for students of various instructional approaches tried by faculty.

The University of Wisconsin, Green Bay, became much-heralded as an innovative institution during the late 1960s, and an Office for Educational Development was established to aid the evaluation and implementation of the academic plan. The small staff, which has been headed by Eugene L. Hartley, conducts four distinct programs: (1) to monitor students' educational experiences from the time they enter as freshmen until after they graduate by means of surveys of their values, views of the school, satisfactions, and educational benefits, (2) to obtain reactions of students to their courses, (3) to provide a variety of services for instructional improvement, including seminars, workshops, and videotaping of classes, and (4) to conduct special studies on aspects of the academic program. This office operates like a research project on student development, a center for the evaluation of teaching, and an institutional research office combined. Faculty are informed of the results of the various studies about students' experience in their courses and in the institution in general by the circulation of short summary reports and by the seminars and workshops in which they participate.

Another example of programs designed to sensitize faculty to the needs of students is the summer institute hosted by New York City Community College that was devoted to improving the skills of two-year faculty from business and technology programs to work effectively with minority students. Emphasis was on helping faculty understand the problems, viewpoints, and aspirations of the minority students who were expected to enter the university through the open admissions program and to incorporate that understanding into their teaching. Fifty two-year faculty members from ten institutions in the City University of New York participated in the two-week summer institute and follow-up program and prepared demonstration instructional projects which were implemented during the fall.

Of course, it does little good to inform faculty about the diversity of students in general or the experiences of students in their own institutions if they are not able to respond in meaningful ways to their interests. For that reason, some programs are concerned with introducing faculty to instructional strategies and procedures by which they may individualize their instruction. Seminars, workshops, and demonstration projects concerning such topics as self-paced learning, independent study, curricular contracts, experiential learning, and criterion-referenced evaluation are used to help faculty members translate a concern for student diversity into their instructional procedures. These efforts to individualize instruction will be discussed in detail in Chapter Three.

This survey of various approaches to faculty development reveals the diversity that pervades this new movement. It is important to emphasize that these new efforts supplement rather than replace traditional forms of professional development. Research support, travel to meetings of professional societies, sabbatical leaves, and the like are necessary but not sufficient for the professional development of faculty today. These several new approaches are promising efforts to improve the quality of teaching and learning.

Chapter 3

▼▼▼

Instructional Development

▲▲▲

If faculty development focuses on faculty members, instructional development focuses on the conditions of learning, particularly courses and curricula, that they foster; and while faculty development emphasizes the improvement of teaching for faculty, instructional development emphasizes the improvement of learning for students. There is, of course, considerable overlap in these two concepts, but as will become apparent, they have different foci, incorporate different goals, and stress different kinds of activities.

Instructional development is a recent academic specialization that may be defined as the systematic and continuous application of learning principles and educational technology to develop the most effective and efficient learning experiences for students.

The specialization of instructional development and its recent application in colleges and universities is the result of the confluence of at least four different intellectual traditions. First, the research on learning which psychologists have been conducting in their laboratories for decades has finally yielded practical application in educational settings. Although the contributions of many scholars have been important, the work of B. F. Skinner (1968) and his followers has been most influential. His central concept is that of *operant conditioning,* which states that if behavior emitted by a person is rewarded, it will tend to be repeated. According to Skinner, a teacher elicits responses from students from course plans, assignments, and classroom activities and can best help the students learn by rewarding correct responses. Although the ability to mete out rewards to facilitate the learning of students contains considerable power, most teachers are unaware of its possibilities and use rewards unsystematically. Considerable research has demonstrated that, generally, learning is faster and more effective if positive reinforcement of correct responses is provided rather than punishment or criticism for incorrect responses and if the reward is provided immediately after the response rather than delayed. Because much of what students are expected to learn, particularly in college, are complex matters such as understanding scientific principles or analyzing a novel, the tasks can be broken down into simpler elements and ordered into a sequence. The method of successive approximation in which a teacher rewards elemental responses that progressively approximate the desired complex performance provides a powerful method to influence the learning of students.

Second is the systems approach (Churchman, 1968), which, like the scientific method, is a set of self-correcting procedures that provide rational control over a large number of related phenomena. Essentially a managerial framework that was fashioned originally to guide the development of extremely complex weapons systems in the Air Force, the systems approach calls for all factors that affect a desired outcome to be identified so that plans may be drawn up to specify precisely how all of the parts can be put together to produce the end product.

Today the systems approach is being applied to produce learning materials and to design the learning experience of students, largely through the advances that have been made in the field of curriculum and instruction, the third major influence.

A set of procedures, summarized as the instructional-development process, that are powerful aids for the improvement of teaching and learning has been developed. They include the specification of measurable learning objectives for students, design and production of learning materials, experiences, and sequences for students to achieve those objectives, evaluation of the attainment of the objectives, and revision of objectives or learning experiences in light of the evaluation. These techniques have been brought to the attention of many faculty members via workshops, courses, and seminars, and they are used in a number of projects to redesign courses or curricula.

Fourth, the most articulate spokespersons for instructional development are educational technologists. Once limited primarily to audio-visual aids, educational technology in recent years has witnessed important advances in television, videotape, and computers, all of which have much potential utility for higher education. Although this potential is largely untapped, the prevalence of media, computer, and television centers on college and university campuses and the growing number of academic and technical staff skilled in these matters are valuable resources for instructional improvement.

The confluence of these four forces has led to the specialization of instructional development. Any particular program may emphasize certain of these traditions and neglect others. On the one hand, the Center for Research on Learning and Teaching at the University of Michigan, under the leadership of Stanford Ericksen, has emphasized the application of learning principles to instructional procedures while underplaying the role of technology and hardware. On the other hand, instructional development at many institutions has been added on to existing media centers, a fact that leads them to place greater weight on instructional technology and hardware. Nonetheless, the influence of each of these separate traditions may be observed in the work of most instructional-development programs.

The concept of instructional development may be more fully comprehended when its major propositions are spelled out. The following are different aspects of the concept distilled from the writings of several of its leading spokespersons, such as Fred S. Keller (1968), Robert M. Gagné (1970), and Robert M. Diamond (Diamond and others, 1975).

1. The improvement of instruction involves primarily the design or redesign of the learning experiences of students, typically in the form of courses. The manipulation of the conditions of learning, including carefully delineating the specific learning tasks required to grasp a body of knowledge, sequencing the tasks, and

making certain that students master elementary learning before they proceed to more advanced levels, can improve the quality of education.

2. The systematic application of the instructional-development process can lead to the improvement of a course. This process, in simplest terms, involves the specification of learning objectives for students, the design of learning experiences, and the evaluation of student achievement of the objectives.

3. Learning objectives can and should be stated in specific and measurable terms that make clear to students and teacher alike what level of performance is expected of students. When the desired behaviors are clear, it is more likely that students will learn them.

4. Accurate evaluation devices that can assess the extent to which students achieve the objectives of the course should be used; the clear specification of objectives in measurable terms allows instructors to construct such tests.

5. The most effective courses are those in which the objectives, learning experiences, and evaluation of students are consistent with one another. This consistency increases the probability that the objectives will be attained.

6. Effective teaching is that which brings about student learning. Efforts to change the classroom behavior of teachers are likely to be most beneficial when such changes are linked to improved student achievement of objectives.

7. A complex activity such as learning a body of material or acquiring intellectual skills may be broken down into its component parts. Learning may be facilitated when these component parts are learned to a specified level of mastery and in the appropriate sequence.

8. The effectiveness and efficiency of many courses may be improved by the use of more and different kinds of media and technology.

9. Many conditions of learning may be embodied in prepackaged learning materials, which may supplement or even replace traditional classroom sessions. These materials may be delivered to students in various forms including programmed texts, audio- and videotape, television, and movies.

10. Courses may be individualized so that students may

proceed through the various segments at their own pace. Procedures for them to study modules, test their understanding, and either to proceed on to the next step or obtain assistance provide the basis for self-paced, flexible, and competency-based learning.

Process

The instructional-development process has been described by many (Robert Glaser, 1965; Ivor K. Davies, 1971; Robert M. Gagné and Leslie J. Briggs, 1974), and several different models have been reviewed by A. Maughan Lee (1972) and James G. Buterbaugh (1971). An inspection of the models that have been advanced indicates that the approaches to the systematic development of instruction range from simple procedures to elaborate processes with several different steps. But all formulations include four steps that are the core of the process: formulation of objectives, design of instruction, evaluation of results, and revision of objectives or instruction in light of the evaluation.

Few people would quarrel with the notion that objectives ought to be formulated before instruction occurs. However, there has been considerable professional attention directed toward the nature of objectives, the way they should be formulated, and the functions they serve in the design of instructional sequences (Mager, 1962; Eisner, 1969; Popham, 1969). Several points of agreement have emerged.

First, objectives should describe precisely what is expected of a student. Typically, when they are mentioned at all, objectives are stated in terms of teacher behaviors, teacher-student interactions, or assignments rather than in terms of student competencies desired. For example, to say that students will read Plato's *Republic* and discuss portions of it in class may describe planned activities, but it says little about what the students are supposed to gain from those activities. It would be more to the point to specify that students will be expected to recognize the major features of Plato's theory of the state or to identify four central features of his view of art.

Second, insofar as possible, objectives should be stated in behavioral or measurable terms rather than general or vague terms. To say that a student should *learn, understand,* or *appreciate* something says little about exactly what a student is supposed to do after a course that he could not do before it. By stating the objectives with a high degree of specificity, it is possible for everyone involved to recognize the behavior that meets or fails to meet them. An example of a specific objective would be the ability of a student to analyze a substance chemically and list all its elements and their percentages.

Third, the statement of objectives should indicate how well a student must perform in order to be judged successful. The actual criteria from which the degree of success will be inferred, such as the degree of accuracy or the number or proportion of correct answers on an examination, may be stated.

Fourth, the statement of objectives should describe the context and conditions in which the performance will be expected to be demonstrated. That is, it is not as helpful to indicate that students are to understand psychoanalytic theory as it is to specify that they will be expected to state three similarities and three differences in the psychoanalytic theories of Freud and Jung on an essay examination given in class without the use of books or notes.

One instructional developer declares, "Many faculty members with whom I work do not even know what they are trying to do." By this he means that they are unable to state their own objectives in a clear way, that is, consistent with the above criteria. To be sure, these criteria are somewhat stylized, and it may be that some objectives cannot be specified in this way, but the inability he mentions is widespread, as anyone who has conducted a faculty workshop on instructional objectives can attest. However, it is both a skill and a way of approaching the design of a course that can be learned relatively easily.

There is a hard line and a soft line on the use of behavioral objectives. The hard line is articulated by Popham (1969), who advocates a very high degree of specification of objectives for every course so that teaching strategies can be chosen to increase the chance that important outcomes will be achieved. In taking a soft line position on this matter, Eisner (1969) points out the practical difficulty of specifying all behavioral objectives for all the classes one teaches; using a reductio ad absurdum argument, he indicates that such an exercise could theoretically consume virtually all the available time for instruction. But both agree that the more specific the teacher can be about what students are supposed to achieve as a result of the course, the better he or she will be able to choose the subject matter content, select methods and media for presenting the content, sequence topics, decide on the amount of time alloted to each topic, and evaluate the results of instruction.

As is usually the case when specialists address a topic, a number of distinctions have been made by scholars in the area of educational objectives. The terms *behavioral, performance,* and *measurable* objectives have been used interchangeably to denote the end behaviors desired as a result of instruction. But soon after those terms gained currency, it was recognized that some learning builds on prior learning, and it was necessary to talk about *instrumental* or *enabling* objectives, things a student has to learn as a precondition to learning more advanced material. Eisner (1969) offered *expressive* objectives to indicate the situation in which both the teacher and learner encounter material to explore its meaning and implications but for which specific student outcomes cannot be known at the outset. A comprehensive taxonomy of educational objectives has been developed by B. S. Bloom and others (1956), who hold that learning may occur in three different domains: cognitive, affective, and motor. In this work they distinguish between cognitive objectives that vary in terms of complexity and sophistication: knowledge of factual information; comprehension of knowledge; application of knowledge and understanding to specific situations; analysis of complex ideas into their component parts; synthesis of disparate items into a whole; and evaluation of the consequences of actions. The affective domain subsequently has been categorized by Krathwohl, Bloom, and Masia (1964). Gagné (1970) discusses learning hierarchies and identifies eight types of learning that differ in regard to the conditions under which they are best learned. Although some objectives are too elementary for most purposes of higher education, the top four are quite relevant: *verbal* association refers to learning of information or facts; *concept* learning refers to understanding terms or ideas that are used in a subject; *principles* involve learning relationships between concepts; and *problem solving* requires finding ways to cope with problems which lack clearly defined solutions. Despite all of these classifications, in practice the objectives that are most frequently chosen in instructional development projects tend to emphasize the mastery of cognitive content of a course. But regardless of how the objectives are conceived or categorized, the essential point remains: the more clearly they are stated, the easier it will be for the instructor to plan his instructional activities to achieve desired objectives, for students to direct their learning to the specified goals, and for teachers to prepare tests to assess the extent to which objectives are achieved.

The second step of the instructional-development process is that of deciding on the instructional procedures that will be employed to achieve the objectives. Once the objectives are carefully delineated, it is possible to consider a wide range of instructional procedures, from lectures and seminars to learning contracts and simulation, that may be effective in helping students attain them. Whatever method or combination of methods is chosen, it should be chosen because it can be expected to lead to the objectives that have been specified, not because it has been used before or because the professor prefers some particular approach. It is this requirement that gives the instructional-development process power and leads its users toward innovative approaches; after an objective is formulated, it often is apparent that the traditional lecture or seminar format is only one—and not necessarily the best—procedure for facilitating the desired outcome.

Many instructional methods, in addition to the familiar lecture and discussion approaches, are available for the interested faculty member. These include independent study, contractual study (in which a learning contract detailing a plan of study is agreed to by the student and a faculty member or committee), tutorials, audio and visual media, experiential learning (internships, field study, practica, cooperative education, and the like), simulation (manipulating elements of a model of real-world problems), games, role-playing, community-action projects, and self-paced instruction. Most faculty members will be unfamiliar with these alternative forms of instruction, but they may be helped to learn how to use them. Seminars, workshops, and course-development projects are used to help faculty members broaden their repertoire of instructional styles and methods so that they choose from a larger number of alternatives the methods best able to achieve their objectives.

No single method will be equally effective in achieving all

objectives. A professor may decide that basic factual knowledge in his subject may be best mastered by reading or working through a set of programmed materials, developing concepts by small group discussion, thinking critically through debate or simulation, and creating awareness of practical problems or application of ideas by field experiences. But again, the specification of objectives is important because it encourages more variation and richness in instructional procedures than is typical, variation that may pique the interest of students as well as lead to improved quality and efficiency in instruction.

In practice, however, the use of audio-visual media and development of self-paced instruction are most frequently the methods preferred by persons working in instructional-development programs, perhaps because many individuals favoring this approach come out of educational media and technology backgrounds and because many instructional-development programs are mounted by media centers. This process may lead to more innovative teaching when it is applied by individuals with less interest in hardware.

Whatever instructional procedures are decided on, their adequacy will become apparent in the third step of the instructional-development process, that of evaluation. The evaluation focuses on the extent to which the objectives are realized by students. Although few persons would quarrel with the notion that students should be evaluated to determine what they have learned, there has been considerable professional debate directed toward the nature of this evaluation, a debate that in some respects parallels the one over the specification of objectives.

In particular, the debate revolves around the relative merits of two different forms of evaluation that are technically referred to as *norm-referenced* and *criterion-referenced*. These days students typically are evaluated in relation to one another rather than against absolute standards. Most standardized tests of intellectual ability or educational achievement calculate and report the score of an individual in relation to the scores of some appropriate comparison group, and many faculty members grade on a curve. Because these procedures yield scores that are interpreted by comparing an individual's score with the results of a normative group, they are called *norm-referenced*. Such procedures are useful, particularly if one wants to know how a student performs in relation to his peers, for instance, when a teacher assigns different grades to the students scoring higher and lower on examinations. However, critics of this procedure point out that this comparison is often not the most important one in educational matters, that it is often more important to know whether a student learns the material than to know how he performs relative to others in a class. For instance, it usually is important to determine whether a student can apply Boyle's law or not; it matters little that he knows more or less than his peers, who themselves may or may not understand the subject matter. Tests that are designed to indicate whether an individual student has performed to some designated criterion, whether he has realized the objectives regardless of how well his peers perform, are called *criterion-referenced*.

The implications of criterion-referenced evaluation for education are quite profound. First, good norm-referenced tests should have considerable variability in the scores so that differences in the amount of learning between students will become evident; those with the highest scores receive an A, those lower a B, and so on. In contrast, a criterion-referenced test may have little variability; in fact, if the instruction is effective in realizing the objective, everyone could receive an A grade. The essential point of criterion-referenced evaluation is that the test should accurately reflect the extent to which each individual attains the performance objectives that have been carefully specified. Second, if, as is frequently the case, new courses are designed so that a student must master one segment before he goes on to more advanced levels, it is possible that all students will achieve the objectives of the segments they complete to the desired criterion level, although it may take some students longer to reach that level than others, and some may go further in an instructional sequence than others. The logic of this approach is that it would be better to give all students the same grade—a measure of the quality of learning, and vary the amount of credit—a measure of quantity of learning—they receive rather than the usual approach of giving all students the same amount of credit and varying the grade. This logic is behind the movement toward competency-based curriculum, which holds that students should be expected to master certain competencies regardless of the length of time they require to do so. Further, the increasing use of self-paced instruction that embodies these ideas is cited as one of the reasons behind the grade inflation that is occurring in colleges and universities.

Although the technical differences between these two forms of evaluation transcend the scope of this report, it should be mentioned that, as Popham and Husek (1969) have indicated, criterion-referenced evaluation requires new approaches to test construction, new definitions of standard statistical terms such as reliability and validity, and new ways to report and interpret test results. For this reason, faculty often need to learn how to use this kind of evaluative tool in their work.

Although the differences between these two forms of evaluation have been drawn sharply in this discussion, neither one enjoys an innate superiority over the other; both have their uses and limitations depending on the questions one wants to have answered. It is possible to use either form of evaluation and derive useful information from it. Yet, it is increasingly clear that criterion-referenced evaluation has advantages over norm-referenced procedures, particularly in assessing the achievement of specific learning objectives.

The instructional-development process may become self-correcting at the fourth step, in which the results of the evaluation indicate the extent to which the objectives are realized by the instruction provided. If the evaluation indicates that something is lacking, it may be that the instructional procedures or materials need to be revised; a determination of the particular objectives that were not realized, especially when supplemented by reports from students, can help pinpoint the area where revision is needed. Or a poor evaluation may mean that the objectives may need to be reconsidered; perhaps they are unrealistic or assume prerequisite knowledge or skills that students do not actually possess. In this case the objectives may need to be revised, perhaps to include the additional ones that assure students are adequately prepared to tackle the original purposes.

An evaluation plan that provides information useful in revising and improving an instructional sequence must transcend measures of student learning, as important as they may be. It is also important to obtain from students their judgments about the utility or value of the course, reports of the enjoyment and satisfaction they derived, opinions about the teacher and the study materials, and suggestions about ways in which the course may be improved. All of this information will be helpful in deciding whether and how each part of the instructional procedure will be revised.

The important point is that this systematic process provides a dynamic interplay between learning objectives, new forms of instruction, and evaluative information. The application and repetition of this process provides a mechanism for continued improvement in the quality of instruction.

Programs

The first major application of the instructional-development process in higher education occurred in 1963 when the University of Michigan and Michigan State University established instructional-improvement programs. Since that time numerous colleges and universities have established units with the responsibility of improving the quality of learning, largely by applying the instructional-development process. Because of its pioneering character, Michigan State may be a particularly apt example of the way these programs work. The following description draws heavily from a recent annual report (Office of the Educational Development Program, 1973).

The Educational Development Program (EDP), a division of the Provost's Office, was established in 1963 for the purpose of improving undergraduate education. It is a small organization staffed by a director, an associate director, and a secretary. It relies on three closely coordinated subunits to provide consultation and assistance to faculty as they plan and implement a series of projects. First, Learning Services, with two professional staff members, "consults with any department or faculty member on increasing the efficiency of student learning. It brings to bear on each problem current knowledge regarding variables which influence the learning process . . . and it assists in the design of instructional procedures that make use of all appropriate media and relevant techniques." Second, the Instructional Media Center "is responsible for the coordination and development of instructional applications of audio-visual media, including closed-circuit television, and the improvement, through research and development, of programs and materials designed for instructional purposes." This office employs nine faculty members of varying ranks as well as a technical staff. Third, Evaluation Services, with its eleven faculty and four technical staff members, provides assistance in the "evaluation of student and faculty performance and the improvement of course examinations" (p. 5).

The EDP operates on a project basis; instructional-improvement projects are proposed by faculty members and are supported by a special university fund. Projects typically are supported only during their developmental or experimental phase, rarely more than one or two years; after that time the departments are expected to maintain successful projects. The procedure usually begins with a faculty member who has an idea and approaches the EDP office; he or she is referred to one of the consultants from the Learning Services or the Media Center to prepare a proposal. Proposals are evaluated by a panel of faculty members from throughout the university against four general criteria:

> 1. *Number of Students Affected:* In general, EDP is concerned with those undergraduate courses and departments which serve the largest number of students.
> 2. *Experimental or Innovative Approach:* The project must evidence an experimental or innovative approach to curriculum or instruction. EDP does not seek to promulgate traditional procedures but instead seeks new and improved methods of solving instructional problems.
> 3. *Generalizability:* The techniques, procedures, or materials developed must seem potentially applicable to other academic areas in the University.
> 4. *Capability for Evaluation:* The project must be designed in such a way that outcome can be evaluated. Procedures for evaluation are built into all projects and faculty are required to submit final reports describing project outcomes [p. 6].

During its decade-long history, the program has worked closely with faculty members on hundreds of individual projects. Its recent report of a single year of activities contains descriptions of projects in nineteen different departments as diverse as accounting, art, biology, English, history, mathematics, music, physics, and psychology.

Different colleges and universities have utilized the instructional-development process in different ways. Some place an emphasis on the production of learning materials that may be used in courses; others design or redesign whole courses; some help implement whole curricula by working with faculty; others seek to inform professors about various aspects of the instructional development process; and still others rely largely on providing consultative services to individual faculty members about a variety of issues and concerns.

Producing learning materials. Frequently a faculty member will have a problem about presenting some particular material in a course, and he will request assistance from an instructional-development program. For example, a nursing instructor may want to prepare a series of videotapes to demonstrate ways to obtain a thorough medical history, procedures to conduct physical examinations, or ways to conduct home visits. In consultation with instructional-development personnel, the faculty member may decide that the original request would not really solve his problem or that procedures he had not considered may be more effective, less time consuming, or more economical. As psychologists have learned in other areas, sometimes a request by an individual masks a different, occasionally a deeper and more serious, problem. Conversations between the faculty member and the instructional-design consultant may identify or clarify the reason for the request, the learning objectives the material will serve, the ways it will be incorporated into the course, and how it will be evaluated. Once the developer is satisfied that the proposal has merit, he may arrange to help the faculty member prepare the material.

A wide variety of media may be used to prepare the new material, each of which has advantages and disadvantages that are familiar to the instructional designer. Videotape, films, audio recordings, filmstrips, programmed texts, computers, and illustrative material such as transparencies, graphs, and charts may be used to achieve certain instructional objectives. Although these materials may be produced in many media centers around the country, the thing that makes an instructional-development program different is that the staff do not simply fill the request of a faculty member.

Rather, they discuss his request in a professional manner to help him make certain that he is aware of the alternatives and that he chooses the alternative that best suits his instructional needs. Often the faculty member is not sufficiently informed of all available options, and he is not able to make the best judgment about what he wants until after talking with the designer.

In some cases a faculty member may want to prepare materials that can be used in an entire unit of instruction. In this case a greater degree of academic planning is involved, and the project becomes more substantial in terms of the amount of academic content as well as the amount of time and expense that is involved. For example, the Division of Instructional Research and Service at Florida State University assisted a biology professor to prepare transparencies, printed materials, and laboratory exercises for use in modular units for training students in microscopic observation and in microscopy skills. It also facilitated the preparation of tapes and slides by a professor of English to provide supplementary materials on the historical and cultural background of the nineteenth century for his course in American literature. Typically, a single instructional designer is assigned to work in collaboration with a faculty member on a project of this sort, and he, in turn, involves the production specialists in the media center to produce the materials that he and the professor agree will make the best presentation.

One modular approach that has gained a good deal of attention is the "audio-tutorial approach" devised by S. N. Postelthwait at Purdue University (Postelthwait, Novak, and Murray, 1969). Originally used to develop modules that individualized learning among the large numbers of students in an introductory botany course, the audio-tutorial approach has sometimes been used for whole courses. It consists of a series of self-instructional materials designed to provide more individualization and more efficient learning as students proceed at their own pace through the materials. Typically, a student goes to a specially equipped carrel in a library or learning resource center where an audio tape guides him through a sequence of learning activities that involve a number of assembled materials. The learning experiences may consist of such activities as reading texts, listening to discussions, conducting brief experiments, and analyzing data. This approach has been widely adopted in other schools for all types of subjects.

Postelthwait has supplemented the audio-tutorial approach with a "mini-course" concept. Traditionally the curriculum has been divided into specific courses, and this approach involves simply subdividing each course into small units, each of which may be considered a mini-course. There are five basic components of the mini-course.

1. Audio tape. Rather than being a lecture on tape, this is a medium that allows a teacher to serve as a tutor to each student as he discusses exercises, makes observations, and gives directions to guide the student.

2. Tangibles. Specimens that are being studied are provided whenever possible so that students can make their own direct observations.

3. Visuals. Some material may be highlighted in diagrams, photographs, color slides, and films.

4. Printed materials. Study guides contain instructions about each unit, questions to be answered, and a summary of the lesson.

5. Human interaction. Although most of the work done by students is performed alone, an opportunity for the student to meet with the instructor to gain assistance with his specific problems and needs is built into the mini-course.

The mini-course concept has been used to develop modules in many universities for subjects as diverse as the historical and cultural background of Chaucer and medieval literature, the geography of a state, and black music. Of course, several of these mini-courses put together may become a single course, or they may be used to teach only a portion of it.

Designing courses. An instructional approach similar to those discussed above is known variously as the Keller Plan (after Fred S. Keller, who developed the procedure) or the Personalized System of Instruction (PSI). In his seminal paper, "Goodbye Teacher," Keller (1968) lists five ways in which his kind of course differs from a traditional one. It is a self-paced, mastery-oriented, student-tutored course that relies on study guides to communicate information to students and involves a few lectures by teachers primarily to motivate students. The entire course is divided into units, and the students proceed through the units in the prescribed sequence; however, they are not allowed to continue to the next unit until they master the material in the previous unit. The instructor chooses and plans the course content, writes the study guides, and prepares the examinations following each unit. The tutor grades the examinations and helps students who may need assistance with particular problems. The Center for Personalized Instruction has been established at Georgetown University to assist college teachers who want to use such individualized instruction. Its programs include regional conferences, workshops, publication of a newsletter, and distribution of literature on the Keller Plan.

An extensive literature on the evaluation of Keller Plan courses in a wide variety of disciplines and institutions has appeared, and a review of these studies (Kulik, Kulik, and Carmichael, 1974, p. 383) is quite positive. It reaches the following conclusions.

> 1. The Keller Plan is a very attractive teaching method to most students. In every published report, students rate the Keller Plan more favorably than teaching by lecture.
>
> 2. Self-pacing and interaction with tutors seem to be the features of the Keller courses most favored by students.
>
> 3. Several investigators report higher-than-average withdrawal rates for their Keller sections. The conditions that influence withdrawal and procrastination in Keller courses have been studied, and it seems possible to control procrastination and withdrawal by course design.
>
> 4. Content learning (as measured by final exams) is adequate in Keller courses. In the published studies, final examination performance in Keller sections always equals, and usually exceeds, performance in lecture sections.
>
> 5. Students almost invariably report that they learn more in PSI than in lecture courses, and also nearly always report putting more time and effort into Keller courses.

This evidence documents the value of Keller courses for at least a portion of a student's education, especially that where mastery of subject-matter content is a goal. For those courses or sections of courses that seek to promote personal growth, increase awareness, provide enriching experiences, or change attitudes or values, this structured individualized approach probably is less effective.

Florida State University has two funding programs that are administered by the Council for Instruction of the Academic Senate to support both the development of learning materials and the redesign of whole courses. The Summer Awards are given typically to faculty for the purpose of developing tools or materials that promise to make a course more effective. A large portion of these funds is used to pay faculty salaries during the summer quarter as they work on their projects. The Academic Year Program supports efforts of faculty members to redesign entire courses. These funds may not be used for faculty salaries, but they may be used to obtain student assistance, fund travel, purchase supplies, and support the development of necessary materials. Recipients of either award are expected to work closely with an instructional designer to design, implement, and evaluate the results of their projects.

Robert M. Diamond and his colleagues at the Center for Instructional Development at Syracuse University (1975) have developed an individualized instructional system that is more flexible than the audio-tutorial and Keller approaches. They have concluded that these systems are not sufficiently adaptable to the needs of individual students and have listed six key features of a truly individualized program of study.

1. Flexible time frames. Since students learn at different rates, the instructional program should allow them to move through it as rapidly or slowly as they need to meet the objectives.

2. Diagnosis, remediation, and exemption. Students enter any course with a wide range of educational backgrounds. The entering level of competency should be diagnosed; students who have deficiencies should be helped to correct them, and students who already possess certain desired competencies should be allowed to omit the sections dealing with them. The usual method of remediation or exemption on the basis of the entire course should be replaced by a more targeted, unit-by-unit approach.

3. Content options. Most courses, particularly large intro-

ductory ones, enroll students with a range of interests, and options that allow a student to relate the subject matter to a particular field of interest may heighten the interest and value of the course to him.

4. Alternate forms and flexible time for student evaluation. Not only is it necessary to have a series of tests for students to take as they move through a learning sequence, it is desirable to allow each student to choose the way he wants to demonstrate competence.

5. Choice of location. Not all learning occurs in the classroom, and an individualized system should provide various options as to where a student can learn.

6. Alternate forms of instruction. Different students learn in different ways, and alternative learning experiences, as well as the opportunity for students to choose among them, should be available.

Although they recognize that it is not always possible to build each of these features into every course, Diamond and his colleagues believe it is possible to include most of them in most courses. They contend that their approach is superior to those of Postelthwait and Keller in its provision for diagnostic evaluation, content options, alternate evaluation techniques, and alternate instructional techniques.

The movement from Postelthwait, to Keller, to Diamond— merely three among many instructional development approaches— represents historical shifts in the application of the systems approach to the improvement of instruction. Each successive step provides greater options, builds in more student choice, and relies less on hardware with its inherent constraints, all of which make instructional development more attractive to faculty and more useful to students.

Implementing whole curricula. The logic of the instructional-development process extends beyond the production of learning materials and the design of isolated courses to include the design and implementation of entire curricula. Competency-based curricula are particularly compatible with instructional-development approaches. The basic idea behind competency-based curricula is that a college education should not be just the accumulation of a certain number of credits or courses but a means by which students may acquire a number of competencies that are the marks of an educated person.

College courses as currently constituted may well provide a general
vehicle by which a person can achieve those competencies, but in
most courses some parts are irrelevant to desired competencies and
other parts may not be the most effective route to those attainments.
A number of colleges and universities are actually seeking to transform their curriculum, or a portion of it, to this new basis.

But what is actually involved if a college wants to redesign its
educational program in such a way as to systematically promote the
attainment of specific competencies? The case of Sterling College is
informative, as revealed in a recent report (Meeth, Hodgkinson,
and Brownlee, 1974). The first step was to develop a set of
competencies that graduates were expected to have. A curriculum
task force developed an initial list that was presented to the faculty
in late 1971, and the faculty elaborated items with more specific
objectives, clarified their language, considered evaluation criteria
and methodology, and designated the kinds of experience students
could use in achieving competence. As a result of this process the
school decided that "a graduate of Sterling College: (1) comprehends the Christian heritage and its relevance to his life and community, (2) is aware of his own values and commitments, of others'
values, and of alternatives, (3) knows how to acquire knowledge
and use it, (4) understands the artistic and aesthetic dimensions of
culture, (5) comprehends the relationship of man to his physical
and social environment, (6) demonstrates proficiency in at least one
discipline in depth, (7) is competent in verbal communication, (8)
demonstrates physical skill in one or more recreational activities,
and (9) is able to work in groups, studying, analyzing, and formu-
lating solutions to problems and in acting on them" (p. 2).

This list of educational goals could appear in most college
catalogues, but what makes these competences distinctive is that they
were used as targets for the redesign of the entire curriculum. One
approach was for a group of faculty members to develop new
interdisciplinary courses that would meet the specific objectives of
these competences; after working for a year and a half, they devised
a total of ten new or redesigned courses with such titles as Values,
Society, and the Individual; Methods of Inquiry; Whole Earth; and
Personal and Group Development. Furthermore, out-of-class learning experiences are recognized as an important route to some

competencies; participation in the campus chorus, attendance at a series of seminars on science and values, field trips, and attendance at a special drug education workshop are all designed to supplement more formal curricular experiences and to lead to certain competencies. In addition, faculty members are continuing to attend workshops and work individually as well as with consultants, colleagues, and administrators to develop competency-based majors; eight departments hope to be ready to start changing to their new program in fall 1975. Outside funding permitted the preparation of four competency-based interdisciplinary majors also. Of course, a change of this magnitude has required changes in other areas of the college, including student advising and orientation, supportive resources and services for students and faculty, college policies, procedures to evaluate students, and the reward structure for faculty.

And it required a good deal of work with the faculty. On-campus workshops were held to further faculty understanding of the total curriculum, to help them redesign their own courses and methodologies, and to give them an opportunity to consider the changing role of faculty. Several faculty members went to off-campus workshops on teaching disadvantaged students and using technological tools, and they returned to apply their ideas at Sterling. Consultants were brought in to work with groups of faculty and with administrators, a host of group meetings were held, and much individual work was done on the campus. Similar efforts to revamp entire curricula are underway at institutions such as Alverno College in Kansas, Mars Hill College in North Carolina, Governors State University in Illinois, and the Curriculum of Attainments project at Florida State.

Informing teachers. Rather than develop products and learning materials, design courses, or implement curricula, some persons believe that a better strategy is to develop people who have knowledge of and sympathy for the instructional-development process. By encouraging individual teachers to have favorable attitudes, diagnose student needs, set objectives, use various teaching strategies, and evaluate their instruction, an instructional-development program may be able to stimulate a process of continuous instructional development that will have more impact on student learning than any single product, whether a module, course, or curriculum. This approach is captured by Michigan's Stanford C. Ericksen (1974, p. viii), who declares, "Projecting one's voice to the back of the room and projecting visual images to the front are judged to be less important for teaching than is the instructor's ability to make sense to young adults, to challenge their curiosity, and to provide the resources for learning."

This approach is very similar to the faculty-development concept discussed in Chapter Two, since both seek to help faculty become more knowledgeable and effective instructors. The difference, when one exists, is partly a matter of emphasis on courses rather than faculty members. Also, some instructional developers regard this as an endeavor to develop favorable attitudes of faculty toward instructional development and systematic instruction.

The University of Redlands, in addition to a varied program of activities during the academic year, had a summer workshop in which thirty-five professors, about one-third of the entire faculty, assembled to consider such topics as course planning, organizing instruction, motivating students, leading class discussions, meeting special needs of minority students, utilizing audio-visual instruction, and evaluating student achievement. The workshop was evaluated quite positively, with many faculty members reporting they gained ideas they would put into use.

Frank J. Vattano, Assistant Academic Vice President and Director of Instructional Development at Colorado State University, operates an instructional-development lecture series. During the academic year nationally recognized experts are invited about once a month to discuss topics of concern to the faculty. Recently, Billy Koen spoke on PSI, John Valentine gave a series of talks on nontraditional study, contract learning, and the open university; Samuel Gould discussed the report of the Commission on Non-Traditional Study which he chaired; Paul Dressel discussed independent study; Wilbert McKeachie talked about research on effective college teaching; and a panel of local faculty members who had used innovative teaching methods reported on their experiences.

Other institutions rely heavily on consultation with individual faculty members. James E. Stice at the University of Texas, Austin, reports that consultant services offered by his Center for Teaching Effectiveness have been among the most valuable of all services provided. Four consultants, from the departments of physics, psychology, and education, have one-fourth-time appointments with the center and are available to provide assistance to individual faculty members on a variety of teaching-related topics. Their services to any faculty member may continue as long as the relationship is beneficial, making in-depth assistance possible to those faculty members who desire it.

The way this one-to-one consultation works in a somewhat different context is described by Frederick H. Gaige, who directs the professional-development program of the Kansas City Regional Council for Higher Education (personal letter, May 12, 1975):

> I sit down individually with faculty members (and administrators) to assist them in identifying professional problems and articulating professional development plans. I then attempt to assist them in solving problems and moving ahead with their plans. This often involves no more than putting them in touch with some kind of specialist and an honorarium for that assistance. It sometimes involves providing them with small amounts of money to attend workshops and conferences or to undertake teaching-related research. It sometimes involves sitting in a class and assisting faculty members to evaluate [their] teaching. There are almost an infinite number of ways I can work with individual faculty members with regard to their teaching and broader professional and personal interests and activities.

Medical and dental schools frequently have an office staffed by instructional-development experts who help prepare programmed and individualized learning materials. But Arthur King of the College of Dentistry at the University of Florida has carried the process one step further. He has prepared a four-part self-instructional syllabus, with the appropriate acronym CAVITIES, with which to instruct faculty about their new teaching roles in the modular curriculum the school has adopted. The syllabus has four modules, each with several objectives, descriptions about self-instructional materials available for teachers to reach each objective, and information about where and when the materials may be obtained.

A more extensive approach to preparing self-instructional materials for the improvement of college teaching has been undertaken by Roderick Hart and Gustav Frederick at Purdue University. They and several colleagues have developed a series of twelve audio tapes and related study guides on the following topics: behavioral objectives, knowing students, innovations in college instruction, lecturing as communication, teaching through discussion, instructional technology, philosophy of classroom testing, and test construction. These materials are available for use in instructional- and faculty-development programs at other institutions. Although they are substantively sound and of high technical quality, it remains to be seen how many faculty members will use them to pursue a self-instructional course of study.

The potential uses of the instructional-development process are numerous. Although some institutions emphasize one or another application, it is possible for a single program to embrace several. At the Center for Research on Learning and Teaching at the University of Michigan, a group of faculty members who had used these services were working on diverse projects. Jon Rush spoke of the proliferation of media in sculpture and the need to instruct students about the characteristics of each medium and the basic principles for working with clay, wood, and metals in his sculpture course. With help from the center he videotaped several different introductory comments about the characteristics of each medium, a practice that he said allows him to prepare the best descriptions and demonstrations of which he is capable, while freeing him for working with students as they try to apply those ideas. Robert Bishop talked of the traditional drudgery of teaching basic principles of writing to students in journalism and of how a computer-assisted instructional program provides a more effective and enjoyable method of performing much of that task. Harvey Bertcher told of preparing a mini-course on the development of empathy which he uses in his course on drug counseling in the School of Social Work. William Durham, a graduate teaching assistant, described the seminar that has been set up in the zoology department to help graduate students consider aspects of their new teaching assignments. And Buzz Alexander told of his problems teaching Introduction to the Short Story to large numbers of students and how he has created several student-led discussion sections to provide an opportunity for greater intellectual and personal engagement. This range of people, subject matter, needs, and educational approaches suggests various ways by which a single center can assist different faculty members to achieve their own instructional purposes.

Despite the singularity, even simplicity, of the instructional-development process, there are genuine differences of opinion among practitioners of the art over a number of issues. Some of the most crucial points of difference are the following.

1. Product orientation versus people orientation. Some institutions place greater emphasis on the development of products, various kinds of learning materials, while others place greater emphasis on the development of competencies among faculty.

2. Technology as hardware versus technology as principles of instruction. Some regard technology as hardware, equipment, media, and computers, while others see technology as software, particularly principles of learning and their application to instruction in higher educational settings, often independently of hardware.

3. Concentrated versus "shotgun" approach. Some people argue that a concentration of resources on certain key projects, such as large undergraduate courses, has most long-term impact, while others believe that less intense and short-term relationships involving more faculty members and courses are most beneficial.

4. "Hard core" versus "soft core" instructional development. Some persons emphasize the need to adhere rigidly to the central features of a systematic instructional-development process, arguing that consistency between objectives, instruction, and evaluation is critical. Others believe that it is better to regard the process as only a general guide that can be adapted to a number of concrete situations and supplemented by other efforts to improve teaching.

Despite the variations that exist in the understandings and applications of the instructional-development process, this movement has been closely allied with media centers on most college campuses. Although the organization of instructional-improvement programs is the subject of Chapter Six, this relationship deserves some consideration here. Ron J. McBeath (personal communication, August 15, 1974) has commented that the media center at San Jose State University "became involved in teaching development as a natural outcome of its activities in helping faculty select, produce, and use media in their instructional programs." Indeed, there is a national trend for media centers to become instructional-resource centers with instructional development as one of the services offered to the faculty. One director of the newly renamed Instructional Resources Center confided that he sought the name change as the first step toward adding an instructional-development program, obtaining staff positions, and changing the character of the center. Staff members of media centers long have been second-class citizens in academia, and they see this change as an opportunity to upgrade their status and to get closer to the academic mainstream.

However, media centers that have undergone this metamorphosis find it difficult for a leopard to change its spots. The director of an instructional resource center at a major university lamented that he had "instructional development aspirations but media center personnel," implying that the process of consulting with a faculty member or team to redesign a course or to develop learning materials requires a different set of competencies than are required to work in a media center that merely maintains equipment and distributes materials. (See Chapter Nine.)

But even if a center makes the transition and has staff members that are fully competent in instructional design, it still may encounter problems. The director of one of the leading instructional-development centers reports that even though it is organizationally separate from the media center, it is still seen as a glorified media center by many of the faculty. This misconception may result from the professional background of some key staff members or because their work sometimes involves developing instructional materials using various media. But it could also be that the faculty simply do not comprehend the precise nature of instructional development and fail to differentiate it from the work of the media center. These considerations led Dartmouth College (1973, p. 8) to declare in a proposal to the Alfred P. Sloan Foundation that their proposed Office of Instructional Services "will not be a mere audio-visual or technological ghetto as has happened in so many other universities."

It is significant in this regard that medical and dental colleges have embraced instructional development with an enthusiasm rare among arts and sciences colleges. This may be so for several reasons. First, medical and dental students are required to master large amounts of factual knowledge, which is needed for sophisticated medical practice today, and instructional development is regarded as an important aid toward that end. Also, it is relatively easy to state the specific learning objectives for students in these fields and to assess precisely the extent to which the desired knowledge and skills have been achieved. Another factor is the relative affluence of medical schools, which permits them to make greater investments in the systematic development of courses, modules, and learning materials than can most baccalaureate institutions. Finally, faculty members in medical schools may be more amenable to receiving help with their instruction. Unlike faculty members in departments of English or sociology, for instance, physicians have their primary professional identity outside the academic world, and they may therefore be less defensive about receiving assistance with their teaching.

Instructional developers have had considerable difficulty convincing faculty members of the value of their services. (See Chapter Seven.) Part of this difficulty may be traced to the knee-jerk reaction of many faculty members who dismiss any idea that emanates from media centers; disdain for technological "aids" and "educationist" notions runs deep in the faculty culture. Stanford Ericksen provides a rule of thumb based on his experience at the University of Michigan: wherever "training" is a good word, as in a professional school, these aids are welcomed; wherever it is a bad word, they are not. This differential receptivity probably reflects the greater ease of applying the instructional-development process to more structured subjects where particular competences and sequences of learning experiences are more easily formulated than in the less structured disciplines. But there is also the matter of the language of instructional development with its roots in systems theory and educational technology—language that might appeal more to persons in engineering and science because of their familiarity with such terms. A faculty member said, "I don't understand the jargon of educators"; the fact that the language of instructional development has become quite technical and stylized probably turns off some persons who might otherwise be interested in these forms of innovative instruction. Whatever the cause of this antipathy between some humanists and some instructional developers, it is a two-way street. One developer commented that "conservative humanities faculty consistently oppose instructional development." Notwithstanding this dynamic, there have been many successful projects in such fields as English, history, art, and foreign language. As the many examples cited throughout this chapter illustrate, instructional development has potential for use in any area of the curriculum, or for reshaping the curriculum in its entirety.

Chapter 4

▼▼▼

Organizational Development

▲▲▲

Organizational development, the third major approach used to facilitate the improvement of instruction, not only has merits of its own but may overcome some of the deficiencies of faculty and instructional development. For instance, faculty development tends to focus on single individuals, and practitioners may neglect the fact that faculty members dwell among colleagues and in departments, divisions, schools, universities, or multicampus systems, each of which has its norms, standards, and policies affecting instruction. Faculty who acquire new sensitivities and skills in workshops or retreats may revert to old habits when they return to their familiar haunts—unless the social situation is also changed to support them. Organizational-development spokespersons insist that individual change must receive support from group policies and procedures if it is to be sustained and point out that organizational changes may stimulate more effective teaching and learning among individuals.

Instructional development may focus so narrowly on the tasks of developing learning materials or redesigning courses that it neglects the larger context of the institution. Organizational development, however, places emphasis on the interpersonal aspects of teaching and learning. Instruction is a social as well as an individual activity, and advocates of organizational development assert that efforts to improve instruction must attend to group processes and institutional functioning as well as to the more specific teaching or learning tasks.

Organizational development takes whole institutions or their subunits as its focus and seeks to improve their overall functioning, primarily by systematically applying principles of group process and change. It has been defined in one of the standard texts (French and Bell, 1973, p. 15) as an "effort to improve an organization's problem-solving and renewal processes, particularly through a more effective and collaborative management of organization culture— with special emphasis on the culture of formal work teams—with the assistance of a change agent, or catalyst, and the use of the theory and technology of applied behavioral science."

The several elements of this formal definition may be clarified by amplifying them. Organizations—like individuals—resist change; frequently a consultant can help group members take stock of themselves, examine alternative ways of working together, and make changes that improve the functioning of the group. Because the formal work groups—departments, divisions, or classes in an academic setting, for instance—are the heart of the institution, these groups often serve as the focus of organizational-development efforts. Drawing from the perspectives and theories of the behavioral sciences, organizational-development specialists use a variety of techniques designed to improve communication, enhance morale, and increase the achievements and satisfactions of individuals. In these ways persons may become aware of the culture of their organization and may manage it in ways that allow the group to achieve their common purposes and promote the development of individuals.

The intellectual roots of this approach may be traced to sociology (specifically organizational theory and organizational change), to management, and to social psychology (particularly group dynamics and processes). Its assumptions, concepts, and values are articulated by its seminal thinkers, including Chris Argyris

(1962), Rensis Likert (1967), Douglas McGregor (1960, 1967), and Warren G. Bennis (1969). The concept of organizational development may be better understood if some of the basic assumptions and propositions emanating from these scholars are specified. The following propositions represent a variety of their views and my application of them to colleges and universities.

1. The environment is basic; more than anything else it determines the behavior of individuals. Individual behavior may be changed most effectively by modifying the environment, and individual changes induced apart from the natural environment must be supported by parallel changes in that environment.

2. An organization is a dynamic system of interrelated components; a change in any part of a system requires a change in other parts. Efforts to improve the quality of instruction within a university and to enhance the professional and personal development of faculty members must find support in parallel changes in the functioning of other parts of the institution.

3. Work groups, such as academic departments, not individuals, are the basic building blocks of an organization. Therefore, improvement depends on changing the character of these groups and the relations among their members.

4. Synergism occurs in small groups. Classes, whole departments, and campus teams permit individuals to express their opinions and feelings, get reactions from others, and participate actively in the work of the group. Energy and ideas are unleashed, even generated, in small groups of people who share their experiences and views.

5. Between persons in most organizations barriers develop over time that interfere with their work. Steps may be taken to overcome these barriers and get all individuals to work together to accomplish common goals.

6. Training programs and learning exercises can help individuals learn to work more productively with their colleagues. Various training programs may help leaders to identify needs of the group and develop strategies for satisfying them, assist participants to contribute more effectively to the progress of the group, and aid groups to set goals and devise policies and procedures to achieve their goals.

7. Department chairpeople are the front-line administrators with responsibility for maintaining a climate that facilitates teaching and learning. Because their academic training—usually a doctorate in some academic discipline—does not give them any special preparation to assume these responsibilities, they can benefit from learning ways to improve the functioning of their departments. Central administrators as well as faculty leaders also can benefit from learning more about how to manage the institution.

8. Most organizations can be improved by a periodic review of their functioning and by initiating a process of planned change. The several steps in such change include diagnosing a problem, devising a plan that will solve the problem, implementing the plan, evaluating the effectiveness of the effort, and revising the plan in light of the evaluation.

Process

The broad character of organizational development means that it may be applied to any kind of organization, and indeed, the approach has been applied in such diverse institutions as business, government agencies, and hospitals. Insofar as it has been used in education, elementary and secondary schools have been most commonly involved (Schmuck and Miles, 1971). It is only recently being used in post-secondary education (Boyer and Crockett, 1973).

Raymond E. Miles (1974) has provided a brief history of training programs that have been used to improve organizational productivity, primarily in business and industry. During the early part of this century, training programs were for front-line workers, and they attempted to provide "immediate job skills required to operate an emerging rationalized organizational technology" (p. 172). Later the concern moved upward to include first-line supervisors, such as foremen, and expanded to include human relations problems, such as providing leadership, meting out discipline, and responding to complaints and grievances. Following World War II, concern shifted to management to help executives manage large and increasingly complex organizations; during this time several universities developed programs which included both human relations and problem-solving aspects. Sensitivity training, developed from workshops in Bethel, Maine, in the late 1950s, became popular during the 1960s. The practice in these programs was to put leaders from different organizations together in "stranger groups" where they could increase awareness and responsiveness to immediate inter-personal relationships apart from the press of daily affairs and the constraints of their co-workers. By the late 1960s and early 1970s the difficulty of transferring sensitivities gained in groups of strangers in nonwork settings to conditions of regular work and colleagues became apparent, and organizational development recently has emphasized natural work groups, helping members to examine the way they deal with ordinary, day-to-day problems. Miles (1974, p. 176) comments that "today it is not uncommon to find organiza-tions which may have moved step by step from the practice of send-ing individual executives to off-site T-groups, to the practice of placing numerous executives from different organization units in the same T-group, to the current practice of on-site team training." Yet the historical shift continues as on-site team training has also en-countered problems. "A host of incidents in which work group development efforts were damaged if not destroyed by organizational forces external to the group . . . led to widespread agreement among training specialists that the development target should be not the individual manager or even the work group, but must be the organization as a whole" (Miles, 1974, p. 176). This means that training of individuals and groups must be supplemented by institu-tional structures, policies, norms, and procedures which support individuals and teams. Such is the way most practitioners think of organizational development today.

These various efforts have attempted to improve the func-tioning of many different kinds of organizations. But what makes for effective organizational functioning? According to the leading scholars of this field, an organization is most effective when: trust-ing, open, and honest relationships are found among participants; widespread participation in setting goals and making group decisions is the rule; egalitarian relationships among individuals prevail; members share feelings and ideas and give one another useful, non-threatening feedback; individuals are self-directed and assume re-sponsibility for their behavior; conflicts among individuals are ex-pected, faced, and managed creatively and thoroughly; support for individual growth and development is found in organizational policies and practices; and respect for diverse opinions, work patterns, and life styles is widespread. While these ideals are applicable to a wide variety of organizations, they are particularly appropriate to colleges and universities where academic freedom and a concern for the development of individuals are salient values.

But how can an organization be assisted to develop these qualities? Particularly, how may these qualities be realized in large organizations governed by bureaucratic principles where individuals are expected to "fit in," give up part of their autonomy, and submerge their individuality? There are a number of tools of the trade for organizational developers; those most commonly used have been compiled by The Conference Board (1973), a nonprofit institution concerned with improving business practices.

1. Techniques for setting clear and realistic goals for groups and for individuals are frequently utilized. The goals may be in the area of the major tasks of the organization, such as increased profits for a corporation or improved teaching and learning in a university, or they may be in the personal or interpersonal arenas that are thought to facilitate the realization of the major goals.

2. Setting goals is but the first step. Procedures, including those subsumed by the phrase *management by objectives,* are used in helping leaders work toward the achievement of the identified objectives, prepare criteria and measures of achievement, and monitor progress toward the objectives.

3. Action research, frequently including attitude surveys or interviews about such topics as job satisfaction, superior-subordinate relations, group policies and procedures, morale, and interpersonal relations, is a common approach. Such surveys may identify problems, determine satisfactions or dissatisfactions with many aspects of group life, and indicate the kind of actions that might improve group functioning. Actions undertaken by the group may be evaluated by these research methods.

4. Another class of techniques centers around participative problem-solving in the group. The problems may be either short term or long term, and the techniques used are both rational-intellectual (that is, acquiring more information about the problems)

and experiential (that is, learning new ways to deal with the problems).

5. Improvement in communication is the target of another set of exercises. Using internal or external consultants to serve as group facilitators, many organizations seek to make communication clear and effective among group members, between different levels in the hierarchy, and between different work groups in the organization.

6. All organizations have conflicts; sometimes these conflicts are handled so as to be creative and productive, while other times they become destructive and debilitative forces. Techniques are used to identify conflict, to teach individuals to confront and resolve or accept problems, and to help leaders improve their ability to manage an organization which recognizes and respects individual differences.

7. Job redesign to produce greater satisfaction includes such diverse techniques as enlarging or enriching the nature of a job, clarifying and creating incentives, and establishing "leaderless" or autonomous work groups.

0. Evaluation of the work of the change procedure itself is quite common. The self-conscious examination of planned change efforts not only helps because it leads to understanding of the adequacy of intervention approaches and the learnings of group members, but it serves as a model to help group members become more aware of themselves and their interactions.

These various procedures and techniques, some of which have become quite stylized, are carried out by both internal and external consultants or facilitators. The consultants serve primarily as catalysts for change and use these various techniques as ways of helping group members acquire the sensitivities, knowledge, and skills that will enable them to enhance the effectiveness of the organization on a continuous basis.

Programs

As the foregoing discussion indicates, organizational development is a relatively new concept which grows out of a history of experience in nonacademic settings. This approach rests on a common set of assumptions, conveys a configuration of values about what constitutes an effective organization, and involves a "bag of tricks" by which facilitators practice their art. However, as Boyer (1974, p. 1)' points out, "Applications of organizational development theory and techniques in universities have been very limited. Moreover, the 'state of the art' is quite primitive compared to that in industrial settings where O.D. practice has developed considerable sophistication over the last few years."

Part of the reason why organizational development has not been extensively used in colleges or universities is that they are quite different in character from the business corporations and other organizations where the basic work has been conducted. In particular, the goals of a college or university are less specific and clearcut, involving such intangibles as the education of students and the advance of knowledge rather than the production of goods or services or the generation of profits; academic institutions generally have a more horizontal structure than businesses in that decentralized units such as departments have much authority and responsibility for realizing organizational goals; and the professional staff (professors) consists largely of autonomous experts, each with somewhat different purposes and methods of operating. Given these basic differences, the use of the industrial model for describing academic institutions is a matter of some controversy. On the one hand, conservatives, particularly members of boards of trustees, argue that schools are not run like businesses but they should be; if they were, they would be both more effective and more efficient. On the other hand, radical or liberal students and faculty complain that schools are run like businesses but they ought not to be; students are mass produced by educational factories in which faculty are the workers, department heads the foremen, administrators the managers, and all dehumanized. The great bulk of academics tend toward the latter view and distrust the application of approaches and techniques developed in corporations to their own institutions.

Yet, colleges and universities *are* organizations, and they do function like other organizations in many essential respects. Just as physicians have come to accept that hospitals can be more effectively operated by using management principles and by employing persons with expertise in these areas, so will academics have to recognize that their schools and departments are not so unique that they are immune from organization and management procedures and techniques. However, the concepts, values, and techniques of organizational development do need to be modified to reflect the distinctive character of colleges and universities and to help them achieve their own purposes, which are quite different from those of businesses. This work is presently going on in a number of schools around the country, and the remainder of this chapter will discuss some of these endeavors.

The University of Cincinnati uses two quite different strategies. The Institute for Research and Training in Higher Education has utilized a "bottoms up" approach since it was established during the late 1960s, largely to assist the implementation of affirmative action programs. The staff provides training, consultation, and research services to faculty, administration, staff, and students on matters related to organizational development for instructional improvement. Boyer (1974, p. 8) recounts the work of the institute in this way: "We have been primarily 'bottoms up' change agents who have over a period of years gradually worked our way up through the hierarchy (most theories of O.D. recommend a 'tops down' approach). Initially our only clients were faculty and students, later we worked with whole departments, and recently we have begun work with Deans and top administrators. Now we have some clients at virtually every level and location in the University."

Since Warren Bennis, one of the leading figures in organizational development, became president in 1972, the university has also used a "tops down" approach; a steering committee coordinates the work with the top administrators including the president, vice presidents, and deans. Using internal and external consultants, confidential interviews are conducted with administrators, extensive training sessions held, several follow-up meetings scheduled, seminars organized, and follow-up consultation provided. The "bottoms up" or "tops down" approach—rarely both—is found at increasing numbers of schools.

The program of the institute has placed emphasis on three areas—improving the teaching-learning process, facilitating the organization and management development in various administrative units, and administering an equal opportunity graduate intern-

ship program—as well as engaging in other activities including
assistance to the long-range planning committee of the university.
The way the institute has worked with whole departments during
several years may be illustrative of the application of organizational
development. "As is usually the case with O.D. approaches," Boyer
(1974, pp. 5–6) states, "we attempt to avoid pushing preconceived
solutions, raise the department's organizational knowledge and
awareness of options, and emphasize the use or development of
client resources to solve the organization's problems." The usual
sequence begins when the institute is approached by a department
head for some assistance. Initially the chairperson meets with a staff
member who attempts to get a general understanding of the situation, build a trusting relationship, and establish a clear, mutual
understanding about their relationship. Then data are collected by
means of lengthy interviews (about one and one-half hours), with
all faculty and possibly students, and a questionnaire covering such
issues as departmental priorities, decision-making procedures, social
climate, and interaction among individuals. Feedback of the results
and discussion of their implications occurs in two stages. First, staff
meet with the department chairperson to continue the process of
leadership education begun at entry to help him understand the
data and think about its relevance for himself and the department.
Second, the total department meets for at least three hours to discuss the data and their implications as agreed on at the outset. Follow-
up activities are possible depending on the outcomes of the study
and discussions and may include continued consultation with the
department head on his leadership style, helping the faculty improve
their problem-solving effectiveness, assisting in the revision of the
undergraduate curriculum, and consulting on ways to secure greater
student participation. The institute has worked with departments
from six months to as long as two years, periodically reviewing their
relationship and the benefits derived. It may be significant that this
work disproportionately has involved departments which have a
business rather than a liberal arts thrust, such as architecture, business administration, economics, and nursing; the arts and sciences
departments have been less inclined to these approaches.

The kinds of activities which are a part of organizational
development fall into several major categories.

Utilizing work groups. Departments, schools, committees, and task forces are important work groups in colleges and universities, and the performance of individuals may be facilitated by improving the functioning of these groups. Programs for enhancing work groups may function in either an on-campus or an off-campus environment.

A few off-campus programs utilize a team approach. Perhaps most successful have been the Danforth Foundation Liberal Arts Workshops which bring small groups of faculty members and administrators together for about three weeks. The teams hear lectures, participate in seminars, meet with consultants, and share ideas with other team members as a basis for preparing specific plans for change in some aspect of their institutions.

The use of on-campus teams for renewing colleges and universities is becoming more common, and this approach has perhaps been most thoroughly tested by Walter W. Sikes, Lawrence E. Schlesinger, and Charles N. Seashore (1974). They worked on a five-year National Training Laboratory Institute project, training teams for a wide variety of campus changes. The assumption underlying the project was that "teams using a collaborative action-research strategy could best improve the quality of campus life for themselves and for others" (p. x). Although utilizing off-campus workshops with both experiential and cognitive components, the primary work of the ten- to fifteen-person teams was on their own campuses. While they worked on quite different projects, each of the volunteer teams had the following characteristics:

1. It uses some form of calculated data collection and analysis for diagnosis and action planning.

2. It consciously examines its own functioning.

3. It basically is collaborative in its functioning and in its change strategies.

4. It tries to implement change rather than merely make recommendations to others.

5. The learnings and the relationships of members are viewed as important and valuable outcomes.

6. It often utilizes consultants.

7. It may be initiated in several ways: by administrators, by advocate groups, by departments [p. 54].

The teams sought, with varying degrees of success, to work toward goals as diverse as improving student services, increasing the relevance of a psychology program, improving instruction, and changing a grading system

Training campus leaders. Just as faculty members are given little preparation for their instructional roles, so are administrators and faculty leaders left lacking in formal preparation for their professional responsibilities. It is obvious that a doctorate in French, for example, does not prepare one to be the chairperson of the French department much less the dean of a college. This is not to say leaders are incompetent, but it is to say that most of them acquire their art largely by trial and error, and they understandably ground their work in the folklore of the academy and their own limited experience. This despite the fact that the *raison d'être* for education is to provide cognitive principles that improve on trial-and-error learning; it has been demonstrated often that the folk wisdom of any group of people is only a partial, and sometimes quite distorted, guide to reality. To remedy this state of affairs a number of in-service programs have been established to help administrators learn concepts, acquire skills, and improve techniques of administration and management.

As with early experience in business, the earliest efforts involved administrators going away for some specialized training. For instance, the American Council on Education operates Institutes for College and University Administrators, including separate programs for presidents, deans, and business officers; the National Center for Higher Education Management Systems at the Western Interstate Commission for Higher Education in Boulder, Colorado, conducts seminars for administrators interested in learning to use the information, management, and planning systems they have developed; and the several Kellogg Leadership Centers operated by universities around the country provide preservice and in-service education for community college administrators.

Although many of these off-campus programs focus on fairly specific and practical matters, some are more wide-ranging. The first annual Workshop for New Academic Deans, sponsored jointly by the American Conference of Academic Deans, the Association of American Colleges, and the Council of Colleges of Arts and Sciences, for example, brought together forty-one deans and vice presidents for six days of intensive work with several consultants. Combining lectures, formal discussions, informal discussions, and experiential exercises, the workshop focused on such issues as definition of institutional missions, innovations in the undergraduate curriculum, resource allocation and long-range planning, staffing policies, faculty development and evaluation, the process of change, and new developments in learning. An evaluation which I conducted documents the importance of this kind of workshop. Over three-fourths of the participants said they had never before had an opportunity to consider these several aspects of their work in some depth with colleagues in other schools and with experts in each area. They unanimously said they would "recommend a workshop like this to other new deans." When asked to indicate what they gained from the workshop, the deans said the following benefits were the greatest: "confirmation of previous ideas or policies; information about resources, materials, information, consultants, etc., for use at your institution; development of your concept of the deanship; awareness of political strategies and tactics; and personal growth or renewal."

Even though these are considerable benefits from a mere six days of work, one must wonder how much carry-over value they have. Judging from other programs that take people out of their natural work settings for short periods of training, there is likely to be some slippage in transferring learning back home. The establishment of campus-based programs for administrators and faculty leaders has occurred recently. These have the advantages of making the transfer of learning easier, providing more frequent and continuing training, and being less expensive.

David Whitcomb, a faculty member and member of the Counseling Center on the Long Beach campus, while on temporary assignment at the Chancellor's Office of the California State University and Colleges system, established a system-wide organizational-development project. A group of about twenty persons from campuses throughout the system with expertise in organizational development were identified and met to explore system needs and to prepare a plan for a series of workshops to meet some of the needs. A communication network was created so that these resource persons could compare notes about effective strategies and techniques. A series of

workshops centering on department chairpersons and deans—
strategic campus leaders—was planned and implemented with the
assistance of the resource persons who served as staff. The early
workshops emphasized team building, skills in conducting meetings,
techniques to manage conflict, conceptualization of administrative
roles, development of leadership styles, development of problem-
solving skills, and understanding of system-wide needs.

Department chairpersons are the front-line administrators for
teaching and learning in a college, and some schools have set up
programs to help them perform their work more effectively. John
Noonan at Virginia Commonwealth University, for instance, is
directing a department chairperson program. In early workshops
each person was interviewed about his attitudes toward chairing a
department, assumptions about teaching and learning, conceptions
of leadership, and professional aspirations. After the results of
these interviews were reported to the workshop group, a series of
small group sessions and exercises designed to help them specify their
assumptions, clarify their values, and enhance their leadership styles
were held. Consultation with individual department chairpersons
and follow-up work that might involve all members of a department
were provided for those units which were interested.

Providing training in interpersonal relations. Campus leaders
not only need concepts, skills, and techniques of management, but
they must be able to cope with the human side of their organization.
Indeed, there are those who argue that this is their most important
task. Programs to increase self-consciousness, sensitivity to other
people, and interpersonal skills operated by such places as the National Training Laboratory in the East and Esalen Institute in the
West have attracted hundreds of executives and professionals from
every field of work. Although the evaluations of sensitivity training
are inconclusive (Back, 1972; Lieberman, Yalon, and Miles, 1971)',
it is clear that they have lost much of their popular appeal recently.

Academics seem particularly suspicious of "process" training
techniques where the content is the group interaction of "stranger
groups." They seem to be more amenable to "task-oriented sensitivity groups," those that focus on the assumptions, feelings, values,
and other noncognitive aspects of their work. These groups require
that individuals expose their feelings and values only insofar as they

pertain to the task or mission of the work group. A number of programs help administrators cope with the affective side of their work.

Workshops and seminars are held among the administrative staffs of several institutions to help individuals give useful, nonthreatening feedback to others, manage productively the conflict which exists in virtually any group, identify and develop their own leadership styles, build trust, and encourage free and open communication. The Office of Staff and Organizational Development at Miami-Dade Community College worked with the top administrative staff for two years on such procedures as management by objectives, setting goals, designing programs, and evaluating goal achievement. Carol Zion and her colleagues met regularly with the administrators and led the group in a series of training exercises designed to help them share their feelings and thoughts openly, create a climate of trust, and learn from one another. Thus they improved their interpersonal relationships and engaged in teambuilding at the same time they learned a number of management concepts and techniques. Subsequently, this approach was extended to include the faculty and modified to emphasize the issues of concern to teaching faculty.

When Zion was asked about the impact of the program at Miami-Dade, she related the following. In March of 1969 she started by meeting with the chief administrative officer on the campus to plan a program which could be implemented with support from a forward-looking state-funded Program for Staff and Program Development. (See Chapter Eight.) Five years later, after countless workshops, seminars, retreats, consultations, and other activities, they had just concluded a workshop to prepare another five-year plan. There were now thirty persons involved, ranging in status from the chief administrative officer to first-year faculty members. Before the group broke for lunch one day, a young faculty member asked for the participants to "process" the discussion they had had, that is, to analyze the progress of the group and their ways of working. Zion was able to note the changes over the five years. These participants were sensitive to the process of interaction and able to "process a group"; the younger persons felt free to ask for the group to analyze the interaction among individuals; and individuals expressed their feelings freely and nonthreateningly. Improved interpersonal relationships were widely attested to by many persons throughout the college and much credit for this change was attributed to this program.

There is a perfectly respectable theory that holds that when relationships are improved among top administrators and between administrators and faculty, they will lead to an improvement in relationships among faculty members and between faculty and students. Although there is little solid empirical evidence to support this theory as applied to academia, it does make sense that faculty members who are treated with respect and dignity by their administrative staff will accord these same courtesies to their students, solicit student views, and respond to student interests.

Facilitating faculty development. Deans and department chairpersons are in key positions to facilitate the development of faculty members in their units. If the most important educational resource is the faculty, and if they truly seek to create a "talent pool" among their staffs, they must play a special role in nurturing the professional and personal growth of individual faculty members. This means that administrators must know the faculty well enough to identify their needs, be aware of the resources—both material and less tangible ones—they have control over, use the resources to support the efforts of individuals, and create a climate where individuals learn from one another.

A common academic tragedy is that administrators often do not know their faculty colleagues well enough to know what they need. Some large departments have over one hundred faculty members, and presidents and vice presidents of moderate or large universities seldom have more than superficial contact with most of the faculty members; the large scale of many institutions has depersonalized higher education not only for students but for faculty and administrators as well. But even where size permits frequent and personal contact, real understanding is hindered by the traditional barrier between administrators and faculty members and the guarded communication that occurs among persons differing in status or power.

In this situation some administrators, like Richard Gross, Vice President and Dean of the Faculty at Gordon College, interview each faculty member each year (see Chapter Six). Their conversations center around the professor's strengths and weaknesses, and they include a consideration of ways he may seek to improve some aspect of his work during the coming year. Then individualized "growth contracts" are prepared by the instructor, detailing the goals, procedures, and bases for evaluation of his own professional-development plan. The administrator is responsible for providing the resources to allow the individual to implement the mutually agreed-upon plan.

What resources do administrators have at their disposal for supporting and encouraging faculty? More than most are aware of. They include the obvious power to recommend retention, promotion, and salary increases, dispense travel money, give research support, make extension or summer teaching assignments, and provide graduate or clerical assistance. But they also include the authority to make teaching assignments in terms of courses, hours, and times of day, the ability to call attention to the contributions of individuals, and even the opportunity to thank an individual for a special contribution he makes to the life of the school.

Faculty members are a peculiar breed in that, more than most workers, they have an intrinsic interest and are highly ego-involved in their work. Perhaps more than anything they want to be recognized and appreciated for their professional competence. At a meeting of organizational-development specialists assembled recently, this fact became crystal clear. One individual from the nearly twenty present who does extensive consulting outside his university confessed that this was the first time he had been asked to contribute any of his professional expertise to his own institution, and one after the other of those present confirmed the observation with their own experiences. Here were several "experts" who were willing—even eager—to contribute to their schools and be recognized as professionally competent, and it was the first time any of them ever had been asked.

So administrators need to learn how to use their resources to support and encourage faculty. But they also have a responsibility to obtain material resources and to help faculty obtain their own resources. Often this means allocating one's budgeted funds or making a case before superiors on behalf of a faculty member with a worthy project, but it also may mean seeking outside funding.

Faculty members are notoriously poor at writing proposals for funding educational projects; they are likely to be much better at
writing proposals for research projects in their discipline. Thus, one
part of professional development of administrators is learning how
to obtain external support for worthy projects and help their faculty
learn how to write good proposals.

Forming institutional policies. Some persons, such as Victor
Baldridge of California State University, Fresno, argue that although
workshops for campus leaders or team building among work groups
are of value, the best approach to the improvement of instruction
is a well-administered university. That is, clearly stated and well-
implemented institutional policies which emphasize effective teaching
and support faculty and instructional development are the best route
to an effectively functioning university. Accordingly, some institutions focus their efforts on reviewing existing personnel and academic
policies and procedures and revising them where necessary.

Fresno, for example, in addition to holding workshops for
top administrators, faculty leaders, and department chairpersons,
has created a presidential Task Force on Faculty Development. This
task force is working with appropriate academic senate committees
and university administrators to make a comprehensive review of all
major personnel practices, including promotions, tenure, sabbatical
leave, and salary practices. The goal is to revise and systematize all
personnel practices so that appointments, promotions, and tenure
practices will emphasize the importance of faculty development and
instructional improvement. One of the early results is a new set of
guidelines governing sabbatical leaves. The new guidelines encourage faculty to use such leaves for activities leading to the improvement of instruction and retraining in areas of new student demand
as well as continued mastery of one's field of specialization. And,
although these are not a radical departure from past practices, the
Vice President for Academic Affairs and the Personnel Committee
are requiring closer review, better justification for proposals, and
wiser use of sabbatical leaves.

Institutional policies surrounding the advancement procedures have been the focus of attention at many schools. It is common knowledge that effective teaching, innovative instruction, and
self-improvement efforts have not been given adequate recognition

at many schools. But there is some evidence that this situation is changing. The survey of directors of instructional-improvement programs and centers conducted as one phase of this study reveals the strong sentiment that the "overall climate at (their) institutions in regard to teaching improvement" has become more favorable over the last couple of years. Reasons given by the directors include the reduction of external research money available to faculty, declining student enrollments, administrative leadership, and tightening of the advancement system to require greater evidence of teaching effectiveness. This configuration suggests that the external pressures of money and students already have been translated by central administrators, those individuals with a major responsibility for communicating between the institution and the larger community, into more rigorous advancement procedures.

Yet the task is unfinished. Faculty members are seldom given release time to work on instructional- or faculty-development projects, and unless they see some payoff for themselves, voluntary efforts will be difficult to sustain over the long haul. (See Chapters Six and Seven.) Some schools report that not only do faculty often not get "brownie points" for improvements efforts, they are sometimes "punished" for paying too much attention to their teaching. At Florida State University, the academic senate is considering a resolution supported by the Division of Instructional Research and Service to regard a learning module or a course prepared by a faculty member equivalent to a publication in the advancement system, if it is an "inheritable" product which, like a textbook, may be adopted without modification by other instructors. While this proposal is hanging fire, the Florida legislature has contributed to the matter by debating the proposal that every state employee must be given a job description and be evaluated in light of that description. Although seemingly benign, this law—if enacted—may be expected to have a profound impact by specifying that a major portion of professors' jobs involve teaching, and an evaluation of their performance would legally require that comparable weight be given to their teaching effectiveness.

The advancement system affects the work of instructional-improvement efforts in another way. Directors and staff members of such programs often have joint appointments in an academic department, and they sometimes find their own advancement blocked by these departments. One center for the improvement of teaching lost its director because his department in the humanities failed to recommend tenure, arguing that directing the university-wide program has nothing to do with scholarship or teaching of the academic specialization. At another center, staff members with joint appointments in the psychology department have not been able to get promotions or tenure largely because the substantial and high-quality research they have done in teaching and learning is not viewed as the kind of research acceptable to "hard core" psychologists.

Although faculty- and instructional-development staff are obviously interested in these matters and are sometimes sought for formal or informal advice, they generally try to work independently of the reward structure so they can continue to work with faculty in a nonthreatening context. But organizational-development programs do examine and strive to improve the reward system. One outcome of such work may be seen at Miami-Dade where participation in instructional-improvement activities counts toward advancement. Faculty members are given a number of points for attending seminars or workshops on such topics as course development, student learning styles, and interpersonal dynamics. When a certain number of points are accumulated, the faculty member qualifies for a promotion and salary increase. This system places in-service education for instructional improvement on an equal footing with course work taken in the subject matter at a university insofar as promotion and salary are concerned.

These, then, represent beginning efforts to apply organizational-development concepts, values, methods, and techniques to colleges and universities. Improving the functioning of work groups, training campus leaders, providing training in interpersonal relations, helping administrators learn how to facilitate faculty and instructional development, and developing supportive institutional policies are all efforts to make colleges and universities effectively functioning organizations. Collectively these separate thrusts add up to a promising approach to the renewal of colleges and universities and to the improvement of instruction.

Chapter 5

▼▼

Overview of
New Programs

▲▲

Having discussed the changing concepts of instructional improvement and having treated in some detail the different approaches of faculty, instructional, and organizational development, we can now step back and consider these programs from different perspectives. First, up to this point each approach has been treated separately, largely to provide conceptual clarity about the many different activities carried on by each. But operational instructional-improvement programs frequently include faculty, instructional, *and* organizational components, and this fact deserves to be discussed. And, second, differences between the three approaches have been implicit in earlier discussions, but they can be more sharply drawn and summarized.

The extended treatment given to each of these three approaches in Chapters Two through Four may lead some to think that all programs are based on well-formulated assumptions and principles, embody a careful analysis of the precise outcomes desired, and engage in those activities consciously designed to achieve those ends. This is simply not true; people and programs are not as rational as these descriptions make them appear. Most actual programs are the result of a confluence of several factors besides a program plan, such as the particular talents or skills of individuals, the interests of specific faculty members and administrators, the availability of funds for certain activities, and the inevitable vicissitudes of campus politics. Few colleges or universities have a coherent, logical, and consistent program of instructional improvement, because the events surrounding the preparation, adoption, and implementation of such a plan almost surely result in compromises that make its actual operation more responsive to the practical needs of people and politics and less conceptually pure than it might be.

Yet, the terms—faculty, instructional, and organizational development—are useful. This is partly because they are empirically derived; that is, they are used by many individuals who staff instructional-improvement programs to characterize their work. Also, they provide a conceptual framework within which the various assumptions, goals, and activities that are part of different programs may be comprehended. Together, they provide an understanding of the intellectual bases on which various instructional-improvement programs are built. Following are examples of programs using more than one approach.

Although the previous discussions have been focused on either faculty, instructional, or organizational development, several programs—indeed some of the most exciting—combine elements of each in a comprehensive program. Recall the description of the College Center of the Finger Lakes contained in Chapter Two, where a concern for individual, instructional, and organizational development was manifest at the outset. Although few new programs begin with such a comprehensive vision, some have set their sights high.

In addition to consciously designed comprehensive programs, other programs that are narrowly focused on instructional, faculty, or organizational development tend to reach across these categories to embrace the others. Indeed, there appears to be a natural tendency for programs in each area to broaden their concerns and encompass the other two areas simply as a means to the realization of their own goals.

Robert Diamond, for example, in his presentation at the National Conference of the American Association for Higher Education in 1974 discussed the instructional-development program at Syracuse University. After describing the way instructional development is practiced there, he pointed out that it is necessary to have an institutional climate favorable to such a program if it is to be successful. Syracuse established a Center for Instructional Development with adequate staff and budgetary support, but it also supported the program in a number of other tangible ways. First, it budgeted special funds to support instructional-development projects including reduced teaching loads or extra employment for the faculty involved. Second, a variable credit procedure was adopted to provide a high degree of course flexibility for the individualized study programs the center produced, thereby allowing a student to get credit for just the portion of the courses he completes. Third, a continuous registration procedure was implemented to permit students to start and end courses at their own pace. Additionally, a copyright policy that protects the interests of both the faculty member and the institution was devised concerning materials produced by the projects. Diamond's active leadership in effecting these organizational changes has been important in creating a climate supportive of the individualized learning systems his center has helped faculty to create. Similarly, the faculty members who became involved in the work of the center have had to learn new ideas and new ways of working with both students and colleagues in designing and implementing the individualized courses. Diamond claims that such new learning has led some faculty members to make rather dramatic changes in their teaching styles, changes that are associated with greater student learning. Thus, an instructional-development program may entail organizational and faculty development if it is to succeed in its own terms.

While working from the framework of faculty development, John Noonan at Virginia Commonwealth University has found it necessary to go beyond a concern for the individual faculty members and to work on organizational components. As was mentioned in Chapter Four, he is working with department chairpersons, whom he regards as critical front-line administrators, and has held work-shops of entire departments as a way of enhancing the effectiveness of many departments. Similarly, a large portion of the center's program focuses on topics directly related to instructional matters. A weekly series of on-campus workshops feature such topics as setting objectives, conducting evaluation, and considering the various teaching styles of faculty and learning styles of students. Thus, to realize its own purposes of developing faculty members, this program has included organizational and instructional components.

The efforts of Ronald Boyer, Anthony Grasha, and their associates at the University of Cincinnati in organizational development are similar. Their institute was concerned largely with organizational development, and as was discussed in Chapter Four, has provided several organizational-development services to the academic departments and to the central administration. However, they found out early that if they could offer some assistance to the departments in improving the instructional program, a service with high face validity, that provided a good entree to work on other organizational matters. And, of course, studies of departmental functioning and workshops emphasizing group processes engage faculty members and affect their development as individuals as well as group members.

Even though they focus on one approach, each of these exemplary programs incorporates aspects of the other two. Each in its own way has found it necessary to develop into a comprehensive program, one that transcends the narrow definitions previously given to faculty, instructional, and organizational development.

Two forms of comprehensive programs have been mentioned, those designed to be holistic and those that branch out from either faculty-, instructional-, or organizational-development approaches to embrace the others. A third form, a decentralized one, is found at California State University, Long Beach. There, three different programs are operated out of different campus settings. James Robinson has directed the Faculty Career Development Center which sponsors a series of workshops for faculty, provides feedback to faculty concerning their teaching by means of videotapes, and publishes a newsletter. Frank Christ, Coordinator of Learning Assistance, has developed a Learning Assistance Support System to mobilize existing campus and community resources for learning and to help develop self-paced instructional programs. David Whitcomb, working out of the Counseling Center, provides workshop and consultation services to several departments on campus to facilitate organizational renewal. This kind of organizational arrangement allows the university to operate each type of program but to avoid some of the difficulties of having such different approaches under the same roof.

Any college or university has a great diversity of faculty members, and a comprehensive program seems more capable of meeting the diverse needs of faculty at different stages in their lives and careers and with different educational philosophies and personal styles than any more narrowly conceived program. Further, a comprehensive program is capable of making a more holistic and integrated impact on faculty than a single-purpose one. If it is important for faculty members to function effectively as individual professionals, as instructors, and as organization members, than all of these features need to be incorporated into a comprehensive instructional-improvement program. This is precisely why the new concepts of instructional improvement have so much power: they embrace several aspects of academic life that have relevance for the central activities of teaching and learning. Any of the three different approaches, individually or collectively, if followed to their logical conclusions, would lead to far-reaching changes in academic life, changes designed to improve the education of students.

Although comprehensive instructional-improvement programs have been established, and faculty-, instructional-, and organizational-development programs have a tendency to become more comprehensive as they pursue their distinctive goals, each of these various programs also tends toward exclusiveness. It has been pointed out that programs of faculty, instructional, and organizational development have different foci, seek different ends, draw from different intellectual traditions, and have different conceptual frameworks. These differences are so great that they tend to function as separate conceptual paradigms (Kuhn, 1962); practitioners often see the world through one of these sets of glasses and are unable to sympathize with the other approaches, thus presenting a barrier to the inclusion of alternative approaches.

The differences extend beyond concepts into language and

lexicon, as each group has developed its own jargon. Faculty-development persons tend to talk in terms of "teaching effectiveness," "professional development," "personal growth," and the "acquisition of classroom skills and techniques." Instructional developers are partial to the improvement of "instruction," the design of "instructional delivery systems," "learning materials," and "individualized or innovative instruction." Organizational development specialists talk fondly of "team building," "problem solving," "leadership training," and "communication skills" and favor other terms that emphasize the interpersonal processes of academic life.

The prevalence of these terms that have taken on special meanings for persons working in instructional-improvement programs has posed continuous problems in conducting this research. At the outset I was ignorant of the significance of the different words and phrases used by individuals at the schools I was studying. In preparing a questionnaire for directors of instructional-improvement programs and centers, for instance, I settled on the general and innocuous term of "teaching resource unit" to characterize the kinds of places I had in mind, and explained that "this questionnaire is designed to gather information from a variety of *teaching improvement* efforts in different schools." One director of an *instructional*-development program wrote a marginal note on the returned questionnaire saying that "we should differentiate instructional development from faculty development. All questions have been answered in terms of instructional development in its broadest sense, *not* teaching effectiveness which is but one element of ID as we define it." It eventually dawned on me that several common words had taken on special connotations, in some cases technical meanings, by the practitioners of these new arts, and it became necessary for me to develop a linguistic self-consciousness that allowed me to use the "in-house" terms when talking or corresponding with persons of each persuasion but to use nontechnical language and avoid pet phrases of any camp when addressing mixed audiences.

The differences between faculty, instructional, and organizational development are conceptual and linguistic, to be sure, but they are even more deeply rooted than that. There is a sociology involved too. Although evidence is limited, it seems that proponents of these various approaches tend to come from different educational backgrounds, to have different professional memberships and ties, and to read different journals. Instructional development, perhaps because it has been the first of these approaches to be practiced in higher education and is, therefore, the most professionally advanced of the three, appears to have the most distinguishable profile in these matters. Instructional developers tend to come from fields of education, educational psychology, and instructional media; they frequently are members of the Association for Educational Communication and Technology, especially its Division of Instructional Development; and they read about their craft in such journals as *Educational Technology, AV Communication Review,* and *Audiovisual Instruction.* This association and these journals hold little interest for persons who think of themselves as working in faculty organizational development.

Faculty-development experts tend to come disproportionately from psychology, particularly with specialties in clinical, developmental, and educational psychology, and to a lesser extent from among assorted academic departments throughout the university; although no association has yet created a special division devoted to their interests, they often look to organizations such as the American Association for Higher Education, the American Psychological Association, and the American Educational Research Association for professional colleagues; and they frequently read psychology journals, such as the *Journal of Educational Psychology,* education journals, such as the *Journal of Higher Education* and the *American Educational Research Journal,* and assorted other periodicals in applied behavioral science.

Organizational development in higher education is even less formalized than faculty development, although it is more widespread as an approach in other social institutions. Its practitioners, more than those in faculty and instructional development, tend to have emphasized group processes and organizational functioning in their psychology, sociology, and business administration backgrounds; they frequently are members of the American Psychological Association, American Sociological Association, and American Educational Research Association; and they rely on publications such as the

Journal of Applied Behavioral Science and the *Administrative Science Quarterly* as well as other periodicals concerned with applied behavioral science in higher education.

This characterization of the sociology of instructional-improvement efforts should not be construed as a series of absolute statements. There are individuals who do not fit these generalizations. Douglas Alder, a historian, has provided leadership for Utah State's instructional-development program, Carol Zion with a background in English and business administration has established a fine organizational-development program at Miami-Dade, and Stanford's David Halliburton in comparative literature as well as historian Stephen Scholl of the Great Lakes Colleges Association have provided sound leadership for their institutions' faculty-development programs. Nonetheless, there are important differences in the professional backgrounds and practices of persons operating these different kinds of instructional-improvement programs. Even this brief excursion into the sociology of the matter indicates that the differences between the various forms of development are deeper than mere differences of terminology, opinion, or personal preference. Despite important overlaps, the basic professional structure of each approach functions to keep them separate from one another.

This discussion of differences between the three approaches to instructional improvement is of more than academic interest, because they have implications for the future of such programs. For example, those attending a meeting of directors of instructional-improvement centers and programs hoped to share common concerns and learn from one another. Although there were many similarities, it soon became apparent that there were fundamental differences among participants. People were talking right past each other—not an unusual occurrence at professional gatherings, to be sure, but quite unexpected among people who were brought together because of their common interests. Although all were interested in instructional-improvement programs, participants held quite different views about what the problems were and about how they should be addressed. The fact that several persons used words with the kinds of special meanings discussed earlier merely added to the confusion.

Not only do these differences create confusion among professionals and laymen alike, they also occasion competitiveness, suspicion, and even conflict within this burgeoning movement. Leaders in the area of *faculty* development have confided that *instructional*-development advocates seem to be trying to build "mechanical systems" that "any boob can manage" and that efforts to get faculty to use new "techniques, gadgets or gimmicks" are trivial unless they are grounded in his or her own personal approach to teaching. And *instructional developers* often press faculty- and organizational-development specialists to demonstrate that their seminars or workshops have a clear and beneficial impact on student learning, a nearly impossible feat. Some instructional developers argue that it is at worst "dangerous" or at best "irrelevant" to try to change professors or institutions unless the effects on student learning are specified.

Further, each type of development may appeal to different kinds of faculty, and each type probably turns off other kinds. In the California State University and Colleges system there are practitioners of each of the three major types of development, and there are benefits in each. But also individuals have said, "So and so is a nice enough person, but I don't think that approach is very helpful," or "Our faculty would never buy that approach." The practical lesson is that a variety of approaches may reach more persons than any single approach, largely because of the diversity among faculty members and students. Surely, no single approach will meet the needs of all; panaceas have been no more common in education than in any other area of social life.

Also, practitioners of instructional improvement need to gain an appreciation of the broad spectrum of activities that are being conducted at colleges and universities around the country under rubrics different from their own. But merely being aware of these differences is not enough; a sympathetic tolerance of these different approaches, based on an understanding of their basic rationales and intentions, is also needed. After all, faculty, instructional, and organizational development may enhance the impact of any single approach.

Chapter 6

▼▼▼▼▼▼▼▼▼▼▼▼▼▼▼▼▼▼▼▼▼▼▼▼▼▼▼▼▼▼▼▼▼▼▼▼▼

Organizing for Improving Teaching and Learning

▲▲▲▲▲▲▲▲▲▲▲▲▲▲▲▲▲▲▲▲▲▲▲▲▲▲▲▲▲▲▲▲▲▲▲▲▲

"During the past several years," Lawrence T. Alexander and Stephen L. Yelon wrote in 1972 (p. 1), "in response to increasingly widespread dissatisfaction with the quality of undergraduate education, several colleges and universities have created a unique kind of agency whose function is to assist college faculty improve their instruction. These agencies may vary in the scope of their activities from one institution to another, but they all have one goal in common: to contribute to the development of improved college instruction." The most visible sign of the growing importance of instructional improvement is the creation of such centers, offices and divisions in all kinds of colleges and universities, state systems, consortia, and educational associations.

Actually there are many ways to provide organizational support for faculty-, instructional- and organizational-development ac-

tivities, depending on the kind of institution, the purposes of the
program, the resources available, and the interests and talents of the
existing staff.

Administrative Leadership

Central academic administrators—vice presidents, provosts,
deans—often assume the leadership in focusing attention on teaching
within their units. Kenneth E. Eble (1971; 1972) has discussed
several ways administrators of departments, divisions, colleges, and
whole institutions may foster faculty development, but the work of
three persons may illustrate the range of activities in which they
engage.

Charles Neidt (1974), Vice President for Academic Affairs
at Colorado State University, argues that there are three loci of responsibility if an institution is to have an effective program for
faculty members and administrators. First, the responsibility for
professional development rests ultimately with each individual; all
development in the final analysis is personal and cannot be imposed
on another. Second, the responsibility for providing opportunities
and resources for individuals seeking improvement rests with the
chief administrator of each unit, that is, the department chairperson
or the dean of the college. Third, the responsibility for establishing,
testing, and maintaining a comprehensive professional-development
program, including the establishment of policies, the allocation of
fiscal resources, the securing of professional expertise, and the provision of opportunities for on-campus and off-campus experiences,
rests with the institution. Neidt himself is active in each area. He is
attentive to his own professional development by continuing to be
active in his academic specialty of personnel work, which is intimately
related to this aspect of his administrative work. He seeks to obtain
and provide resources for faculty renewal to the units for which he
is responsible. For instance, an Assistant Academic Vice President
for Instructional Development, Frank Vattano, has been appointed
to coordinate several learning resources, instructional-improvement
grants have been provided, and a faculty seminar has been instituted;
these services are in addition to the usual travel money, research
support, and sabbatical leaves that are provided. But perhaps most
important, from his role as vice president, Neidt is helping the

institution create a comprehensive program for individual development. By working through the various schools and their several departments, he has managed to prepare and obtain endorsement of a statement of institutional goals. Using this goals statement, he has asked each school and department to create long-range plans for their units which are consistent with the institutional missions, including provisions for the growth of the faculty. These several plans have recently been accepted after much discussion, revision, and refinement, and collectively they constitute a five-year plan for the university. Presently he is working on an institutionwide faculty-development plan which will be needed if faculty members are to implement the academic plans that have been made. This ambitious approach is illustrative of the way a single administrator may take the lead in fostering professional development.

A somewhat different approach is used by John Bevan (1974), formerly academic vice-president at Davidson College and now vice president for academic affairs at the College of Charleston. Bevan combines a clear vision of an abstract ideal with an acute sense of the practical needs of specific individuals. His ideal is embodied in the concept of a faculty as a resource pool. Each faculty member has certain talents, some of which he needs to maintain, others of which he needs to improve, and still others which may continue to be undernourished. Bevan sees that it is his job to stimulate, encourage, and support individuals in the development of their various talents, and he pursues this goal aggressively. He finds money to send a French teacher on her first trip to France, and she returns excited, wiser, and more experienced in her subject matter. He hires emeritus professors part-time to serve as supervisors of student independent study projects, which draws retired faculty into the college community and augments their incomes while giving students access to sustained attention from faculty members for their individual projects, and all at modest costs. He helps faculty members turn their ideas about educational programs into proposals for grants to support their instructional interests, which, they discover, is quite different from writing a research grant proposal. These and countless other actions constitute one-half of Bevan's day-to-day approach to faculty development.

The other half of the vision is that each faculty member is

seen not only as a developing individual but as an integral part of the college community. This means that each person has a responsibility to share his talents with others in the community, and it gives each person the opportunity to tap the knowledge, experience, wisdom, and fellowship of the entire faculty and use it to his advantage. Thus, individual development contributes directly to the development of a rich community which, in turn, contributes to individual development. To implement this half of the concept Bevan interviews at length every faculty member before he is hired to inculcate a sense of what the college is like, indicate what he will expect of the individual, and discover what that person may bring to the school. This interview helps to "define the situation," as W. I. Thomas used to say, to set expectations which will lead to the kind of sharing Bevan thinks is essential in an institution devoted to liberal learning that transcends the usual barriers of academic specializations and departments. Then he actively finds ways to bring people with common interests together or to put a person with a need in touch with a colleague who can assist. One outcome of this effort is an interdisciplinary educational effort to study the social, economic, and political factors that affect the life of a river basin. The active collaboration of faculty whose interests meshed, along with Bevan's support, led to this novel field study program for several students. Efforts to combine individual development with the creation of a college community make sense, particularly for a small liberal arts college, and they command the attention of other program planners.

To Neidt's planning and Bevan's creation of a resource pool among faculty may be added the approach of Richard Gross, Vice President and Dean of the Faculty at Gordon College in Massachusetts, which emphasizes individualized growth contracts. A pilot program is based on the principles of diversity of human strengths, opportunity for individualization, comprehensiveness that encompasses all faculty roles, self-imposition of goals and means, measurement of growth, continuous and systematic planning and assessment, and relationships to the reward system and personnel decisions. The program requires each faculty member, in consultation with his department head and in the context of a statement of the above principles, to devise a development plan which includes the following information (Gross, 1974, p. 4):

A. An assessment of strengths and weaknesses

B. His intended areas of contribution to the total role responsibilities of the faculty

C. A specific statement of goals and plans for personal improvement and professional growth

D. A plan of evaluation for B and C above including (1) measurable criteria, (2) an evaluation committee, (3) length of the plan and time(s) at which evaluation will be made. Periodic assessment and continuing feedback to the faculty member is an essential aspect of the plan.

At the conclusion of the plan the evaluation committee and the faculty member prepare a written summary of the plan which becomes a part of his dossier. Gross has taken the lead in implementing this plan by writing his own growth contract and sharing it with the faculty. Thus a development program is tailored to the needs of each individual while meeting institutional needs.

There are doubtless many individuals in the administration of institutions of higher learning who engage in a wide variety of development activities, but the sad fact is that the initiatives of Neidt, Bevan, and Gross are the exceptions rather than the rule. Whereas at one time the dean was regarded as an intellectual and educational leader of the faculty, the first among equals, the dean's role has too often become bureaucratized, routinized, and trivialized, insofar as meaningful work with the faculty is concerned. There are good reasons why deans, provosts, and vice presidents seldom function as faculty- or institutional-development facilitators. Burdened with paper work, committee work, and many other institutional responsibilities, even those academic administrators with institutional responsibilities and personal inclinations to do development work with faculty members seldom have time to do so. Further, line administrators do not necessarily possess the professional expertise or personal qualities to facilitate the growth of individuals. Finally, and perhaps most important, they occupy positions of authority over the faculty. Just as Freud long ago pointed out that a person who occupies an authority relationship to a patient cannot provide effective psychotherapy, so have many administrators learned that academics hesitate to reveal their weaknesses, fears, concerns, or needs to a person in a position of authority over them; such a person may hold such information against them in other situations. These limitations indicate that however effective some line administrators may be in providing leadership for the development of faculty and the improvement of instruction, additional programs may provide useful supplementary benefits.

Faculty Groups

Groups of faculty members are another vehicle for conducting faculty-development programs. Many institutions have something like a Committee on Teaching, and some have created new Faculty Development Committees; either of these would appear to be a logical means for planning and coordinating an instructional-improvement program. For example, the University of New Hampshire established a Teaching/Learning Council consisting of eleven faculty members, nine students, two administrators, and a faculty member as half-time chairperson. Under sponsorship of this council, a universitywide system of student rating of teaching was instituted, a newsletter was published, an inventory of all new and experimental courses was made and published, symposia on teaching-learning issues were held, a regional conference on teaching was hosted, and small grants to faculty members for course- or teaching-improvement projects were made.

The forty-two schools which participated in the first phase of the Faculty Development Project of the Council for the Advancement of Small Colleges built small groups of faculty members to provide the core of their faculty-development work. Three faculty members, the dean, and the president attended a week-long summer institute in 1974 after which the groups of three faculty members were expanded to nine. Team building and development of procedures to develop and utilize human and material resources of the campus were objectives of follow-up workshops and consultations. The teams engaged in a wide range of activities including conversations about teaching and learning, planning new incentive structures that give more weight to teaching effectiveness, realigning the faculty workload, giving critiques of one another teaching class, learning about the research on effective teaching, and discussing one another's special intellectual interests.

This approach, which relies on the work of teaching faculty, has high face validity; they are the front line of the instructional program and in a fundamental sense know best what they and the program need most. Further, this approach also has important strategic benefits; teaching faculty may secure the involvement of colleagues in a way that administrators and "experts" are unable to do. However, faculty groups have several disadvantages. Members have little time to devote to this demanding task, particularly since they seldom are rewarded for their efforts; they have little expertise or experience in instructional-improvement programs, a condition that may constrict their imaginations; they often are unaware of resources they can draw on for their programs; and continuity in the face of changing committee or team membership may be difficult. But perhaps the most important problem is that the faculty may conceive of development too narrowly and in traditional ways, for instance, merely enhancing subject matter competence through research grants, sabbaticals, or travel to association meetings.

That these problems may be overcome is illustrated by Cleveland State University. The Innovative Teaching Group, a collection of faculty who met together informally, fostered an intense dialogue about teaching and learning. Although not a formal committee, they planned and eventually established a Center for Effective Learning so that some of their members could acquire expertise in this area and sustained attention would be focused on the improvement of instruction throughout the institution. Unlike most such centers, which are administratively located in the office of the dean or academic vice-president, it is governed by a steering committee composed of twelve full-time faculty drawn from each of the five colleges; it shapes policies, supervises their implementation, and approves professional staff hiring. Under the leadership of the center, a wide range of instructional-improvement activities are conducted.

Individuals with Specialized Appointments

A third way of organizing is to assign responsibility for development of faculty, instruction, or the organization to persons who occupy one of a number of specialized academic positions. Because colleges and universities are complex organizations, they have many kinds of positions and employ persons with diverse talents who might provide leadership for faculty-development efforts. In addition, new positions have been created specifically to facilitate the improvement of teaching. Some of the positions from which various individuals have provided leadership in campus professional-development activities are listed below.

University Professor. Several institutions have created university professorships and appointed a few specially selected senior faculty members to such positions. The appointment typically permits faculty members to teach courses in any department of the university and take the lead in several institutional innovations. Such faculty members are widely respected for their effectiveness as teachers and are a potentially valuable contribution to an instructional-improvement program. For instance, Parker Lichtenstein took a leave from Dennison University to become the first director of the instructional-development program initiated by the University of Redlands in 1972. After two years he returned to Dennison, where as university professor he currently is devoting a portion of his energies to coordinating the campus faculty-development program and serving as the campus liaison person for the Faculty Development Program of the Great Lakes College Association in which the school is participating. Several younger colleagues at Redlands commented that they appreciated not only discussing their instructional concerns with a knowledgeable and sympathetic person but benefited from the wisdom and perspectives that such a senior statesman like Lichtenstein could provide.

Educational Development Officer. A position conceived by the Regional Educational Laboratory for the Carolinas and Virginias, an educational development officer presently can be found at dozens of schools, mostly in the Southeast, to facilitate a wide range of educational innovations. Selected individuals from several colleges have been given special training to be "change agents" on their campuses. Robert Knott, who occupied such a position at Mars Hill College in North Carolina, helped to develop a competency-based curriculum and worked with his faculty colleagues to help them implement the new curriculum, particularly assisting them to acquire skills and procedures for the assessment of students.

Staff Development Officer. This is a new position created by several schools who employ individuals to work with their faculty members. In California community colleges, Hayden Williams is doing instructional-development work at Golden West Community College with such a title, and Chester H. Case, Jr., is the Professional Development Facilitator at Los Medanos College. Terry O'Banion, a professor at the University of Illinois, is supervising several graduate students who are studying to prepare for such positions. It seems certain that this specialization will become more common as staff members themselves are subjected to pressures to become more professionalized.

Individual Faculty Volunteer. At California State University, Fullerton, the faculty senate voted to support the idea of establishing a faculty-development center, but resources were not available to launch it. Operating with no funds and about the same amount of authority, Frank Collea volunteered to provide leadership in this area and has conducted several productive workshops for interested faculty members and for department chairpersons designed to improve listening skills and to improve intellectual development of students. In addition, with the assistance of the media center he helped make a film, *People Who Teach,* that portrays the differing styles of several outstanding teachers on the campus for use in additional workshops.

Internal Consultant. Stanley Nicholson has worked at the University of California, Santa Barbara, for three years as a Consultant on New Ways to Teach. With background in education and measurement, he has administered a mini-grant program for faculty to try alternative instructional strategies, consulted with individuals and departments about teaching-related issues, organized workshops, and staged conferences on the improvement of teaching. Individuals with idiosyncratic titles and serving consultative—or perhaps gadfly— roles are found at several schools.

External Consultant. The University of Puget Sound has launched a three-year faculty-development program, a key aspect of which is a departmental consulting program. External "experts" are invited to consult with departments to discuss new curricular and instructional developments, help identify areas for curricular and faculty development, assist in the introduction of new programs, and advise individual faculty of specific opportunities for professional and personal development. Although external consultants to departments are the heart of the program, their visits are coordinated and supplemented by the campus project director, Stephen Phillips.

Counseling Center Staff Member. Although counseling staff often hold nonacademic appointments and have little authority with faculty members, there are exceptions. For instance, William Latta from San Diego, David Newman of San Jose, and David Whitcomb at Long Beach in the California State University and Colleges system provide organizational-development assistance to interested groups in their institutions. Workshops to acquaint faculty members with principles and techniques of counseling and advising are offered by counselors in a number of institutions. The program mounted by Eckerd College in Florida, which was discussed in Chapter Two, was designed in part to sensitize faculty to students and help them to be more effective counselors and has been credited with helping to reduce student attrition significantly.

Short-Term Projects

Short-term instructional-improvement projects administered by one of the established divisions of the university are another organizational form. Projects are usually set up, often with external funding, to meet certain specific needs of the institution. They have the advantages of being able to secure the services of experts and focus sustained attention on a problem for a short period of time. However, their chief drawback is a limited life span, usually no more than three years, after which they often are abandoned. A good example of the project form of organization is that funded by the Division of College Support, U.S. Office of Education. This division provides aid to "developing institutions" for a variety of purposes, including hiring temporary faculty members through National Teaching Fellowships, supporting advanced graduate work to increase the proportion of doctorates on the faculty, funding travel to meetings of learned societies or to visit other institutions, and securing consultants to conduct workshops on instructional topics. These projects appear to meet genuine needs, but one wonders what will happen to the various needs of the schools after the projects terminate; little is being done to assure continuation of needed programs. Unfortunately, this condition may be a necessary evil, given the vagaries of federal funding.

Instructional-Improvement Centers

Although many instructional-improvement activities are conducted by administrators, by faculty groups, by persons with specialized appointments, and by staff of special projects, many institutions have found it useful to establish more formal organizations. Indeed, instructional-improvement centers are becoming the newest entry on the organization charts of many colleges and universities.

What exactly is an instructional-improvement center? It is an organization that is charged with the responsibility of facilitating the continuing development of professional and personal competencies of faculty, particularly those that lead to the improvement of teaching and learning. It may be distinguished from similar programs operated by many schools in the following ways.

1. It is a centralized organization. Because of its central position it can transcend the limited concerns and narrow perspectives of individual departments and focus attention on a variety of teaching-learning issues which face faculty members engaged in a number of different educational tasks.

2. It has a professional staff, a program, a budget and other marks of an established academic division. As such it can provide the specialized expertise and concentrated attention to a wide variety of instructional-improvement activities that individuals with other responsibilities cannot. And it can provide continuity which is missing in short-term projects.

3. It focuses on improvement within the institution. Organizations such as federally funded research and development centers or institutes for the study of higher education, which serve primarily a national or regional clientele, may be mistaken for an instructional-improvement center, but unless they have definite programs to serve their own institutions, they function quite differently.

4. It has an in-service rather than a preservice emphasis. Although several universities are implementing programs to help their graduate students prepare for teaching roles, this does not necessarily

make them instructional-improvement centers. If they also serve regular faculty members, such programs may be regarded as the kind of organization being discussed here.

5. It focuses on higher education. Continuing education for teachers of elementary and secondary schools, which is provided by schools of education, are different from instructional-improvement centers, which serve college and university faculty members.

6. Its clients are primarily faculty members. Although students, administrators, and even community people may be involved, organizations which serve primarily these other clientele, such as most learning resource centers, are a different species.

7. It is not a media center. Although some instructional development is done by staff members of media centers, and although some instructional-improvement centers are responsible for supporting mediated instruction and providing media services, an instructional-improvement center should not be confused with a media center. The instructional-improvement center is more concerned with human than material resources, provides a wider range of instructional services, and provides more consultation concerning academic issues than the usual media center.

It should be clear that an instructional-improvement center is *not* defined by its size; some are "one-person shops" while others are quite large. Nor is it defined by its organizational structure; function is more important than structure after a certain minimal level of organizational form has been provided. Nor is it defined by its location in the hierarchy of the institution; it may operate under the authority of a faculty committee, a school of education, or an existing service unit. The point is that all instructional-improvement centers are engaged in "centering" attention on certain key issues in teaching and learning, bringing generalized and specialized resources of a university to the service of individuals and groups, developing understandings and competencies concerning teaching and learning, and helping to place effective teaching and learning at the center of the academic life.

The Center for Improvement of Undergraduate Education at Cornell University is an example of this kind of organization. It has a permanent professional staff of modest size, administers a small grant program for instructional innovation, provides consultation to

interested faculty, works with teaching assistants, and generally acts
to emphasize the importance and improve the quality of teaching.
Although most are small, some centers are large and comprehensive
organizations that contain several specialized divisions. For example,
the Office of Instructional Resources at the University of Illinois is
organized into four principal divisions. The Measurement and Research Division scores, analyzes, and consults with faculty on examinations; it administers and researches a teaching evaluation procedure; and it conducts research on instructional effectiveness and
student achievement. The Television Unit helps prepare new
instructional materials, copies films and videotapes for course use,
and consults with faculty on the use of instructional television. The
Division of Instructional Materials distributes information about
media, materials, and equipment; assists faculty to use media in
their courses; and designs and produces instructional materials. The
Course Development Division attempts to develop strategies for
applying learning principles to instructional programs; it assists
faculty to analyze instructional problems, select appropriate instructional techniques, and evaluate learning outcomes. A total of forty
persons are employed in professional, technical, and clerical capacities.

Single institutions are not the only setting for instructional-
improvement centers; consortia, multicampus community college
districts, state systems, and educational associations have established
centers to service member institutions. In some cases the multicampus
unit conducts a program of activities in which individuals from
member campuses participate. For example, the workshops on
faculty development and instructional improvement conducted by
the College Center of the Finger Lakes involved faculty from member colleges. In other cases a multicampus center assists member
institutions to establish their own professional-development programs to improve teaching and learning; the Center for Professional Development in the California State University and Colleges
system functions in this way. It works closely with six campuses to
utilize different approaches to instructional improvement, provides
information to campuses about other programs, trains campus staff
members, secures consultants for campus activities, coordinates an
evaluation of separate programs, and disseminates results to other
schools in the system as well as beyond.

However they are structured, most centers have several organizational features in common. First, most of them report to the chief academic administrative officer, such as the provost or academic vice president. Most directors of centers find this a desirable situation because it gives them access to an administrator with authority to emphasize the importance of instruction, and it helps them secure the necessary financial and material resources to operate their programs. In practice, the relationship between some directors and their superiors is very close and effective, while in other cases the directors have difficulty getting the kind of attention and support they would like. However the actual relationship develops, this structure is one generally favored. The reciprocal of this arrangement is that the director is often given the title Assistant Academic Vice President, which provides him with formal authority and accents the degree of administrative support of center activities, both of which may help the center gain acceptance.

In addition, most centers have an advisory committee or policy board that oversees their work. If the relationship with the administrators provides a vertical link with the power structure, the advisory committee serves as a horizontal liaison with persons throughout the institution. Such a committee usually serves several functions including setting policies, helping to gain faculty support and involvement, and facilitating the spread of information about the work of the center. Again, in practice some committees are more effective than others depending on their composition, the time members devote to their assignments, and the roles they play in the work of the program. Nonetheless, effective linkages "up" and "out" are keys to a sound organizational structure of an instructional-improvement center.

Regardless of their location in the structure of the institution, centers almost invariably function independently of the formal advancement system of an institution. Although there are sound reasons for integrating the work of the instructional-improvement program with the reward structure and institutional decisions about personnel matters, most centers are deliberately set up quite independent of the advancement procedure. This arrangement assures that the staff will not be in an evaluative relationship to the faculty clients but will be able to function more in a professional helping relationship. It helps faculty feel free to express negative feelings and concerns so that they may be dealt with, and it also permits the staff members to devote attention to the welfare of the client rather than having to subordinate the interests of the client to those of the institution.

Finally, centers have to come to grips with the school or department of education. The education school is the repository of much expertise about teaching and learning, and those resources must be tapped, yet many faculty harbor negative stereotypes about professional educators. In addition, it may be self-serving for a department of education to establish a center for improving instruction for the benefit of the faculty in the rest of the institution. It is possible to have solid universitywide programs that are administered by the school of education—the Clinic to Improve University Teaching at the University of Massachusetts and the Center for the Teaching Professions at Northwestern University demonstrate that. However, several schools have found it advisable to establish their centers independent of the education department and to regard that department just like any other.

Most centers are of recent vintage, and their growth seems to be accelerating currently, even in the face of fiscal and staffing cutbacks elsewhere. Not all of them are brand new, however; a few of them have been in existence for more than a decade. These various centers and their staffs have accumulated some experience about the ways of working with faculty to improve their instructional effectiveness; they have identified some key issues involved in working with faculty and have gained a certain amount of wisdom, some of it the hard way, about effective means of proceeding. The principles they have learned have relevance beyond their own organizational settings and might be of value to other persons interested in faculty, instructional, and organizational development. A survey of the directors of these centers as well as visits to several of them were designed to tap their experiences and learning, and they provide the basis for most of the remainder of this book.

Guidelines

It is apparent that instructional-improvement programs come in all sizes and shapes. The organization of any single program reflects the size, character, and traditions of the institution, the purpose, history, and nature of the program, and the interests, abilities, and personalities of the persons involved.

Despite the fact that there is no one best way to organize a professional-development program, there are several good ways. The following generalizations are borne out by programs, and they can serve as useful guidelines to institutions that want to establish such programs.

1. Although individual administrators and faculty members sometimes can facilitate the professional development of faculty members by themselves, the creation of a program that is separate from their regular activities will greatly augment their efforts.

2. A comprehensive program or center can provide the continuing structural base, the authority and responsibility, and the expertise for the improvement of instruction.

3. In most instances, the center can best be established directly under the chief academic officer of the university so that it can be identified with the academic activities of the institution, serve a campuswide constituency, and have strong administrative support.

4. A faculty advisory committee is useful to establish policy, assure faculty guidance for the campus activities, and assist in the implementation of the program.

5. Although there are cases where the program is effectively lodged in the school of education or the media center, such a location generally should be avoided. This is because such organizations call forth negative stereotypes among many faculty members and because such existing centers may be constrained by their own vested interests, which may limit their effectiveness in working with faculty.

6. As a rule, the campus program ought to be headed by a faculty member who is regarded as an effective teacher, who is knowledgeable about teaching and learning, or who has been a leader in innovative education.

▼▼▼▼▼▼▼▼▼▼▼▼▼▼▼▼▼▼▼▼▼▼▼▼▼▼▼▼▼▼▼▼▼▼▼▼

Chapter 7

The Politics of
Improvement Centers

▲▲▲▲▲▲▲▲▲▲▲▲▲▲▲▲▲▲▲▲▲▲▲▲▲▲▲▲▲▲▲▲▲▲▲▲▲▲

The basic political position of an instructional-improvement center is as a new organization seeking to bring about changes or reforms within an established institution. Furthermore, it occupies a unique position; it is neither a typical administrative unit, though it administers a program, nor an academic department, though it offers an educational program. In providing an in-service program, in effect teaching the teachers, the center must obtain support from the faculty as well as from the administration, and it must be supported by institutional policies and procedures. Each of these foci of the political life of instructional-improvement centers will be discussed in this chapter.

One staff member observes, "We have a condition of high need but low demand for our services." This comment aptly characterizes the state of affairs in many instructional-improvement programs. By definition, a faculty-development program can succeed only if it obtains the support and participation of the faculty. But how can this be accomplished?

A precondition to reaching the faculty is to know how they perceive this new concept of professional development and the organization that implements it. Typically, faculty have a cautious, skeptical, or critical initial reaction, which stems from several sources. For one thing, there is the implied criticism inherent in the terms that are used. Professors often react defensively to the term *faculty development* and ask, "What's wrong with me the way I am? Who wants me to 'develop,' in what ways, and why?" Some centers seek to avoid waving this particular red flag by not using that direct and possibly threatening term and by substituting less direct words like *professional, instructional,* or *learning* for *faculty* and words like *improvement* (since we can all stand to improve in some ways) or *facilitation* (because we are all interested in facilitating learning) for *development*. Although these concerns may be dismissed by some as an empty exercise in semantics, the preferred choice of terms in an institution will avoid conjuring up harmful images in the minds of potential clients.

Another common initial reaction is for faculty to perceive that the center may be setting up a remedial program for bad teachers. In point of fact, this is one reason given by some administrators who support instructional-improvement programs, although it is soon apparent to all that there is no magic that will transform poor teachers into good ones. One faculty member who eventually became the director of a new campus center for the improvement of instruction revealed that when he first heard of the proposal, he thought it was a remedial program designed by the administration to help poor teachers and that it would surely fail. Only after he more clearly understood the concept and the opportunities it offers both to faculty members and to the institution was he persuaded of the value of the program.

Sometimes faculty conceive of instructional-improvement programs as akin to a "methods course" offered by the school of education, and that image elicits negative educationist stereotypes, particularly among those in the liberal arts disciplines. Because faculty members tend to share the conviction that the best teacher is the one who knows the most about an area, the emphasis on methods and techniques tends to be resisted. This resistance can be intensified by beliefs that traditional ways of preparing teachers for the elementary and secondary schools, which have placed a heavy emphasis on methods and techniques, have not proved to be very effective and ought not to be introduced at the higher level.

Finally, faculty may try to turn an institution-wide instructional-improvement program into a more content-oriented one administered by the departments. At the University of Redlands the chairman of the Board of Trustees offered to make a sizeable grant to the institution for a centralized instructional-development program. The faculty was more than willing to take his money but asked that it be parceled out to the various departments and used to improve subject matter competence through travel, use of subject matter consultants, research support, and the like. The potential donor was not willing to support these activities. Very little progress was made for about a year until the faculty finally decided that it might be able to benefit from the program as originally proposed. Naturally, one of the first tasks of the new director was to allay fears, build trust and respect, and secure the involvement of faculty in the initial programs.

Although initial faculty reluctance is widespread, it is by no means universal; there are many faculty members in virtually every institution who are interested in improving their instruction and who can be counted on for support. And the initial resistance usually is not a deep one; most frequently it is based on incomplete knowledge and may be overcome by clear articulation of the program. Included in this articulation should be information about what the program entails and also what it does not. The assurance that participation will be voluntary, that it will be disassociated from the advancement system, and that it will serve the needs and interests of the participants usually makes the program acceptable to even out-and-out critics.

Instructional-improvement centers are in a position to provide assistance, expertise, and in some cases modest financial support to faculty members, but by design they are separate from the power structure of the institution that ultimately determines the faculty members' teaching assignments, retention, promotion, salary, and tenure. Thus the centers must find ways of inducing faculty participation without resorting to the usual institutional rewards and punishments. Indeed, not only do the centers lack power over the faculty members, but the reverse is a more accurate statement. The faculty retains ultimate authority over the academic affairs of the institution, and individual faculty members have authority to teach in the way they consider best. Thus, the centers must employ strategies to secure the support of the faculty who in a real sense have power over them; if the faculty are not well served by a center, it eventually will wither and die from lack of support. If, as has been pointed out, it is difficult for a person in a position of power to help one subordinate to him, it is an equally delicate matter for a person to induce change in persons with power over him and his programs.

These political realities help to shape the strategies of the centers in working with faculty members. These strategies are used in many situations by persons who have little power but much influence. Sexual imagery is often used by staff members to indicate their way of obtaining faculty support. For example, one woman said that she tried to "woo" the faculty, and Claude Mathis of Northwestern University has written a paper entitled "Persuading the Institution to Experiment—Strategies for Seduction." In a very real sense the practical task for the center is to convince faculty members that it can assist them, whether this process is seen as educating, wooing, seducing, or persuading. The following specific strategies are used by centers to gain faculty support.

1. Develop an outreach program. One of the best ways to assure little faculty interest in instructional-improvement activities is to merely announce that the center exists and offers certain services. There is a need to obtain visibility for the center, to describe the nature of the services, and to explain the way of operating. Face-to-face discussion is far more effective than distribution of written materials, and visits to department meetings, conversations with faculty committees, and individual conversations with department chairpersons, college deans, and committee chairpersons are important, if time-consuming, ways of establishing the presence of the center on campus. Such discussions may help faculty to clarify the nature of the program, overcome initial fears, and learn what they might gain from participating in the activities.

2. Start small and prove yourself. Large and growing pro-

grams have always led to suspicions of empire building among academics, and particularly during the present time when faculty positions are being reduced, there are good reasons to be sensitive to this concern. Any expanding program is likely to be the target of those whose own budgets are constricted, particularly if it is a new program that has not yet demonstrated its value. Therefore, most centers begin as modest efforts, often with just one or two professional staff members. After the programs are established and their value demonstrated, they may be enlarged to meet a growing demand.

3. Keep a low profile. An abundance of new educational and social programs accompanied by much fanfare have been launched in recent years only to be abandoned a few years later when their high expectations could not be realized. A low-profile, low-key approach keeps expectations at realistic levels and provides a better basis to begin working with faculty. A "hard sell" tends to alienate or intimidate many faculty members and thereby to create difficulties in working with them later.

4. Start where the faculty are. Mathis (1974, p. 8) has emphasized the importance of working within the faculty member's framework. "Anyone who develops strategies for helping faculty improve their teaching should recognize the importance of accepting the goals which faculty establish for themselves. Just as there is no one set of criteria which defines a successful teacher, there is no one correct method to be used in teaching. While some methods may be more efficient in specific instances, the motivation and enthusiasm of the teacher is a critical factor in determining the success of any method." Other persons supplement this pragmatic rationale with the philosophical belief that the faculty member should retain ultimate authority over the purposes and conduct of his courses.

5. Be eclectic in approach. Reform movements attract extremists who offer new techniques as panaceas for educational problems. But the complexities that abound in the teaching-learning process, the course of adult development, and the consultant-client relationship assure that no single procedure, including the now popular competency-based curricula and self-pacing procedures, whatever its merits, will become the saviour of higher education. The very diversity of faculty members, the variations among the disciplines, and the complexities involved in helping faculty to improve their

instruction require that centers employ various techniques and approaches.

6. Start with a small group of volunteers, and let them "sell" the program to their colleagues. However much skepticism there may be initially about a program, there are always many individuals on any faculty who are interested in participating in instructional-improvement activities. Because the early participants are volunteers, they tend to be above average in interest, enthusiasm, and effectiveness as teachers. These people are likely to contribute the most and to gain the most from the program, and their descriptions of their own experiences and of the benefits they derive in their conversations with colleagues are a valuable way to increase participation in the program.

7. Go with winners at the outset. First impressions are important, whether in personal relationships or in establishing an instructional-improvement center. Several new programs have gone to great lengths to do all they can to assure that initial seminars, workshops, and retreats are well received. Nothing breaks down faculty resistance or wins their favor like success. The more daring or controversial projects can be postponed until a firm foundation has been established.

8. Administer a small instructional-improvement fund. Many institutions have allocated a fund to support a variety of instructional-improvement projects. (See Chapter Eight.) If this small-grant program is administered by the campus center, many faculty members with motivation and ideas may surface, and their proposals may provide a specific task on which both faculty and center staff members can jointly work. Center staff members had highly positive comments about the value of such a fund in their work.

These are common strategies, but there is no guarantee that they are the right or the best approach for any particular institution. Further, although instructional-improvement centers have little power themselves, their strategies for securing faculty involvement must necessarily rest on a careful analysis of the formal and informal power structures of the institution. Mathis (1974, p. 6) points out:

> Any strategy for initiating improvements in teach-
> ing should emerge from . . . a pragmatic assessment of

the leverages of institutional power which can be used
to motivate faculty involvement in the process of change.
These critical pressure points are not the same in all
colleges and universities. The explicit distributions of
power on a college campus between faculty, administration, students, and alumni often have little resemblance
to the implicit relationships and actions when power is
exercised. An analysis of the academic culture of the institution can save much time in determining the right
tactics to move faculty.

Not only can it save much time, but a careful analysis of the academic culture of an institution is necessary to avoid serious mistakes
and to identify those opinion leaders who can play a key role in
creating a positive view of the center.

This matter of gaining faculty participation in their programs
has high priority among directors of instructional-improvement
centers, as is borne out by the responses to a survey of fifty-five
directors of instructional-improvement centers conducted as a part
of the project that led to this book. Thirty-seven of the respondents
checked "increasing faculty awareness of the need for improved
teaching" as a "high priority"—the most commonly checked item
listed as a possible concern. Close behind was "stimulating faculty
interest in and use of (center) services," which was checked by
thirty-five persons. Nineteen regarded "overcoming faculty opposition
to teaching improvement efforts" as a high priority. Although this is
a rather large number, it is a minority of all centers surveyed and
one of the lesser concerns. Even though active opposition may be
both vocal and disruptive, the greater problem seems to be the quiet
lack of interest shown by the faculty.

This conclusion is reinforced by responses to another item on
the questionnaire. Directors were asked to estimate the proportion of
faculty who viewed their centers in certain ways. "They don't even
know the unit exists" received a median estimate of 9 percent of the
faculty; "they are opposed to the work of the unit" was estimated
to describe 8 percent of the faculty; and "although they are not
opposed, they don't use the unit very much" received the highest
estimate, 31 percent. The other categories were faculty who received

little or much of benefit from the center. Again, it appears that among the centers studied, the matter of obtaining faculty participation is a major one and that the strategies described above are only partially successful.

These results mean that the strategy so widely espoused—to start with a small group of volunteers and let them bring in new clients by word of mouth advertising—is only partially effective, in part, perhaps, because participants in instructional-improvement programs, even if they have derived considerable benefit, may support the program without proselytizing on its behalf. But these results are also indicative of the relative size of the institutions and the centers. Most centers are small, and most of those included in the questionnaire portion of this study are located in large universities. It is almost impossible for a small center to provide services to more than a modest proportion of a moderate or large faculty. And because most of these centers are young organizations and tend to concentrate on serving a small group of faculty for strategic reasons, they simply have not been able to reach out to include a large proportion of the faculty. Indeed, if they had generated that much interest among the faculty, they would simply be unable to respond effectively to the demand.

In light of the importance they attach to arousing faculty interest and securing their participation, one might expect that centers would have conducted careful analyses of faculty needs. Indeed, about half of the centers surveyed have conducted a formal "needs analysis." Twenty-seven directors said they have "conducted a systematic survey or other analysis of faculty interests and need in regard to improving their teaching"; on the other hand, twenty-eight said they had not done that. An examination of the actual procedures used revealed that with few exceptions, the kind of analysis most often used has been a short, general questionnaire to determine faculty *interest* in possible center programs. Although this procedure may be quite useful, it does not necessarily reveal what faculty *need* to learn. The effort to determine and stimulate faculty interest may override the equally compelling requirements of grounding the program in something more basic than individual desires.

Professional-development programs may be based on a com-

prehensive analysis of the goals and priorities of the institution, as
was discussed in Chapter Six. Or they may be responsive to student
educational experiences. For instance, Parker Lichtenstein, when
he was at Redlands, analyzed student ratings of teaching across all
faculty. He found that the faculty as a whole scored highest on
items concerned with the mastery of subject matter but lowest on
items having to do with arousing student interest, encouraging student participation, and demonstrating relevance of the course content
to students. These deficiencies became the targets for some of the
ensuing instructional-improvement programs. Programs may also be
based on future trends, projections, or plans. Today, for example,
there is a strong trend for institutions to emphasize adult learners
who have different learning needs and styles than the familiar
eighteen- to twenty-one-year-old students (Cross, 1971). Instructional-improvement programs to prepare faculty to work with a new
clientele or to implement a new curriculum could well be a great
need that would not appear on an interest inventory. And finally,
research on the impact of college on students (Wilson, and others,
1975) demonstrates that certain teaching and learning practices are
more likely to have significant impact on the lives of students than
other practices. Stimulating courses were one factor, but out-of-class
interaction, discussions about a range of value-related issues relevant
to college youth, effective educational and vocational advising, and
reading materials with personal and social overtones have all been
shown to be particularly effective experiences for students.

Although focusing on faculty interests, institutional goals, or
student needs may facilitate formation of an institutional-improve-
ment program, it would be as foolish to design a program to meet
student or institutional needs that were of no interest to faculty as it
would be to respond to faculty interests apart from student or institutional needs. Hopefully, some compromise can be devised.

Michael DeBloois and Douglas D. Alder (1973) introduce
a differential and progressive dimension into the discussion. They
advocate a strategy for stimulating faculty readiness for instructional
development based on an ascending ladder of faculty interest.

The bottom rung might be labeled *awareness activities;* the second *faculty support activities;* and at the

top, *instructional development activities.* A major purpose behind the graduated structure is to engage the
faculty member where he is, regardless of his predilec-
tion for instructional improvement and offer meaningful
service at his level. Close on the heels of that first objective is the second one, of helping the faculty member
move a step closer to initiating meaningful instructional
improvement. The ultimate goal is to have each member
of the faculty initiate a major development effort in
courses (or modules of activity) for which he or she has
responsibility.

According to the authors, awareness activities may consist of
distributing information about educational innovations, announcing
seminars on topics of interest, distributing request forms for individual assistance, and preparing a handbook with teaching suggestions. Support activities might include mini-grant competition to
support limited efforts to improve instruction and individual
consultation from instructional design and evaluation personnel.
Instructional-development activities consist of full-scale redesign of
a course subsidized by release time for the faculty and supported by
a design team consisting of experts in media, evaluation, or other
specialties.

The paper by DeBloois and Alder raises the question that
centers are increasingly starting to encounter: What can a center do
after it has developed programs that appeal to the initial self-selected
group of faculty? Assuming that it does go with a winner and that
initial participants do spread the word to several of their colleagues,
what next? The original program, such as a seminar, workshop, or
grant support program, may be repeated for a new group, of course,
but a repetition of the program will not likely be of much interest to
the original participants. Furthermore, after the second group has
gone through the program, it becomes increasingly difficult to enlist
the interest of additional faculty.

The answer is that the instructional-improvement program
itself must develop; it must change to meet the changing conditions
which it helped to foster. This need is characteristic of all centers
with the possible exception of those which seek to provide a major
redesign of a few courses. These focused efforts may be repeated on

one course after another almost indefinitely in a large university. However, all other centers must devise strategies to sustain the interest and involvement of the early participants (who are likely to be key opinion leaders) and to reach the nonbelievers.

One useful way to maintain involvement of the early participants is to recruit them to provide leadership or to be resource persons for future activities. If several persons have redesigned their courses, they may be asked to share their experiences, benefits, or problems; persons who have developed special knowledge in areas such as evaluation of teaching, use of simulations in the classroom, and experiential learning can be asked to pass it on to their colleagues.

The involvement of faculty also may be sustained if they deepen their interests, enhance their competencies, and perhaps specialize in some area of education. For example, Michael Scriven, a prominent philosopher, has become a leading figure in educational evaluation. Of course, a faculty member need not abandon his own academic specialization, but may graft a serious study of some area of higher education onto his earlier specialty. This combination can make the instructor more sensitive in his teaching role and provide additional expertise of use to the institution. It will also help to make discussions among faculty members about higher education more sophisticated and informed than they are at present, perhaps eventually as rigorous as discussions about the content of their academic specialties.

Additionally, a center may build variation into its program to maintain interest. In a large school this variation may be provided by a comprehensive program of several different instructional-improvement activities, including those discussed in Chapters Two through Four on faculty, instructional, and organizational development. A small school may introduce variation and increase comprehensiveness by changing the focus of the program from year to year, or it may participate in a consortium which has a broader base and justifies a more diverse program than any single small institution may mount.

Even though many original participants may remain closely associated with the center, there is a continuing need to involve additional faculty. Because these persons are likely to be somewhat less enthusiastic, to have more traditional ideas about professional development, and to have more reservations about the benefits of such a program, special strategies may be needed to reach them.

The center may hold a series of highly targeted seminars or workshops that appeal to specific persons. For instance, a workshop on practical matters of immediate utility, such as how to motivate students, or a discussion of alternative evaluation and grading practices, may meet the needs of some faculty members and help arouse their interest in other activities. One faculty member confided that he was initially skeptical about the center on his campus, but he attended a discussion of ways to motivate students and found the idea of positive reinforcement intriguing. He tried increasing his use of positive and rewarding comments to students and reducing the number of his critical or negative responses and was amazed at the increased motivation of students to participate in class discussions and at the improved quality of the dialogue. He became a strong supporter of the center and an active participant in later activities.

Another strategy is to supplement universitywide programs with programs tailored to the needs of persons in specific departments or divisions. Some faculty opposition to instructional-improvement programs stems from the belief that certain instructional techniques are inappropriate for use in their disciplines. This concern may be countered by offering a program for an academic department or division that emphasizes the special qualities of that field, embraces the values of those faculty members, and uses the idiom of that field. These practices may help demonstrate the value of professional development to individuals who could not, or would not, translate ideas into their own settings.

Subject matter experts in one's own discipline often have more credibility to a professor than colleagues in other fields; C. P. Snow (1959) writes about the clash of two cultures, and subsequent research (Gaff and Wilson, 1971) shows important differences among faculty from different departments. Cases abound where faculty members or groups were advised to take a certain action but rejected that advice until they heard it from an acknowledged scholar in the subject matter. Individuals with expertise both in an established field and in some instructional area are valuable for reaching those persons with reservations about accepting the word of "outsiders."

Finally, several centers try to elicit interest by offering a number of small, and in some senses insignificant, services which may entice faculty into greater involvements. For example, one center offers to make slides or graphic reproductions which allow a professor to present a greater range of visual material in such fields as art, biochemistry, or anthropology. One important part of this strategy is to make it easy for a person to request assistance, and another is to take advantage of this show of interest to find out other ways the center may serve that person.

Although the need to obtain and maintain the willing involvement of faculty is a paramount concern, instructional-improvement centers must also secure administrative and institutional support. This includes commitment to the center, institutional policies that support effective teaching and instructional improvement, and provision of adequate financial resources. (Fiscal matters will be discussed in Chapter Eight.)

Administrative leadership is critical in establishing instructional-improvement centers. The survey of center directors asked whether "the climate (in regard to teaching improvement) is more or less favorable than it was a couple of years ago." Twenty said that it was "much more" and twenty-six that it was "somewhat more" favorable; only three said it was less favorable. When asked the major reasons for any observed change, they gave responses that indicate the key role played by administrators. One set of factors mentioned is external forces, including the decline of federal support for research, the current poor job market for faculty, and demands for accountability. Another set concerns recent changes within the institution, including the tightening up of the advancement system, the requirement that faculty document their teaching effectiveness, and the prevalence of student evaluations of faculty. Active administrative leadership is another factor mentioned specifically, and administrators must play an important role in bringing about these other changes in the climate of the institutions. Certainly they are prime movers in establishing several instructional-improvement centers.

Because administrators are sensitive to the interests of the faculty, probably the best course for maintaining administrative support is to maintain a broad and strong base of support among the faculty. A program that produces benefits to a significant portion of the faculty will be hard to scuttle, and no wise administrator would want to do so.

Another way to maintain administrative support is to avoid creating opposition in key segments of the institution. The awarding of grants, particularly, is a sensitive matter and can generate suspicion and resentment if there is any reason to believe that decisions were made in an arbitrary or heavy-handed fashion. One center director told of how he tries to avoid arousing resentment among unsuccessful grant applicants. He never turns down even a poor grant proposal but delays approval while he works with the faculty member to revise the proposed project and increase its chances of success.

Sometimes failures may provide more insight than successes. Although there are few instances of outright failures of instructional-improvement centers, two cases where loss of administrative support occurred may be instructive. In one center the fact that the vice president is seeking to have the director of learning services report to the librarian rather than directly to him, as has been the case, indicates a loss of some administrative support. At least part of the reason for this shift may be traced to the rather doctrinaire—sometimes even messianic—attitudes some of the staff seem to have concerning instructional development. Although the center has had some quite successful projects, its rhetoric has also tended to alienate some elements of the faculty. This opposition seems to have overridden its several successes in the mind of the vice president.

Another center, which was established in 1971, was abolished in 1974, and the primary reason for its demise seems to be the turnover of the top three administrators in the institution. There had been a lack of firm leadership from the top administration during this period of transition. The new administrators did not have the same kind of commitment as their predecessors who had established the center. This case highlights the special problem of institutionalizing the center so that it persists even when individuals leave. Of course, loss of leadership within the center as well as in the administration, particularly when the staff is quite small, poses problems of continuity. Conscious efforts to institutionalize the center before there is a major change in personnel would help it to weather these transitions.

Sometimes an administrator may have a commitment to the center but not be able or willing to back that commitment with the necessary actions. Mathis (1974, p. 7) has observed that "many administrators act as if they believe that the exhortations of the Dean at faculty meetings is all that is needed to interest professors in improving teaching." Sometimes presidents, vice presidents, or deans must be urged to make decisions about the allocation of resources or recommendations for promotion that give substance to their words.

In this connection it is unlikely that instructional-improvement programs will be sustained unless they are supported by institutional policies and practices. It may be possible to launch a program with volunteers who have intrinsic interests and pursue their own agendas, but that is no basis to sustain a program. Three policies seem to be particularly crucial.

First, faculty need to have the time and material resources required to embark on significant new projects. A course cannot be thoroughly redesigned or a traditional course transformed without a great deal of work. Release time, pay for vacation work, student and clerical assistance, and operating expenses are required if a major commitment from faculty is expected.

Second, institutional policies concerning a host of instructional programs may have to be revised. As was mentioned in Chapter Five, Robert Diamond points out that Syracuse University has had to make a series of institutional changes to support the individualized, self-paced courses his center has helped to create. The most important are the following: awarding variable credit to reflect the amount of work a student satisfactorily completes, instituting continuous registration to permit a student to commence and terminate courses when he is ready, designing new space utilization policies to permit a single self-paced course to use the same room for several hours continuously, and revising faculty workloads to permit a faculty member to be credited for actual work performed in his new instructional role. Unfortunately, few universities have made the kinds of institutional changes that support their faculty-, instructional-, or organizational-development programs.

Third, institutional policies and practices that foster security and that accord a sense of professional respect and dignity to faculty members are necessary for an effective instructional-improvement program. For instance, if an institution is faced with the possibility of cutting back faculty positions and faculty members are threatened with the loss of their jobs, that is probably the least hospitable time to attempt to implement a program of professional development. A clear understanding of the staffing plans, including the procedures and criteria to be used in making any changes, creates a sense of security among faculty that can make their participation valuable. Some institutions have built up such resentment among faculty because of their past actions that there may be widespread suspicion of development activities. For instance, when I went before the State-wide Academic Senate to brief them on the newly created Center for Professional Development, the members expressed surprise that the system that had heretofore neglected their interests suddenly had their best interests at heart. "If the Chancellor's Office believes in professional development, where are our sabbaticals? (They had been only minimally funded.) What's in it for the faculty if they participate? Will this be used to get rid of poor teachers?"—these were the kinds of remarks made. Although their initial fears were allayed, and several sound campus-based programs were established with the aid of the systemwide center, these resentments remain a serious obstacle.

If the domestic political affairs of a center concern gaining and maintaining faculty, administrative, and institutional support, its "foreign relations" revolve largely around its relationships with professional-development programs to improve teaching and learning in other institutions. Answers to two items on the survey of directors suggest that most centers are relatively isolated from each other, relatively uninformed about the work of similar units, and desirous of collaborating with their counterparts elsewhere.

It was thought that there may be a few centers that are well known and whose work might serve as models for others. To test this idea center directors were asked to name up to three instructional-improvement centers and their directors in other colleges and universities that "are doing what you would regard as a good job of helping faculty improve their teaching effectiveness." A total of thirty centers were nominated, but few clear "favorites" emerged. The Center for Research on Learning and Teaching at the University of Michigan, the Center for Instructional Development at Syracuse University, and the complex administered under the Educational Development Program at Michigan State University received the greatest number of nominations. Very few centers stand out as exemplary programs among the center directors. On the contrary, there are several places that are regarded as effective instructional-improvement centers by at least one practitioner and which may provide guidance to their colleagues elsewhere.

Nominations may reveal as much about the person making the nominations as about the center receiving them. A close inspection of these data leads one to conclude that center directors lack knowledge about comparable programs in other institutions. Although thirty-six persons did name at least one center, sixteen of these named just one, ten cited two, and only ten listed the three other places that were requested. Fully eighteen—the largest single group— were either unwilling or unable to refer to a single other center. (Since these same persons were willing to respond to other items, it is unlikely that they were holding back here.) Further, some of the centers cited had the wrong directors, and several responses were accompanied by question marks to indicate their uncertainty. One center that had been abolished received a nomination from one center director.

Center directors, on another item, indicated their strong interest in participating in a number of cooperative activities. There was strong sentiment for participating in a clearinghouse to share written materials and information on instructional-improvement activities, attending conferences for staff members to share their experiences, going to workshops to train staff members, collaborating on research on learning and teaching issues, and considering techniques to evaluate their centers. The degree of unanimity in favor of these cooperative activities is striking, and it probably reflects the interest among leaders in this new movement to keep abreast of ideas and events that may have significance for their own work. But it probably also reflects the isolation of instructional-improvement centers and their need to establish important linkages with their colleagues in other institutions.

Center directors were asked on the questionnaire to indicate the most useful advice, based on their own experience, they could give to a person trying to establish a center in an institution like theirs. This open-ended question elicited a host of responses that are more revealing in their diversity than any summary would be. Below are several of the more salient bits of advice that more than a dozen of these veterans of professional-development programs would offer to their neophyte colleagues. Together they provide useful guidelines for politically effective strategies.

Use local talent in workshops and other activities.

Develop the program *with* the faculty, not *for* the faculty.

Operate primarily on hard money, only supplemented by grant funds.

Select an academic director—*not* a media person, librarian, or educationalist.

Be sure to have the center attached to the provost's office or equivalent, and have good funding to start with.

Make all services voluntary.

Don't try to help with one hand and evaluate (or tattle!) with the other.

Be sure the person to whom you report has lots of clout —but *you* come on gently.

Ensure that the center is faculty initiated and supported.

Make sure you have "grass roots" support.

Expect some opposition, but be patient.

Operate a low-profile, service-intensive organization.

Do not threaten the faculty.

Chapter 8

▼▼

Financing In-Service Programs

▲▲

"How much investment does the university make in a tenured faculty member, and how much of this investment can be protected by a faculty development program?" These questions by Victor Baldridge, Assistant Vice President for Academic Affairs at California State University, Fresno, are intriguing and led me to seek some answers. First it is necessary to make a few assumptions. If a thirty-five-year-old faculty member is granted tenure and promoted to Associate Professor this year in one of the California State University and Colleges campuses, as an Associate Professor Step I, he will earn the current salary for that nine-month position of $15,168, plus fringe benefits of approximately 13 percent, or $1,972, plus a cost of living increase. If he serves until age sixty-five, and if his salary increases at the rate of inflation, which may be estimated at 6 percent annually—a conservative estimate by recent standards—then by the academic year 2005–2006, this single faculty member will have

138

earned a total of $1,443,662! Although not all these assumptions may prove to be correct, it is apparent that a tenured faculty member, in crass financial terms, is a very costly commodity.

How much of this investment can be protected by professional-development activities that keep faculty members up to date in their fields of specialization as well as in their teaching effectiveness? Nobody can answer this question with any degree of certainty now, but leaving aside all human concerns, any investment of this magnitude requires considerable insurance that its value will be protected. Although the precise figures are not yet available, it is obvious that faculty-development programs are prudent investments in human capital, the life blood of any university.

Robert deHart (1974, p. 1), president of DeAnza Community College in California, comparing the miniscule investment in the care of human resources with the larger amounts given to the care of physical resources, expresses the need to redress this discrepancy. "We must recognize that despite our tremendous investment in buildings and facilities, they are not our most important capital, the staff is. We plan for depreciation in facilities, and it is even more important that we make at least a modicum of investment in the upkeep of the staff to assure that there is no obsolescence there either. On the contrary, with the right development program, we can expect an 'appreciation' over the years of this most important asset."

Traditionally it has been the responsibility of individual faculty members to prepare themselves for an academic position by obtaining the requisite graduate training in one of the academic disciplines. Although institutions often assist a young faculty member to complete work toward a doctoral degree, it is commonly accepted that the primary expense will be borne by the prospective faculty member. Once the faculty member is hired, it is common practice for the institution to provide support for him to keep up to date in his field of specialization through travel to conferences and meetings of professional associations, research assistance, and sabbatical leaves. The cost of the new in-service programs that focus on the improvement of instruction has also been carried by employing institutions, often with the aid of external funds from private foundations and government agencies. While the motivation for self-improvement must come from the individual, it does seem appropriate that the financial costs be the responsibility of the institution. In virtually no in-service program in other fields of endeavor is the cost supported by the employees. The largest item in most budgets is faculty salaries and benefits, and it is just sound business practice for an institution to budget for expenses that are required to nourish these resources so as to maintain and enhance their value.

The question for many is not *whether* to support the development of faculty but *how*. How much does a quality program cost? How are current programs financed? How are resources obtained to finance long-term needs?

First, it is necessary to determine what costs may be involved in a faculty-development program. There are two major categories of costs, one to staff and operate the program and the other to support faculty participants. Most centers and programs are small operations, the majority consisting of one or two professional persons, secretarial support, and occasionally student assistance. Program costs are dependent, obviously, on the character and scope of the program, but a few thousand dollars will support off-campus retreats or workshops and a few hundred will support on-campus seminars, workshops, study groups, consultants, or task forces, exclusive of the salaries of staff and participants. The production of learning materials, should that be a part of the program, may be somewhat more expensive, but those schools interested in this approach will probably have media centers, television studios and equipment, or computer centers that can devote some of their resources to this purpose. Large schools may need to maintain a somewhat larger program than small schools if they hope to have significant impact. However, the total cost of a program or center usually is quite modest, especially when viewed in relation to the total instructional budget of the institution.

In addition to the cost of the center may be costs for supporting faculty involvement. The National Advisory Council on Education Professions Development (1975, p. 42) points out that "unlike professionals in other fields who may have strong economic incentives to learn about new ways of doing things, teachers have little economic flexibility. They are not independent professionals. While many teachers aggressively pursue courses of study to keep up to date, doing so is often expensive and time-consuming. Special incentives must be provided in any realistic program of in-service professional development." Some activities such as involvement in major instructional redesign projects, participation in the development of a new curriculum, or revision of institutional policies will require substantial amounts of time if they are to be completed satisfactorily. Faculty members may be released from some of their usual responsibilities such as teaching a course or two, given a full or partial leave, or paid for extra work during holidays or the summer. These costs will vary according to the size and ambitions of the programs. Also, as several directors of instructional-improvement centers attest, mini-grants are very valuable in encouraging and supporting faculty efforts toward improvement. It is not true, as the cynic said, that mini-grants buy mini-ideas; very few dollars may be involved in significant projects. The center directors insist that a small instructional-improvement fund, of as little as $5,000 or $10,000, brings handsome returns.

Some numbers can be placed on these abstractions. Directors of instructional-improvement centers were asked to indicate the amount of their budgets for 1973–1974. The Center for Research on Learning and Teaching at the University of Michigan had a total budget of $212,000, and the Center for Improvement of Undergraduate Education at Cornell University had approximately $150,000; a portion of these budgets was "soft" grant money. More modest programs were the Center for Improving Teaching Effectiveness at Virginia Commonwealth University, which had a budget of $37,000 in its first year that has since been supplemented by additional monies from the university and an external grant, and the Hubert Eaton Program of Instructional Development at the University of Redlands, with a budget of about $60,000. In each case, these budgets are only a small portion of the total university budget, seldom more than .5 percent. Of course, these centers do not embrace all of the professional-development activities of these schools; sabbatical leaves, travel money, and research support, without doubt, are far more costly components. But these centers and programs are major efforts to enhance the instructional effectiveness of the faculty. And these examples do give an idea of the number of dollars involved in such programs at schools of varying size and type.

Presently the chief source of funds for instructional improvement is colleges and universities themselves, but often they have been aided by substantial grants from federal agencies or private foundations. The government agencies that have aided the establishment of instructional-improvement programs the most are the Fund for the Improvement of Post-Secondary Education (FIPSE) within the Department of Health, Education, and Welfare and the Division of College Support and the Bureau of Education Professions Development (BEPD) within the U.S. Office of Education. Although each of these programs offers important benefits, none is able to provide continuous or operational support for regular programs. FIPSE has supported a number of innovative projects designed to facilitate instructional improvement. More recently it has launched a program to elevate the importance of teaching by awarding grants to institutions that already have promising programs. The grants will aid the evaluation of the projects and the dissemination of the results for the purpose of publicizing valuable models for the benefit of others. The Division of College Support has financed efforts to upgrade the faculty of developing colleges, including a great number of community and black colleges. Short-term projects such as faculty fellows to fill slots in needy colleges, support for faculty to obtain advanced degrees, and special workshops on aspects of teaching and learning are the most common programs that receive support under this program. To the extent that BEPD supports work in higher education, short-term workshops or institutes for faculty, again largely from the community colleges, seem to be looked on with favor.

Federal funding patterns play a significant role in the campus-based instructional-improvement efforts. The reduction over the last several years of funds for research at colleges and universities has necessitated realigning priorities toward teaching on the campuses. But unfortunately, other funds to compensate for the loss of research monies or to sustain the new emphasis on teaching and learning have not been made available. The National Advisory Council on Education Professions Development (1975, pp. iv–v) calls for a new program to meet current needs, and although the report focuses on a single law, their rationale provides a useful framework for thinking about governmental support.

> Our conclusion is that the Education Professions
> Development Act should be extended but revised to re-

flect changing societal needs, with emphasis on improving the quality of educational personnel. Since 1967,
when EPDA was enacted, we have moved from a general
shortage of classroom teachers to a general surplus. . . .
The emphasis we now face calls for emphasis on quality,
improved productivity, and in-service education, all
within the context of significant expansion of the non-
conventional segment of the educational enterprise.

New initiatives from several government agencies in support of in-
service programs for faculty would be quite appropriate for these
times and would greatly aid instructional-improvement efforts of
individual colleges and universities.

Several private foundations have been active in supporting
faculty-development or instructional-improvement programs. The
Kellogg Foundation has supported several quite different efforts including the Center for the Teaching Professions at Northwestern
University, the Clinic to Improve University Teaching at the University of Massachusetts, and the major innovation of a competency-
based curriculum at Sterling College. The Lilly Endowment has
made a major commitment to faculty development through three
different programs. It has awarded grants to three leading universities to provide opportunities for faculty in liberal arts and community
colleges in their regions to refresh themselves in the disciplines.
About two dozen quite diverse faculty-development projects have
been supported at individual institutions, mostly small private colleges, around the country. And a new pilot faculty fellowship program has been devised; rather than supporting strictly scholarly
research, these new, and at the beginning few, fellowships will be
used to help faculty members gain some experience that will directly
aid their teaching or serve their institutions.

Perhaps the most comprehensive and holistic, if not the most
well-heeled, program of a private foundation is that of the Danforth
Foundation, which is establishing a series of centers for teaching and
learning in various schools around the country. The first are located
at Empire State College, Harvard University, Atlanta University,
and Stanford University; a separate project involving the Associated
Colleges of the Midwest is located at Northwestern. Each center has
a somewhat distinctive mission, but each is expected to work with

the faculty and graduate students at its own school, serve several other schools in the region, and sponsor occasional related foundation programs. A pilot faculty fellowship program also has been initiated and may grow during the next few years.

These several efforts by federal and private groups have played a key role in fostering faculty-development and instructional-improvement programs, but there is no likelihood that they will provide continuous operating support or that they will provide the total amount of financial support needed by colleges and universities to maintain these programs. Even those institutions blessed with grants find such largesse a mixed blessing; what has been given may also be taken away. Clearly, more stable sources—as well as larger amounts—of financial support are needed if this endeavor is to become a permanent fixture of academic life.

A few states and community college districts have established special programs to facilitate faculty development and instructional improvement. The Florida State Department of Education pioneered in this area by establishing a Staff and Program Development support system in 1968. It was planned that 2 percent of the overall budget of all community colleges in the state be allocated to support new staff development as well as innovative program thrusts. Through this special program substantial amounts of money have been expended to initiate several innovative projects in twenty-eight community colleges. This plan has several features that might well be emulated by other states and districts. First, funds may be expended only in accordance with a long-range plan of each school for its staff and program development; a five-year plan for each institution must be reviewed and approved by the director of the Division of Community Colleges annually. Also, funds cannot be used to pay for normal operating expenses; salary payments to faculty are limited to program initiation or improvement rather than expansion of existing programs. Equipment may not consume more than 15 percent of the funds for any year, and that may not duplicate or replace existing equipment, increase existing inventories, or meet regular, ongoing equipment needs. These restrictions are critical to the success of the program. The directors explain that if faculty members at each school were allowed to decide how to use such money, they would probably want to use it to support their advanced training, which would allow them to increase their salaries. They maintain that the basic focus must be the improvement of faculty competencies to operate programs that serve students well, and centralized control is necessary to see that this priority is sustained. Evaluations by the campuses indicate that the overwhelming majority of the projects they have undertaken are valuable and worth repeating. In a study of this program conducted for his dissertation, Adrien P. Beaudoin (1973, p. 125) concluded that the activities that were most successful were "those designed to add new programs and courses, to upgrade professional employees, and improve existing college programs by developing handbooks, syllabi, audio-visuals, and course objectives."

Individual institutions, too, have allocated a portion of their budgets to faculty development or instructional improvement. At the University of Minnesota the academic senate voted to spend 3 percent of the instructional budget to support professional development activities. Although this amount has never been allocated, many instructional-improvement projects have been supported by this special fund. Such initiatives have been taken by the administration as well as the faculty. When Stanford Cazier assumed the presidency of California State University, Chico, he set aside 1 percent of the instructional budget for instructional-improvement efforts. Phyllis Bush was appointed Assistant Vice President to coordinate an instructional-facilitation program that included several assigned faculty positions and support monies. By dividing the positions into fractions, many faculty members have been able to be supported on their pet projects.

Even though colleges and universities have put some of their "hard" money into these new programs, most are not geared to provide substantial financial support for the development of their faculty. Furthermore, most of the money that is available for assisting faculty is set aside for more traditional kinds of assistance, such as sabbatical leaves and travel to professional meetings. A number of "developing institutions," notably predominantly black colleges and small church-related schools, invest a portion of their limited development funds to help individuals obtain doctorates. There is little evidence that these procedures affect the quality of instruction at all, and there is some suspicion that they are used by faculty to enhance their own careers at the expense of institutional needs.

It would be possible for an institution to examine all of these resources devoted to professional development and to consider alternative ways by which they might be used more advantageously than at present. For example, in regard to sabbaticals, there are three common criticisms: they are costly, they are available to only a few people, and they have little demonstrable effect on the instructional programs. Some institutions have decided to act on the fact that the number of persons receiving leaves can be increased significantly if those who remain will increase their workload slightly. The University of the Pacific adopted a new sabbatical leave plan a few years ago in which every member of the faculty—not just the tenured ones—is eligible for a leave every four years. It is now in the process of relating this procedure to a faculty-development plan. The leave and faculty-development programs will be administered by Eugene Rice, who will try to help the faculty make maximum use of the leaves to further their own growth as well as enhance the instructional mission of the university.

A more radical plan has been suggested by Charles Neidt. He suggests that all professional-development money at an institution be aggregated and divided equally among all professional staff. Each person would have "special drawing rights" up to his share of the total, and he could spend it for whatever would promote his professional growth. If he would like, he would be able to leave funds in his account until it was large enough to finance a trip abroad, a leave, or some other large expense. Although the bookkeeping problems would be difficult, this plan would allow more flexible use of all available resources that any institution now provides in this area.

Fringe benefits are a large part of any faculty costs, but the different items are not equally valued by various individuals. A young faculty member who does not intend to remain at a certain school for a long time may prefer to have no pension plan but to have the use of a comparable amount of money to further his career. Educational Testing Service gives each professional employee a portion of his total salary to use in any way he desires; he may use it to purchase a health plan or dental plan, to take a course, to travel, or to otherwise advance himself personally or professionally. This would not increase the resources, but it could make available resources more flexible and therefore more useful to more persons.

Much of the debate around the resources needed for faculty development revolves around time. The professoriate has great freedom to decide how to use its time; only the relatively few hours committed to the classroom, ranging from six to fifteen hours per week, is committed. The redefinition of time usage is one way to obtain resources without needing any more dollars. Hodgkinson (1974b) points out that professors are the only professional group in America that presents its workload in a minimal way. Although everyone recognizes that a professor works more than twelve hours a week when he teaches four courses that meet three times per week, the fiction persists that academics work only a few hours. Several studies (Dunham, Wright, and Chandler, 1966; Keene, 1971)' report that the actual work week averages fifty to sixty hours, which by any standard is a good deal of working time. Hodgkinson argues that much faculty time in many institutions is spent in committee work, a fact that is costly to the institution and resented by the faculty, and he suggests several ways to streamline the committee structure and free more time for faculty members. In many institutions the number of committees can be reduced without any significant loss of sense of participation in the governance of the institution; parallel committees of the administration, faculty, and students can be consolidated; the size of committees can be reduced; ad hoc committees can replace standing committees in many instances; and committee members, particularly chairpersons, can be given training in order to make committees more efficient. Although one must be careful not to lower the quality of decisions or weaken a sense of participation by indiscriminate economizing, the functioning of inefficient committees is a luxury we cannot afford now. And the time savings can well be used by faculty to work on improving their instructional effectiveness.

It is curious that instructional improvement is thought to require time off from teaching. It is understandable that a major course redesign or the introduction of a major new program may require considerable time to plan and to produce learning materials, but much of the activity could be carried out while in the process of teaching. That is, the classroom is the essential laboratory for the improvement of teaching, and all that is needed is to provide opportunity for a faculty member to be attentive to his craft, try out new approaches, assess his effectiveness, and discuss his work with students or sympathetic colleagues. Thus, the redefinition of faculty roles would go a long way toward finding resources to mount an instructional-improvement program.

Mars Hill College has made a complete overhaul of its workload in light of its current needs, and it might be a useful example to illustrate how faculty-development activities may be incorporated within the normal activities of academic employment.

> The workload at Mars Hill College has been historically defined in terms of a course load. Other duties and responsibilities of the faculty have been assumed or, from time to time, rewarded through merit pay. As the goals and objectives of the institution changed, particularly since becoming a senior college, the duties of the faculty have changed. Since 1973 greater emphasis has been placed on internships, independent study, and other experiences offered outside the classroom. New approaches to teaching and learning have resulted in new demands on faculty time in terms of the design of the experience and its assessment. Support programs in communication skills, math, and personal development are important dimensions to the Mars Hill program, and they make new demands on faculty time and college resources. Many programs and duties related to each of the divisions create new demands on faculty time which the traditional definition of a faculty member's workload does not recognize or include [Hoffman, n.d.].

The new arrangement calls for all faculty work to be figured in terms of work units; thirty-two units of work are expected from a faculty member with a ten-month contract. Each department is awarded a total number of units depending on the number of full-time faculty members it has. The needs of the several college programs, including those of the academic departments, general education, and summer school, are determined by the persons responsible for them prior to the issuance of faculty contracts. Department chairpersons assign one to five units to all courses depending on such factors as the amount of preparation time based on such considerations as whether it is a new design, there are any special needs or difficulties, which methods are involved, the size of the class, and whether or not it includes a laboratory. Each individual faculty member is then given a workload that contains time for each of his assignments, including classes, participation on an assessment team, department chairperson duties, special advising, supervising internships, independent study, and directed readings, research, supervision of extracurricular activities, and participation in professional-development activities. This latter item is significant, as the college requires that each faculty member be assigned two units to participate in developmental seminars and workshops. This way, time for teaching-improvement activities is consciously incorporated within the faculty workload, and it becomes a regular part of each person's job description.

Thus there are several efforts to find resources for the new instructional-improvement activities on the part of the federal government, private foundations, states and districts, and individual institutions. But the problem of financing faculty development is larger than any single source and involves a redistribution of those resources that are already available to higher education away from the preparation of teachers to the provision of in-service programs for those already employed. Future projections indicate that the need for new faculty members will be modest, even though the number of graduate school graduates is slated to continue rising. A less abstract and more human example may make the point most effectively. A young acquaintance with solid academic qualifications, having obtained a bachelor's degree from Oberlin College and a master's degree from Middlebury College, and completing requirements for his doctorate in English at the University of Virginia, where he participated in a teacher-training program, wrote recently: "I am still searching for an administrative position in a university system, and I would like to ask your help. If you know of any openings I would be very pleased to hear of them. I enclose another copy of my resume . . . as a guide to my qualifications. It is complete except for the last six months, in which I have been supporting myself as a cashier at the Miramar Hotel." There is simply no need to support graduate students in English, give them graduate fellow-ships, give them teaching experience only to have them work as hotel cashiers. The educational resources of the institutions, states, foundations, and federal government may be better used to enhance the careers and lives of those persons who are already employed through such activities as faculty fellowships, programs for retraining in midcareer, and instructional-improvement activities. If there were a massive shift of existing resources away from the preparation of new teachers and toward the development of existing ones, some of the resource problems would be solved.

Overall, the following guidelines should be useful.

1. Some combination of federal, state, foundation, and insti-tutional support will be necessary if the massive investment in faculty members is to be protected and enhanced through a faculty-develop-ment or instructional-improvement program. A beginning has been made toward funding promising instructional-improvement pro-grams, but far more needs to be done at several levels if large num-bers of faculty and administrators are to become involved in professional-development activities on a regular basis as a regular part of their jobs.

2. Eventually the bulk of the money supporting instructional-improvement programs will have to come from "hard" institutional sources. It is prudent for each college and university to budget a small portion of its expenditures for the renewal of the faculty, the improvement of instruction, and institutional innovation.

3. Existing programs for the professional development of faculty should be reviewed to determine the extent to which they lead to the desired results for faculty members and the institution. Where necessary, policies and practices concerning sabbatical leaves, research support, travel money, and similar matters should be re-vised so that these resources may be used most effectively and effi-ciently.

4. Faculty workload should be defined in such a way that time for participation in professional-development activities is clearly available, and faculty members should be rewarded for their efforts to improve their teaching.

Chapter 9

▼▼▼▼▼▼▼▼▼▼▼▼▼▼▼▼▼▼▼▼▼▼▼▼▼▼▼▼▼▼▼▼▼▼▼▼

Staffing Programs

▲▲▲▲▲▲▲▲▲▲▲▲▲▲▲▲▲▲▲▲▲▲▲▲▲▲▲▲▲▲▲▲▲▲▲▲

The most important ingredient of a successful instructional-improvement program—if a single factor can be isolated—is the staff. Being primarily a service to faculty members, a program or center usually finds that its most important resources are the human ones it has or can assemble to meet the needs of the faculty. This chapter will focus on the people who operate these new programs, on the nature of a staff position, and on the organization of an instructional-improvement center staff.

Staff Background

The question of who teaches the teachers is an intriguing one. In a fundamental sense nobody *teaches* faculty; an instructional-improvement program merely provides opportunities for faculty members to learn and try out new competencies or strategies. The fact is that there are few persons who are competent by virtue of their training and experience to help their faculty colleagues improve the quality of their teaching. After all, until recently there were no instructional-improvement programs and, therefore, no need to train individuals for positions in them. But within the last few years a small group of "experts" has emerged and obtained considerable visibility across the nation; this cadre is in great demand as consultants to help various institutions plan their own programs, to conduct workshops on faculty, instructional, and organizational development, to participate in campus activities, to give speeches, to train campus staff, and to evaluate projects. Additionally, there is a growing number of individuals who are learning these new arts on numerous campuses around the country. After all, nothing that these "experts" have learned about instructional improvement is so mysterious or taxing that it cannot be learned by others. In fact, some persons already have been engaged in these activities under different auspices. One says, "I have been working on behavioral objectives for some time, and all of a sudden I discovered I have been doing faculty development." There are several persons on most campuses, not all of them very visible, who have such experience that can be utilized in instructional-improvement programs.

The professional backgrounds of staff members was examined in our survey of center directors, who were asked to list up to five professional staff members and to indicate the academic discipline, highest degree, and academic rank of each. A total of 142 staff were listed and described. The composite result indicates that the "average staff member" is trained in education or educational psychology, has a doctoral degree, and holds a faculty appointment.

A total of 59 percent have specialized in either education or educational psychology as their academic discipline, not surprising since this kind of work requires playing an educational role vis-à-vis one's colleagues in in-service programs that have long been common in the lower grades. Another 17 percent come from other areas of psychology, and 24 percent come from fields of specialization as diverse as English, history, and engineering. The predominance of education backgrounds among staff members is not to be denied, but this sample may make it appear greater than it is. The larger centers naturally contributed more to the sample than smaller ones, and the former sometimes were comprehensive instructional resource centers with media distribution and production services or evaluation services which employed largely professional educators.

Faculty members from the rank and file increasingly are becoming involved in instructional-improvement programs, which may prevent this movement from being controlled primarily by "educationists," with all the implications of that designation for many faculty members. This will be an excellent way to diffuse knowledge and understanding about teaching and learning issues throughout the faculty, and it will allow for more points of view from different quarters to find their ways into these programs.

The vast majority of the staff members that have been identified, virtually all of the directors, hold doctorates. The 23 percent who do not have that degree include a few who are working toward it as well as some who have particular skills that make them valuable additions to the staffs. Further, 75 percent hold regular academic appointments in various departments; 21 percent are full professors, 22 percent associate professors, 26 percent assistant professors, and 6 percent instructors or lecturers. These facts indicate that, in general, staff members are drawn from the mainstream of academic culture, though they are drawn disproportionately from educational disciplines.

An early report on the Center for the Teaching Professions at Northwestern University states: "Our most important needs at this time, and in the near future, are ones relating to the adequacy of staff. . . . Our concern is not with the size of staff, but with the availability of the type of individual who can relate effectively at a very human level to the problems and needs of teachers and at the same time possess the credentials necessary within the present system of higher education for the maintenance of a professional status as perceived by his academic colleagues." Also: "We have concluded that . . . the personality of staff is as important as the educational background." These views are echoed by many directors of instructional-improvement centers. In discussing the qualities that they thought were important in staff members, they mentioned a number of characteristics frequently, including the following: These staff members are sensitive to people, enjoy working with people, take risks, work hard, are enthusiastic, have high energy levels, are patient (since change does not come overnight), are tolerant of ambiguity, and have broad and eclectic views about teaching that allow them to work with many different people from many different fields. Although there is no particular personality type that is required for this work, these qualities do give a flavor of the personal traits valued by many directors.

Satisfactions and frustrations are some of the best indicators of the kinds of persons that hold a job, and several persons were questioned about these. Naturally, their answers vary with the persons and their jobs, but one common theme is captured by Lichtenstein. "I most prefer faculty members to come in and say, 'can we talk?' " He feels that if they talk for a while and the faculty member goes out to try something, that is satisfying. "The satisfactions come when the faculty member learns something, enthusiasm, insight, or relief, when he says, 'now I know what to do.' These are just like the satisfactions that come from teaching." And indeed, teaching teachers is very much like teaching students, and staff members seem to have been selected for their teaching effectiveness.

Frustrations also run the gamut, but a few seem particularly endemic to this position. One person talks of a "burn out" factor, having discovered, as innovators before her did, that the enormous amount of work required to launch a new and innovative program tends to consume great quantities of time and energy. Another mentions the tendency to become frustrated and eventually cynical or bitter after working for some time with faculty members who cannot (or will not) learn or change. A further general theme is the need to "fight the system"; the difficulty of trying to improve teaching when the reward structure emphasizes research is cited as is the lack of budget and other commitments from the administration. A rare but real tragedy is the failure of an occasional dynamic director of an instructional-improvement program to receive tenure because he fails to publish. Thus, the satisfactions tend to be those associated with a job well done, and the frustrations center around the obstacles to that end.

Position

The newest position in academe is that of staff member in an instructional-improvement program. Although the position requires a person to engage in many different kinds of activity, it is largely that of being a consultant to the faculty in relation to their interests, needs, and concerns regarding teaching. The consultant-client relationship is a familiar one to academics, but it is most common in connection with their research. Subject matter experts are called on to provide advice and criticism about content and methodological issues. The consultation of technical experts such as data processors, computer programmers, and editors has come to be regarded as an integral part of modern scholarship. Further, many academics have been called on to consult with a variety of clients in government, business, and social organizations about the implications of their work. Although the consultant-client relationship is familiar, the use of consultants in connection with teaching is quite new.

Since most programs are campus-based, the position is that of an internal consultant to one's faculty colleagues, which means many difficulties characterize the role. First, previous stances or actions of consultants may have alienated some faculty members. Second, their vested interest in both the maintenance of the position and the future of the institution may make them less detached and disinterested than a person outside the institution might be. And, they will almost surely be regarded as less expert than someone coming from outside the institution; the quip that an expert is someone at least twenty miles away has some basis in practice. At the same time, the position of internal consultant has several advantages for the instructor: the person is regularly available, has an opportunity to provide continuous assistance to an individual or project, and knows the institution far more intimately than an outsider.

Another role the director or a staff member of an instructional-improvement program often plays is that of educational leader, in many cases a role abdicated by the administration. Once, the dean (or provost or vice president) was the first among equals, a respected person who assumed a leadership role in regard to teaching and learning matters. He knew each member of the faculty intimately, tried to bring out the best in them, and helped to formulate and implement a sound curriculum. However, the role of the dean has become enlarged as most institutions have increased significantly in size and more complex as academic administration has taken on many more functions. As a result, most deans spend the bulk of their time and energy in administrative matters, committee meetings, preparing and administering budgets, making long-term plans, handling short-term crises, resolving personnel disputes, supporting the many units under their authority, and the like. From an educational point of view, the dean's role has become reduced in significance. In many institutions the instructional-improvement staff must thus take over the various functions concerning the promotion of effective teaching and learning.

So the position involves being an internal consultant to the faculty on teaching-learning matters and playing an educational leadership role within the institution. But what does that mean in specific terms? Exactly what does a staff person *do*? When asked this question, one individual frankly stated, "I goose, goad, and inspire." A more expansive if less colorful answer comes from Lynn Wood, a staff member of the Teaching Innovation and Evaluation Services at the University of California, Berkeley, who kept a record of her major activities during a six-week period (Teaching Innovation and Evaluation Services, 1974, pp. 12–15). Although it is particular to a single person, a specific program, and a single institution, her list, which is summarized below, illustrates the various activities of a staff member—in this case the second in command. It can serve as a job description of this new position.

She consulted with dozens of individual professors regarding aspects of their teaching, including interpreting student rating forms for an optometry professor, assisting various teachers to prepare grant proposals for instructional-improvement projects, attending class sessions and critiquing the performance of faculty members in history and art history, and helping evaluate several innovative courses. She consulted with individual students and student groups on the establishment of a teaching-assistant training program in mathematics, procedures for the student body to evaluate teaching, the design of an honors thesis by a sociology student, and the preparation of a student-initiated course. She worked with several departments and two schools within the university on such matters as devising procedures to evaluate teaching effectiveness, evaluating newly developed learning modules, assessing various departmental programs, and speaking at a departmental convocation. She worked with the Committee on Teaching to help members review proposals for instructional-improvement projects. She consulted with a nearby community college concerning its teaching-evaluation program, met with a group of students from another campus within the university system concerning graduate teacher-training programs, and attended a conference on the teaching of geography hosted on the campus. And she responded to numerous requests for information, both oral and written, on various topics concerning teaching and learning that came from administrators, faculty members, and students.

Although the range of activities in which a staff member engages is great, it should not be thought that the staff is the whole show. Noonan (1974, p. 2) articulates an assumption that is widespread throughout this field, "A faculty development program that draws heavily upon the talents of the university will have more credibility than a program that relies exclusively on the skills of a centralized staff." Thus, a large part of the job of a staff member involves determining the available resources within the institution, assessing the needs of different faculty members, and brokering the two. This may mean either putting two individuals in touch with one another or planning a group activity such as a workshop or seminar in which several persons may participate and learn from one or more of their colleagues.

The fact that there are many activities in which a staff member may engage suggests another important fact about his role at an instructional-improvement center: there is a large measure of ambiguity. This fact has several implications. First, because the boundaries are not at all distinct and the role can embrace so many activities, it is difficult for individuals to decide how best to spend their time. There are many legitimate areas in which a person concerned with improving teaching and learning may seek to contribute, and the well-intentioned staffer may find himself going in several directions at once, with the result that he has little sustained impact anywhere. Second, the position is a marginal one that is betwixt and between the worlds of the faculty and the administration without being fully within either. Although many staff members have faculty appointments, they are not fully functioning members of a department. And although many have administrative appointments, they seldom have the authority associated with administration. This marginal position is the natural result of decisions to give the office credibility as a faculty-oriented service and status and authority as an administrative unit. (See Chapter Seven.) Third, the indistinctness of the role creates anxiety in the staff member, who is given the general charge to serve the faculty and help them improve their teaching. Having few clear guidelines and, as is generally the case, being service oriented, and knowing that his future will be determined in large part by the quality of service offered to the faculty, he tends to respond to every request. Although on one hand admirable, this posture betrays some confusion about the role, and in turn creates more anxiety when the person, in less hectic moments, wonders whether he is having much impact at all. Fourth, there is no clear path into or out of this role. Most individuals talk of possibly moving on into administration or returning to the faculty, but the effects on one's career of serving on an instructional-improvement center are not at all certain at this point. Thus, the position has a number of tensions built into it.

Organization

Once the staff members are assembled, how do they work as a staff? Perhaps the most important feature of staff is their limited number; our survey of fifty-five instructional-improvement centers found that the median number of professional staff was two. When my associate and I at the Center for Professional Development in the California State University and Colleges met strangers and talked about the center, we often found them conjuring up images of large buildings and huge organizations, and we sometimes had to remind them that the center was little more than the two of us. The one- or two-person shop is quite common, although several organizations, particularly comprehensive instructional resource centers with media services, production facilities, and evaluation services along with an instructional-improvement component, employ several professional persons. Technical specialists and secretarial support are also commonly employed, and about one-half of the centers hire graduate and undergraduate students.

Although they have few staff members, most instructional-improvement centers actually have access to a broad range of talent. The survey questionnaire asked directors, "Does the staff possess, or have readily available to it, expertise" in several specified areas? Over 75 percent of the directors said the following kinds of expertise were available "to a great extent": information about innovative teaching and learning, skill in instructional or course development, and knowledge about media. Between 50 and 70 percent said staff had expertise in evaluation and testing, teaching evaluation, curriculum or program planning, and research methodology. And over 30 percent said they had much expertise in group process facilitation, human development, and counseling.

Of course, not all these competences are found in the staff but may be obtained from individuals throughout the institution. Forty-eight percent of the directors indicated that they rely heavily on a "home grown staff" by hiring faculty members through release time or as consultants to serve as part-time or auxiliary staff. This is a most useful way to extend the range of competencies needed for any program beyond the core staff. And 70 percent replied that they utilize consultants from outside the institution, at least occasionally. Thus, a small central staff can form a network of individuals to provide many different services to faculty members.

Claude Mathis acknowledges that "it is a great temptation to replicate yourself in selecting staff." This is a general human tendency, but it can be a serious problem in instructional-improvement programs where the small central staff must possess as great a range of expertise as possible. The key seems to be not necessarily to have jacks of all trades but to have several different people with particular strengths available for work in the program.

Some new programs have been established to develop new skills and competencies among staff members of instructional-improvement programs. The Council for the Advancement of Small Colleges has launched an extensive faculty-development effort with many of its member schools. Following an initial program that emphasized faculty teams at over forty schools, it has initiated a program to provide sixty faculty members selected from as many different colleges with advanced training in various aspects of professional development. It is expected that these individuals will be able to learn new skills that they can use in working with their colleagues in their several colleges.

When the results of this effort to improve instruction are in, whether it is transitory or permanent, it may well be that the persons who have developed the most will be the staff members. They have made new commitments, pursued new interests, acquired

new skills, broadened their experiences, and often altered their
career directions. The more individuals who can be involved in
leadership positions for instructional-improvement endeavors, the
greater impact the programs may have. That could be the best in-
service education of all.

Guidelines

1. More faculty members need to be trained to serve as consultants to their colleagues on teaching-learning matters. Although
preservice programs would be useful, a quicker and perhaps more
effective approach would be to provide in-service opportunities for
existing staff members to learn the skills and techniques of other
practitioners, share concerns and experiences, and evaluate their
efforts.

2. More persons from outside education and psychology
ought to be recruited and trained. It is understandable that academics trained in these two disciplines predominate among the staffs
of campus programs, but there is nothing so profound about the
current state of the art of improving teaching that others cannot
learn. And by broadening the range of backgrounds of staff members, institutions may obtain more intellectual perspectives and
practical approaches to the complex task of improving instruction
and at the same time help spread the concern for improvement
throughout the various academic disciplines.

3. Most staff members, whatever their special competences,
should be generalists; rather than specializing in and advocating one
teaching method, they should stress an eclectic approach. In order
to be most effective, they should have broad interests and knowledge, be aware of the range of teaching philosophies, strategies, and
methods, and be able to work with many different kinds of persons.

4. The staff should have a wide variety of specialized expertise readily available to it, either among its members and other
faculty and administrative staff or from outside the institution.

5. Insofar as is possible, the faculty should be used to provide
leadership to campus programs. This not only will create greater
credibility but will secure greater involvement and provide useful
training for the faculty.

Chapter 10

▼▼▼▼▼▼▼▼▼▼▼▼▼▼▼▼▼▼▼▼▼▼▼▼▼▼▼▼▼▼▼▼▼▼▼▼▼▼

The Impact of Programs

▲▲▲▲▲▲▲▲▲▲▲▲▲▲▲▲▲▲▲▲▲▲▲▲▲▲▲▲▲▲▲▲▲▲▲▲▲▲

It is too early to expect a full and rigorous evaluation of instructional-improvement programs, since a large number of them are only recent additions to the academic edifice. In many of them, the bulk of time and energy have been spent in start-up activities, that is, developing plans that have widespread support of the faculty and administration, establishing offices, hiring or training staff, pilot testing a few activities, and gaining further political and financial support. As with previous major academic innovations, promoters of instructional-improvement programs have been too busy getting things in motion to worry about evaluating what they are doing.

This early neglect of evaluation is understandable, although unfortunate. As Paul L. Dressel (1961, p. 6) says, "Failure to engage systematically in evaluation in reaching the many decisions necessary in education means that decision by prejudice, by tradition, or by rationalization is paramount." Professional evaluators like Dressel are wont to point out that evaluation can be most helpful if it is built into a program at the outset. As was noted earlier, the specification of measurable objectives—precisely the kind that an evaluator would look for—can help one to clarify one's own purposes. Provision for evaluation also assures that progress toward the most important goals of the program will be measured at an early date so that modifications in the objectives or the procedures may be made. But the fact remains that few programs have been carefully evaluated.

Although thirty out of fifty-four respondents to the survey for this book report that their programs have been "evaluated systematically," most have not received the kind of evaluation that is most needed. Some prepared reports to the administration summarizing their work and indicating their future plans and needs. Also, some of the improvement programs were examined during a visit by an accreditation team, while others received a campus review by faculty committee.

For instance, the Center for Improvement of Undergraduate Education (CIUE) at Cornell was established in 1971 with the stipulation that its progress would be reviewed in three years. In 1974, the report of the ad hoc committee to evaluate it drew on center documents and materials and solicited the views of users of services, administrators of several units in the university, faculty fellows who had received small grants to work at CIUE, outside referees, staff members, and persons originally involved in the formation of the unit. The generally favorable report emphasizes that the center provides the instructional services prescribed, the administration of the program is sound, the users are very satisfied, even enthusiastic, and the staff has earned the professional respect of experts in other institutions.

Indeed, it is important to know the extent to which a unit provides the services it is asked to provide, the quality of its administration, and the satisfaction of clients. And it is important to learn how the staff, accreditation teams, and campus groups view the work of these units. But these are not the kinds of evaluation that yield much information about the impact of a program. It is quite conceivable, for instance, that a center could be well administered, provide certain agreed-upon services, and have a fine professional reputation, but still not make much difference in the quality of education found at the institution. It is the evaluation of the *impact* of the various programs that is sorely needed at this point to demon-strate the value of their efforts.

This absence of careful evaluation is becoming serious. It is apparent that there has been a substantial investment in this new enterprise by institutions, public and private funding agencies, and professional staff members. Yet, during this time of reduced growth, or in some cases of retrenchment, for existing programs to go beyond their current peripheral status and become incorporated within regular operating procedures on the basis of "hard" money, evidence of their benefits to faculty, students, and the institution is needed. Indeed, other institutions that have not yet established programs will be unlikely to do so unless they are convinced of the benefits they may reasonably expect to gain. Despite the lack of evaluative study, several lessons have been learned that may help to assess the value of the activities described in the preceding chapters.

What Programs Will Not Accomplish

Because the rhetoric of many of the proponents of faculty, instructional, and organizational development makes extravagant claims that sometimes cannot be realized, perhaps the best place to start is with a consideration of what instructional-improvement pro-grams will *not* accomplish. First, it should be emphasized that instructional-improvement programs cannot, in all probability, save institutions. This may seem like a curious and possibly unnecessary thing to say, except that many academics have the idea that instruc-tional improvement may, indeed, bail colleges out of rather desperate troubles. This impression was created in large measure by the title of the influential booklet *Faculty Development in a Time of Retrench-ment*. This title, chosen by the publishers of *Change Magazine* to help market the pamphlet, led many to think that faculty develop-ment was the answer to the problems of declining student enroll-ments and financial stringency. In fact, an institution with problems of enrollment and finance will have to solve those problems with more students or greater economies; faculty-development programs may provide several benefits, but it is unrealistic to look to them to keep a sinking ship afloat.

Furthermore, instructional-improvement programs, with few

exceptions, cannot make bad teachers into good teachers. Sometimes administrators or faculty members think of a few individuals who are notorious for being dull and inept teachers, and they think that it would be nice if they could only find a way to transform them into good teachers. Unfortunately, there is no magic dust, whether marketed under faculty development or some other brand, that can be sprinkled on a targeted professor to change him into a first-class teacher. There are, of course, individual cases that can be pointed to at most institutions where a radical change in a poor teacher has been observed. One example is the professor who gave poor lectures, experienced declining enrollments in his courses, and received poor student ratings until he changed his format to use individualized learning approaches, thereby altering his role to that of a manager of student learning, after which he experienced dramatic improvements in his teaching. But such cases are the exception rather than the rule, and nobody ought to launch an instructional-improvement program with the intention of curing sick teachers.

Although there are important exceptions, most programs, as currently constituted, have little impact on the basic structures of learning. They tend to assume the existence of the academic departments, the reality of the classroom, the fact of the fifty-minute hour, and the barrier between the campus and the community; rather than trying to change these fundamental academic structures, most centers try to improve the quality of education that occurs within them. Unlike the reforms of the 1960s wherein structural change figured prominently, the kinds of change that emanate from instructional-improvement programs are more in the area of process, teaching methodology and techniques, learning materials, and interpersonal relationships. And the changes that do occur will probably have more impact directly on individuals and small groups than indirectly through changes in organizations as a whole. The major exceptions to this generalization are where faculty or instructional development is but one facet of a major institutional change, such as the adoption of the contract curriculum at Ottawa University or the introduction of competency-based curricula at colleges like Sterling, Alverno, and Mars Hill. Another exception is the creation of alternative programs within larger institutions, such as the development of individualized learning systems or the formation of clusters of like-minded faculty and students who pursue common, often interdisciplinary, educational interests.

What Programs May Accomplish

What kind of impact may an instructional-improvement program have? Throughout this volume many claims, both explicit and implicit, have been made for various development programs. Benefits for faculty members, students, and whole institutions have been cited by various spokespersons. Listed below are some of the possible consequences for faculty, students, and organizations derived from these claims.

Benefits for faculty members: acquire additional knowledge about teaching-learning issues, develop and use new or improved teaching skills, develop and use new techniques or methods of instruction, clarify attitudes and values about teaching-learning, develop favorable attitudes toward teaching and learning, develop favorable attitudes toward professional development, derive greater satisfaction from teaching and working with students, discuss teaching-learning issues and problems more frequently and with greater sophistication, develop more stimulating and supportive relationships with colleagues, obtain more accurate and favorable feedback from students.

Benefits for students: acquire more knowledge about subject matter, improve thinking skills and cognitive abilities, increase interest in the subject, gain a desire to learn more about the topic, develop more enlightened or sophisticated attitudes or values concerning the subject matter, find learning more enjoyable or satisfactory, increase speed or ease of learning, acquire greater self-consciousness about teaching-learning matters, increase the amount and sophistication of discussion of subject matter, develop closer and more productive relationships with teachers.

Benefits for the institution: increase the number of courses substantially revised or new courses added, increase the range of learning opportunities for students, plan and implement new educational programs, develop more or more effective learning materials, improve relationships between faculty members, students, and administrators, devise and implement policies supportive of teaching effectiveness and improvement, reduce student dropout rate, improve group problem-solving skills, improve leadership abilities of key faculty and administrators, enhance morale and improve the organizational climate.

These are surely not all of the relevant factors that might be affected by an instructional-improvement program, but they are a large number of specific areas of intended change that have been distilled from the literature and activities of many institutions. In addition, as many others have found, programs of planned social change almost invariably bring about unanticipated consequences, some of them antithetical to their original purposes. For a full understanding of this new enterprise, these, too, have to be examined.

In the survey, center directors were also asked questions concerning evaluation. One item was designed to elicit their attitudes toward a number of possible cooperative activities. Most areas of cooperation received widespread support (see Chapter Seven), and there was nearly unanimous support for devising and sharing "techniques for evaluating teaching improvement units." This high degree of interest suggests that the leaders of these programs are not very satisfied with the quality of existing evaluative data at most institutions.

Another item sought to determine their assessment of the proportion of faculty members that benefit from their programs. Although this would not be a disinterested assessment, it was thought the responses of the directors of instructional-improvement centers would be able to provide some useful information about this matter. Their average estimate of the proportion of faculty who "derive considerable benefit from the Unit" was 22 percent; another 26 percent of the faculty were said to "use and derive some benefit." This number seems a bit high, even given the possibility of overexuberance among the respondents, and further analysis reveals some reasons. First, persons from three large, major universities where the proportion of faculty members affected is surely modest failed to answer the question; one indicated he could not even venture a guess. In addition, some instructional-development programs were part of larger resource centers that include media, evaluation, and other related services; in some cases the response was made in terms of the larger unit, thereby artificially increasing the numbers. Still, despite some variability, the majority indicated that from 10 to 25 percent of the entire faculties at different schools derive "considerable benefit." This is a modest portion, but judging from the small size of the operations, the voluntary quality of participation, the few resources that have been allocated to these programs, and the short time many have been in operation, this represents a respectable number.

Principles of Impact

Even though careful evaluations of the impact of campus programs are lacking, much has been learned about the consequences of planned change in education as well as in other areas of life. Perhaps the delineation of a few general principles that derive from evaluations of planned change in educational as well as other institutions and which seem to be supported by at least bits of evidence from instructional-improvement programs may be useful.

First, most social programs, whether in health, housing, or education, reach only a portion of those persons they were designed to serve. The fact that instructional-improvement center directors indicate that most faculty members, although not opposed, do not use the services very much suggests the existence of this common phenomenon. In addition to the general difficulty of designing a single program that is responsive to the needs and interests of many different individuals, instructional-improvement programs have been established in such a way as to virtually guarantee serving only a portion of the faculty. Their small size, modest financing, and reliance on voluntary participation restrict their impact. Of course, this is in many ways a blessing because if large numbers of faculty did come forward seeking assistance all at once, instructional-improvement programs and their institutions, as currently operated, would be overwhelmed and unable to respond effectively.

The voluntary nature of participation virtually insures that the self-selection will result in the involvement of somewhat atypical faculty members. Several staff members have said that they serve a cross section of faculty in terms of department, age, sex, interests, and teaching ability; they try to improve the competencies of faculty whatever their level of interest or ability. However, there does seem to be a tendency to attract disproportionate numbers of persons who are, on the average, more talented and interested in teaching. In a report on the Teaching and Learning Center at the University of Nebraska, Vernon Williams (1973) indicates there was greater interest among the more accomplished instructors. At the same time, there is a tendency for such programs to repel those most in need of assistance. Lichtenstein comments, "Those who need [instructional assistance] least are the most involved; those who need it most won't come near anything you do." Finding ways to provide assistance to those most in need of improvement is a common problem that characterizes not only instructional-improvement programs but also other efforts to provide health, educational, and employment services.

Judging from the experience of several programs, the participants generally find what they come for. The 1974 report of the Cornell Center for Improvement of Undergraduate Education referred to earlier in this chapter gives the results of interviews with users of various services and reaches this conclusion: "In no case where there was active collaboration was CIUE's customer less than satisfied; more often he was enthusiastic. One may conclude that CIUE's contribution, where solicited, has always been evaluated as competent and helpful" (pp. 8–9). The report goes on to acknowledge that "the selection of collaborators—whether initiated by one side or the other—to some extent guarantees a mutuality of interest." This finding of positive benefit to a limited number of self-selected participants is confirmed in other settings. It suggests that another principle, that of accentuation, is present. Kenneth A. Feldman and Theodore M. Newcomb (1969) arrive at this principle as a result of extensive study of the impact of colleges on students. They find that different kinds of students are attracted to different kinds of colleges and that those students whose personal qualities are most consistent with the demands of the institutions further develop those qualities during their college years. The same accentuation of faculty and instructional competencies as a result of instructional-improvement programs seems to be a reasonable expectation.

Impact is likely to be greater in small than large organizations, either small colleges or small units of large institutions. This is so for several reasons. The same number of participants constitute a far larger proportion of the faculty at a small school, and a critical mass may be more easily assembled for any activity. In addition, there are important informal, frequently personal, ties in small units that reinforce formal professional relationships; a series of instructional-improvement workshops in a small school may, therefore, constitute a shared experience that tends to persist and remain a topic of conversation. In a large institution the same experience is more likely to be an isolated one in the lives of a few individuals who may have little or no subsequent interaction. For whatever reasons, it is understandable that several center directors from small colleges report that large percentages of the faculty have derived benefit from center work.

Where faculty or instructional development is part of a larger curriculum or educational program of the institution, there is greater likelihood of producing change. A curricular change that requires faculty to play new roles gives a reason why they should learn new competencies. And, a curricular change places a demand on all faculty members to do their best to implement the change; more persons are likely to become involved. Perhaps most important, a larger institutional change alters the basic condition of the instructor, requires the breaking of old habits and the development of new ones. Mervin Freedman (1973, p. 78) discusses the impact on faculty of their new roles in an experimental college, one that features interdisciplinary content, egalitarian relationships, and student development goals: "Innovative colleges are a qualitatively different educational milieu. Their discontinuity with traditional settings is so great that faculty have to create genuinely new models with little personal experience or educational tradition to serve as bases. However, the turmoil, the sense of discovery, the feelings of community, and the intimacy can be valuable and cherished experiences." Similar findings have been reported by Noonan (1971; 1972). Although faculty members, like other adults, may resist major changes, involvement in new and alternative educational programs can be a most valuable growth-producing experience for them.

Those individuals who make the greatest investment, especially if it has personal and emotional components, are likely to derive the greatest benefits. Again it is difficult to elicit this kind of involvement from adults, because as Sanford observes, they are ensconced in roles and situations that function as barriers to change, but once they are involved at an intense level, they are likely to make greater and longer-lasting changes. At most institutions a small group of deeply involved faculty members can be found to lend support to this generalization. But perhaps the persons who make the greatest commitment to instructional improvement are the faculty members who direct these new programs. For many this involves moving out from familiar orbits in their departments and disciplines and charting, at least temporarily, new career patterns, learning about a host of new educational matters, and learning to administer an office. Predictably, several directors say that, just as a teacher often learns more about a course by teaching it, so they learn more about teaching and learning by planning in-service programs for their faculty colleagues.

From the spate of new social programs that were launched during the 1960s throughout the nation, we have learned how difficult it is to produce any change in individuals and institutions. Wherever possible, it is far easier and more economical to bring about improvements in a faculty member, an activity like instruction, and an organization by matching individuals with institutional needs rather than trying to change either. The radical "changes" in the quality of teaching by a few faculty are largely the result of a strategy to help them find ways of teaching that are consistent with their personal styles rather than seeking to change them in any fundamental way. Of course, some changes are necessary for a person to switch from a lecturing approach to the use of PSI, for instance, but they are relatively superficial and nonthreatening. Helping a person to find his niche and maximize the strengths of his personal and professional styles may produce much improvement with only limited personal or emotional turmoil.

One of the more massive attempts to improve teaching and learning has been at the University of California, where a special million dollar appropriation has been made for this purpose throughout the nine-campus system. Because the appropriation originally was a last-minute add-on item to the state budget, few plans had been made to spend this money wisely; and, as for many government projects, the funds would be available only during the one year. Hurriedly, guidelines were drawn up, campus liaison persons informed, proposals solicited, and projects funded. Three kinds of project were supported: evaluation of teaching effectiveness, summer grants to faculty members for the improvement of individual courses, and seminars or small discussion courses for entering students. An evaluation of the first year of activity was conducted by James Stone and his colleagues at the Berkeley campus (Stone and others, 1974). "The general impression on most campuses is that the fund has been utilized in a relatively effective fashion, given the variety of constraints—particularly the late funding—which were in effect" (p. 19). This preliminary assessment reported further that "there has not been, nor could there have been expected to have been, a *broad-based* impact from the one million dollars on any of the campuses. Rather, the impact has been highly selective in terms of those involved. Thus, for example, students involved in specific projects or in the overall program appeared to have benefited, but apart from handbooks, the larger student body has not, or at least not yet. Similarly, selected faculty who have had a direct involvement have benefited and generally expressed their satisfaction. However, a broad base of faculty has not yet been involved" (p. 20). One of the more intriguing issues in this whole area is the extent to which these new approaches become incorporated within regular academic procedures, and the evaluation addressed that issue, also. "For instructional changes to have a long-lasting impact, at some point they will need to be incorporated in the mainstream departments. There appears to be no substantial effort on any campus to overcome the barriers which prevent this from occurring" (p. 29). Although this report is only preliminary, and the follow-up evaluation is shaping up as somewhat more favorable—in large part because of the continuity that was provided by a subsequent year of state funding—this finding poses a challenge to others to make such endeavors more than one-shot affairs that are merely peripheral activities.

These, then, are some of the kinds of impact instructional-improvement programs are unlikely to have, the kinds of changes they may produce, and some principles that will probably affect their impact. It is important to stress that there has been very little careful evaluation of these efforts and that there are a great many different consequences that may flow from any particular program. However, there is some scattered evidence that lends support to these various conclusions, and judging from the experience of other efforts to change people and organizations, they seem to be reasonable approximations of what may emerge from these new endeavors.

Chapter 11

▼▼▼▼▼▼▼▼▼▼▼▼▼▼▼▼▼▼▼▼▼▼▼▼▼▼▼▼▼▼▼▼▼▼▼▼▼▼

Prospects for the Future

▲▲▲▲▲▲▲▲▲▲▲▲▲▲▲▲▲▲▲▲▲▲▲▲▲▲▲▲▲▲▲▲▲▲▲▲▲▲

Thus far in this examination of instructional-improvement programs, we have discussed the origins and progress of activities colleges and universities are undertaking to enhance teaching and learning. We have noted that most institutions, faced with the prospects of leveling student enrollments, declining faculty positions, and the possibility of becoming "tenured in," are beginning to realize that in the coming decades they will need to rely on their current faculty to provide fresh perspectives, infuse new ideas, and give leadership to innovative programs if they expect to maintain vigorous educational climates. In the midst of a tight job market, faculty members are realizing that their careers may be confined to one institution which must provide the enriching experiences they need to grow professionally and personally.

We have observed in Chapter One that professional development and renewal for faculty is not new, that opportunities for sabbatical leaves, travel to conferences and meetings, and research support have long been available—albeit often at modest levels. What *is* new is that these traditional forms of development are being

173

supplemented by efforts to help professors grow and flourish in their teaching roles. Centers, divisions, offices, and programs have been established by every kind of college and university as well as by state systems, consortia, and professional associations. These offices include both small- and large-scale efforts, and their programs range from narrowly specialized to broadly comprehensive, but they all aim to provide opportunities for faculty members to enhance one or another aspect of their teaching and to increase student learning.

We have seen that despite this similarity of purpose, the programs differ considerably in focus. Depending on what aspects of the teaching-learning process they emphasize, they draw on different intellectual traditions, make different analyses about what ails teaching and learning, and prescribe different solutions. *Faculty*-development programs, as Chapter Two explained, focus on faculty members rather than on the courses they teach or their organizational environments; they stress both professional and personal development of professors over the life span, stemming from their intellectual roots in developmental, clinical, and social psychology and psychiatry. In contrast, *instructional*-development programs (Chapter Three), focus on the design of effective conditions of learning, particularly as provided by courses, emanating from their roots in the fields of curriculum and instruction, learning theory, educational media and technology, and systems theory. And *organizational*-development programs (Chapter Four) focus on the environment within which students, faculty, and administrators work, stemming from research and practice in human relations, organizational theory, and sociology. In Chapter Five we observed that the most successful programs include elements of all three approaches in a comprehensive endeavor.

We noted in Chapters Six through Nine the various ways that campus programs are organized—from the informal efforts of administrators to the creation of self-contained and separately staffed centers, their politics in introducing a new and potentially threatening idea to the faculty, their financing by both external and internal sources, and their staffing by regular faculty and by specially trained staff. In Chapter Ten the impacts which various programs seem to have or not have on faculty, students, and institutions were detailed.

This final chapter takes a broader perspective on these matters. It summarizes the present status of instructional improvement as a new movement within higher education, indicates the future needs of the movement if it is to bring important benefits to the field, and ventures an assessment of its potential significance for higher education as a whole.

The Developing Movement

Although the attention of previous chapters has focused on activities of single institutions, it is apparent that the scope of instructional-improvement activities transcends individual campuses. The host of new programs, their funding by federal and state agencies as well as private foundations, and the appearance of a new breed of academic professional to staff them all attest to the fact that a veritable movement surrounding professional development and the improvement of teaching and learning is underway throughout higher education. From being virtually unheard of before 1970, the idea of professional development for the sake of better teaching and learning has become a social force within higher education that in many ways has a life of its own.

The instructional-improvement movement parallels earlier reform movements in higher education, some of them successful and others not. Within the past two decades, the creation of institutional research offices, the addition of non-Western studies to the curriculum, the organization of ethnic studies programs, and the involvement of students in academic governance have been examples of innovative efforts that have affected the conduct of higher education. Major changes such as these pass through several stages. First, a few critics attack customary practices and offer alternatives to them. Then a few experimental or pilot programs are created amid high hopes and often unrealistically grand expectations. Hailed as solutions to longstanding problems, programs gain national visibility as their founders speak at conferences, consult with other institutions, answer inquiries from interested persons, and host visitors to the campus. If early efforts appear promising, additional institutions begin to imitate them, and a social movement is set in motion as the idea diffuses throughout higher education. Eventually, experience is gained with the new programs, and their consequences, both good and bad, become apparent; this experience tempers hopes and expectations, and more balanced assessments of the movement are possible. Inevitably, the programs accomplish less than their most enthusiastic proponents have promised but more than their doomsaying opponents have predicted. At this point institutions must decide whether to continue supporting the not-so-new programs and to incorporate them into their regular operations even though they are not a panacea or to drop them because their benefits are not sufficient in terms of their costs. If they are retained, the programs in time become traditional themselves and eventually become the subject of attacks by other critics seeking to bring about subsequent reforms.

The instructional-improvement movement is at an important transition point because it has already passed through the early stages of this process. A high degree of consciousness has arisen about the need to provide renewal opportunities for faculty members and to offer effective instruction for more diverse groups of students. Many pilot programs have been created amid much fanfare, and they and their leaders have acquired considerable national visibility for their views and actions. Large numbers of other institutions have either created their own programs or are planning to do so. Henceforth, the progress of the instructional-improvement movement as a whole will have an impact on numerous campus programs as well as be shaped by them.

But actual experience with in-service programs is quite limited: few of them have been in existence long enough to know what their long-range benefits and costs are and to experience what happens after the initial enthusiasm that surrounds almost any new program starts to diminish. Despite the continuing growth of new programs, the idea of systematic faculty, instructional, and organizational development is by no means established as part of the academic mainstream. Colleges and universities that organized some of the early programs with outside funds must now decide whether to incorporate them into their regular budgets and operations. And other institutions, interested in beginning effective programs, await

objective and realistic assessment of existing programs before proceeding. This book seeks to provide one such assessment and to
outline the tasks that institutions must still undertake if the new
approaches to instructional improvement are to achieve their potential.

If successful, the new ideas concerning instructional improvement will bring fundamental and lasting change to academic life.
They can lead to an increase in the importance of teaching among
faculty, the revision of institutional policies and practices to provide
greater support for teaching effectiveness, a redefinition of professional activity to include regular and repeated participation in
in-service education, and the reallocation of resources to finance
instructional-improvement efforts. If they realize even part of this
potential, these programs deserve to become institutionalized as a
regular part of academic life, just as instructional improvement is an
accepted part of the lives of teachers in secondary and elementary
schools and professional renewal through sabbaticals is accepted for
professors. But, if the current efforts fail to improve teaching or
learning, the current flurry of interest in them will be nothing more
than a passing fad, and academic life will return to the way it was
before the notion arose that faculty, instruction, and organizations
can and should be systematically developed.

At this point, when the movement is still young, it could go
either way. While the early steps that have been described in these
pages are significant, the gap between its current status and its
future potential is great, as Table 3 shows.

Future Needs

First, few colleges or universities currently have instructional-
improvement programs; although the number is growing, it still is a
minority of all institutions of higher learning. If present approaches
are successful, most institutions will eventually establish similar programs. It seems reasonable to expect that every state system of
colleges and universities, individual institutions, and schools, divisions, and departments within them will then have carefully prepared
plans for promoting the development of their staff.

Second, thus far, few faculty members at those institutions

Table 3.   CURRENT STATUS AND POTENTIAL FUTURE
OF INSTRUCTIONAL IMPROVEMENT

Current Status	*Potential Future*
Few institutions have programs.	Most institutions have programs.
Few faculty are involved.	All or most faculty are involved.
Participants are primarily volunteers.	Participants feel some external pressure to participate.
Faculty participation is limited and irregular.	Faculty participation is regular and continuous.
Participation is an "overload."	Participation is provided for in normal workload.
In-service development is a peripheral activity.	In-service development is a central activity.
Budgets and resources are modest.	Budgets and resources are adequate.
"Soft" grant monies are a major source of funds.	"Hard" institutional monies are the major source of funds.
Few institutional policies support teaching effectiveness or professional development.	Many policies support teaching effectiveness and professional development.
Few permanent instructional-improvement centers conduct professional development.	Instructional-improvement centers providing professional development are permanent.
Few staff members have training and experience in consulting with colleagues.	Many staff members have training and experience in consulting with colleagues.
Little evidence of effectiveness of programs exists.	Convincing evidence of effectiveness exists.
Impact is limited to selected institutions and faculty members.	Impact is widespread among institutions and faculty.
Modest reforms aimed at better teaching are underway.	Extensive improvements in instruction and organizational operations are made.

with programs have become involved in them, and their participation is usually voluntary, considered as an "overload," and unrewarded. Unless greater numbers become involved, including those who are most in need of help but who elect not to participate under completely voluntary arrangements, the idea will not achieve its full potential. It is quite possible for institutions to establish policies that broaden participation by expecting that all new faculty members or administrators participate in a professional-development program, that each unit prepare and implement a development plan covering all of its staff, or that all professors and administrators participate in at least some self-development activities on a regular basis. This would entail acknowledgement that such activities are a regular part of the faculty or administrative workload and would provide for the reduction of other assignments, a redefinition of the professorial role, or some tangible reward for the expenditure of time and effort in development activities. If participation is not extended in these ways, then it is difficult to see how instructional improvement will become more than a peripheral activity of academic life except as an activity for self-selected volunteers. Although it may be worthwhile to serve these persons, limited participation will not achieve the needed improvements.

Third, budgets and other resources that heretofore have been allotted to instructional-improvement programs are generally modest, sometimes meager. Further, although some institutional resources have been provided to support their efforts, instructional-improvement programs have relied heavily on "soft" grant monies from government agencies and private foundations. Because of the operating principles of almost all such funding sources, there is no chance that these grants will provide continuing support for regular program operations, however successful they may be. At this juncture, it is critical that institutions budget adequate sums of "hard" money for in-service programs if they are to be institutionalized. Some reallocations of funds, faculty assignments, and institutional priorities, such as from preservice graduate programs to in-service faculty programs or from physical planning and maintenance to human planning and development, as well as redefinition of faculty workloads to permit more efficient use of existing personnel may be possible. But ultimately, additional financial commitment from the institution will be required, with institutional resources supplemented by external funds for particular projects or faculty fellowships. Of course, institutions will be reluctant to make such commitments, particularly in these difficult times, unless they have more evidence of the success of instructional-improvement endeavors than is now available at most institutions.

Fourth, because the movement is so new, few institutional policies and procedures support faculty, instructional, or organizational development. Despite the enthusiastic involvement of many present participants, instructional-improvement programs will not succeed unless they are supported by institutional policies in the areas of hiring, promotion, retention, tenure, salaries, leaves, workload, assignment, and retirement that place emphasis on the effectiveness of teaching, the improvement of instruction, and the growth of individuals. Faculty will not persist in activities, no matter how beneficial they may be to themselves, if such involvement does not allow them to get ahead in their institutions and their profession.

Fifth, although some institutions have established formal instructional-improvement centers to serve as an organizational base to enhance teaching and learning, many have merely established short-term projects or designated certain individuals with the responsibility for conducting such activities. Firm organizational structures are needed to give assurance to faculty members and instructional-improvement staff that an ongoing institutional commitment exists for the enterprise. Otherwise many academics will merely wait for the termination of the project or the passing of the designated individual from the scene. Temporary structures, ad hoc arrangements, and individual efforts may be useful to initiate programs, but more permanent structures are needed to maintain adequate programs in most institutions.

Sixth, few existing staff members have training in consulting with their colleagues about teaching and learning, and most are drawn heavily from education and psychology backgrounds. More individuals from more disciplines—particularly those throughout the liberal arts—must be trained to help other faculty so that the fund of expertise about instruction can be extended. Moreover, although there is a growing cadre of largely self-taught persons in this new field, many have little contact with their counterparts in other institutions. They need to share their knowledge, skills, and strategies with one another and to learn from the experience of pioneers in the effort. Since instructional-improvement programs exist to develop the human resources of colleges and universities, and since their most important resources are the human ones they can muster, it is essential that these staff members be carefully cultivated.

Finally, and perhaps most critical to the future of instructional improvement, is the matter of evaluation and impact. Presently little evidence about the effectiveness of campus programs is available, and what evidence exists tends to be either anecdotal or limited to elementary descriptive information about the numbers and types of faculty members who participate in various activities. If more programs are to be established, more faculty involved, "hard" money committed, long-term organizations created, and qualified professional persons attracted as staff from throughout the various disciplines, then convincing evidence of the benefits of faculty, instructional, and organizational development must be adduced. If the evidence indicates that the benefits claimed by proponents are either small or not forthcoming, then present efforts, no matter how promising, will be abandoned—as they should be.

Significance of the Movement

The future of the movement is one thing, but its significance is quite another. It is possible for an innovation to be incorporated into institutions without producing much of significance, particularly in terms of educational benefits for students. The last question in this inquiry that must be raised is: What is likely to be the long-term significance of the movement if it is successful in becoming a continuing feature of academic life?

One way of addressing this question is to note that while virtually all programs attempt to help stimulate better instruction, very few seek to make major changes in the structure of teaching and learning. Unfortunately, most promise only modest changes in the organization and conduct of education. The thrust of most instructional-improvement programs is to work within traditional frameworks—that is, to assume the existence of the college classroom, the conventional academic disciplines, the separation of the campus from the community, and the fifty-minute hour. With few exceptions, they seek to improve learning within these traditional contexts. While such improvements are certainly desirable, the changes in the quality of existing forms of education are likely to be modest at best. The few programs that seek to transcend these basic constraints by emphasizing nonclassroom learning, providing interdisciplinary educational opportunities, expanding the context for learning into the community, and altering the usual student-faculty relationships are likely to have more significance than others. Such endeavors are more likely to bring about fundamental changes not only in the classroom behavior of instructors but in the academic conditions which structure the ways teaching and learning are conducted.

Another way of addressing the question is by pointing out that many programs seem to lack an explicit and coherent philosophy of education. Their preference for a pragmatic approach that permits staff members to help faculty achieve a variety of educational objectives is a valuable political strategy; if the staff allowed their own values free reign, they would be less effective in serving those with different values. But teaching and learning are above all moral and political matters and not simply technical concerns; values cannot be purged, only ignored. Without a carefully formulated philosophy of education, it is simply not possible to answer the question, Faculty development for what?

The only long-term justification of faculty, instructional, or organizational development is that it improves the quality of education available to college students. But what is an effective college education? In regard to teaching, this means more than transmitting facts and knowledge and more than presenting the content of one's academic speciality, however important these may be. It implies a breadth of concern and an attempt to relate knowledge in one's field to other fields of investigation, to the realities in the larger society, and to the personal development of students. Similarly, the kind of learning which should be the fruit of a college education transcends the acquisition of facts, methods, or general principles. It includes acquiring an appreciation of the value of intellectual inquiry, increasing sensitivity and awareness, and developing a personal philosophy and outlook on life. In short, the kind of teaching and learning which is ideally characteristic of a college education is that which makes a difference in the lives of students.

A large amount of research has been conducted on the impact of college on students. The research literature was summarized originally by Phillip Jacob (1957, p. 7); he compiled evidence that "the quality of teaching has wrought but little effect upon the value outcomes of general education . . . so far as the great mass of students is concerned." Feldman and Newcomb (1969, p. 330), writing twelve years later, and surveying greater amounts and more sophisticated research in the area, drew a similar conclusion: "Though faculty members are often individually influential, particularly in respect to career decisions, college faculty do not appear to be responsible for campus-wide impact except in settings where the influence of student peers and of faculty complement and reinforce one another."

Both reviews reached similar conclusions about where the teachers do make a difference in the lives of students. Jacob says, "Faculty influence appears more pronounced at institutions where association between faculty and students is normal and frequent, and students find teachers receptive to unhurried and relaxed conversations out of class" (p. 8). Feldman and Newcomb conclude, "The conditions for campus-wide impact appear to have been most frequently provided in small, residential, four-year colleges. These conditions probably include relative homogeneity of both faculty and student body, together with opportunity for continuing interaction, not exclusively formal upon students and between students and faculty" (p. 331). A research project (Gaff and others, 1975) at the University of California, Berkeley, surveyed faculty members in several institutions and related faculty attitudes and values concerning teaching and learning, teaching practices, and relationships with students to the longitudinal changes experienced by students during their four years. On most campuses important barriers to the significant encounters between students and teachers were found. Those teachers were most effective who found ways to transcend the barriers of age and authority, classroom and content, to confront students as individuals. Those students benefited more from a college education who more aggressively used the learning resources of the school, including their courses and their teachers, to expand their own self-awareness. And those college programs were most effective which, whatever the content or structure of their formal curriculum, created the conditions for close, frequent, continuous and wide-ranging interaction between teachers and students, both in and out of class.

Colleges and universities too often have failed to realize their goals of having a liberalizing impact on the lives of students—goals which are enshrined and fine-sounding catalog statements—largely because they have fragmented the college experience. First, they have fragmented the curriculum; courses, sometimes even those in the same discipline, are unrelated to one another. A vice president of a leading western university has observed, "The History Department in my school has taken all of history and divided it into courses by country and by century." Second, the curriculum is separated from the rest of student life. Students engage in one kind of conversation and focus of concern within the classroom, and they enter a very different world when they go out the door. Third, facts have been separated from values so that it is difficult for students and faculty members to speculate, discuss aspirations, define purposes, or even consider value implications of factual matters. Fourth, the faculty are separated from the students. There are many contrivances, including the formal classroom, especially in a lecture course, that prevent faculty from revealing much of themselves to students and students from revealing their inner selves to faculty; often interaction is more or less stereotyped and routinized so that each may keep a safe distance from the other. Fifth, the campus has been largely divorced from the larger society and the community which surrounds it. The learning experience typically has been confined to the context of a classroom, and the learning resources of the larger community have been relatively untapped. The weight of evidence is that colleges and universities may best achieve their educational purposes when they consciously make connections between these various factors, between elements of the curriculum, between the curriculum and the rest of students' lives, between facts and values, between faculty and students, and between the campus and the community. Only then will the college experience be integrative for students and provide a synthesis of various elements of their lives. Faculty members hold the key to such integration of the educational experience; this fact contains several implications for instructional-improvement programs.

These new programs and their activities will be judged primarily in terms of the impact that they have on the lives of students. On the basis of the scholarship mentioned earlier, this means that instructional improvement programs ought to help the faculty develop the attitudes, competencies, and techniques to realize the following objectives:

1. Interest, motivate, and stimulate students to learn their subject matter by showing them its value and significance for their lives, rather than assuming students automatically are interested. If such significance is absent, then that material should be re-examined to determine whether it is really appropriate.

2. Teach students higher level mental skills rather than mastery of factual details or basic information. Students can easily obtain facts and details from textbooks and other materials, and much of that will be forgotten soon after it is learned, but principles, generalizations, and mental processes tend to be more useful and to have a longer life expectancy.

3. Help students explore and develop value positions which are intimately related to the factual knowledge which they acquire as well as helping them master cognitive knowledge.

4. Carry their teaching beyond their disciplines and the classroom, engage substantive social and personal problems, and reach students in such a way that their lives outside the classroom join with the concerns within the classroom.

5. Become effective counselors in educational, vocational, and personal matters so that the personal lives of students can be effectively related to their educational programs and vocational futures.

6. Implement a curriculum that provides a holistic and integrated experience for students, rather than merely trying to improve individual teaching within a fragmented curriculum.

7. Maintain an informal culture among the faculty and students that supports the formal curriculum and encourages student development as well as the usual kinds of academic learning.

It is apparent that if faculty are to do these several things, they must become embodiments of the well-educated person themselves. Harold Taylor (1958, p. 162), former president of Sarah Lawrence College, has written, "It is the richness and depth of the inner life of the teacher and the qualities that he holds as a man of character and commitment that determine his students' responses to his teaching. We, therefore, need to do everything in our power to arrange the community life of our college campuses in such a way that its elements conspire to produce stimulating and provocative effects in the intellectual and personal growth of teachers." If instructional-improvement programs and centers can take this advice and help arrange the community lives of colleges and universities to have such profound effects on teachers, and if, particularly, those effects can be observed around the range of objectives that have just been listed, then these new programs will help colleges and universities to have significant impact on the lives of students. In that event, faculty-, instructional-, and organizational-development programs will, indeed, be regarded as valuable additions to higher education.

▼▼▼▼▼▼▼▼▼▼▼▼▼▼▼▼▼▼▼▼▼▼▼▼▼▼▼▼▼▼▼▼▼▼▼▼

List of Programs
and Centers

▲▲▲

This list of colleges and universities that operate instructional-improvement programs or centers has been assembled so that individuals interested in faculty, instructional, and organizational development may learn about others who are engaged in similar activities. The list is extensive but should not be viewed as an exhaustive inventory of all such programs; data are current as of mid-1975. References to those programs and centers mentioned in the text will be found in the index.

The centers listed emphasize the in-service education of college teachers and the improvement of their instruction. Not included are faculty-development activities which are conducted regularly by administrators in the normal course of their work and those conducted by separate departments or other small units within colleges. Centers and programs other than those listed here focus on the preparation of college teachers in graduate school, on teacher

188   Toward Faculty Renewal

training for elementary and secondary schools, or on working directly with students to increase their study and learning skills.

Special acknowledgement should go to Loren Williams of Virginia Commonwealth University, who alerted me to many of the programs operated by medical schools, and to James Hammons, who supplied names of many individuals working in community colleges.

ALABAMA

UNIVERSITY OF ALABAMA
Thomas Diener, Director
Center for Research and Services in Higher Education
University of Alabama
University, Alabama 35486

Jack D. Hain, Director
Office of Undergraduate Medical Education
Division of Research
School of Medicine
University of Alabama
Birmingham, Alabama 35233

ARIZONA

PIMA COMMUNITY COLLEGE
Arthur H. Evans, Jr., Coordinator
Curriculum/Staff Development
Pima Community College
2202 West Anklam Road
Tucson, Arizona 85709

UNIVERSITY OF ARIZONA
Sarah M. Dinham, Director
Arizona Medical Center
University of Arizona
Tucson, Arizona 85724

CALIFORNIA

AZUSA PACIFIC COLLEGE
James Holsclaw
Office of Instructional Development
Azusa Pacific College
Azusa, California 91702

CALIFORNIA STATE COLLEGE, BAKERSFIELD
Kim Flachman, Director
Center for Professional Development
California State College 9001 Stockdale Highway
Bakersfield, California 93309

CALIFORNIA STATE COLLEGE, SAN BERNARDINO
Walter Zoecklein, Director
Center for Professional Development
California State College
5500 State College Parkway
San Bernardino, California 92407

CALIFORNIA STATE UNIVERSITY, CHICO
Phyllis I. Bush, Associate Vice-President for Academic Affairs
Learning Activities Resource Center
California State University
Chico, California 95926

CALIFORNIA STATE UNIVERSITY, FRESNO
Carl Kleeman, Director
Faculty Development Program
California State University
Fresno, California 93740

CALIFORNIA STATE UNIVERSITY, LONG BEACH
James C. Robinson, Director
Faculty Career Development Center
California State University
Long Beach, California 90804

CALIFORNIA STATE UNIVERSITY, NORTHRIDGE
Daniel Sedey, Director
Institute for the Advancement of Teaching and Learning
California State University

18111 Nordhoff Street
Northridge, California 91324

CALIFORNIA STATE UNIVERSITY
AND COLLEGES SYSTEM
Clare Rose, Director
Center for Professional Development
California State University and Colleges System
5670 Wilshire Boulevard
Los Angeles, California 90036

COAST COMMUNITY COLLEGE DISTRICT
Bernard J. Luskin, Vice Chancellor
Educational Planning and Development
Coast Community College District
1370 Adams Avenue
Costa Mesa, California 92626

DE ANZA COMMUNITY COLLEGE
David L. Kest, Chairman
Faculty Development Committee
DeAnza Community College
21250 Stevens Creek Boulevard
Cupertino, California 95014

GOLDEN WEST COMMUNITY COLLEGE
Hayden Williams, Director
Learning Resources
Golden West Community College
Huntington Beach, California 92647

LOS MEDANOS COLLEGE
Chester H. Case, Jr., Professional Development Facilitator
Los Medanos College
Pleasant Hill, California 94523

OHLONE COLLEGE
Neil McCallum
Staff and Instructional Development Program
Ohlone College
Fremont, California 94537

PASADENA CITY COLLEGE
    Esther R. Davis, Educational Development Officer
    Pasadena City College
    1570 East Colorado Boulevard
    Pasadena, California 91100

SAN DIEGO STATE UNIVERSITY
    Patrick Harrison, Director
    Instructional Development Program
    San Diego State University
    San Diego, California 92115

SAN FRANCISCO STATE UNIVERSITY
    Francis X. Moakley, Director
    Audio-Visual Center
    San Francisco State University
    San Francisco, California 94132

SAN JOSE STATE UNIVERSITY
    Ron J. McBeath, Director
    Instructional Resources Center
    San Jose State University
    San Jose, California 05102

SANTA ANA COLLEGE
    Donna Farmer, Dean of Instructional Services
    Santa Ana College
    Seventeenth at Bristol
    Santa Ana, California 92706

STANFORD UNIVERSITY
    Robert N. Bush, Director
    Center for Research and Development in Teaching
    Stanford University
    Stanford, California 94305

    David Halliburton, Director
    Center for Teaching and Learning
    Stanford University
    Stanford, California 94305

UNIVERSITY OF CALIFORNIA, BERKELEY
    Robert C. Wilson, Director

Teaching Innovation and Evaluation Services
University of California
Berkeley, California 94720

UNIVERSITY OF CALIFORNIA, DAVIS
Kathleen M. Fisher, Director
Teaching Resources Center
University of California
Davis, California 95616

Theodore C. West, Coordinator
Medical Learning Resources
School of Medicine
University of California
Davis, California 95616

UNIVERSITY OF CALIFORNIA, IRVINE
John Stroessler
Office of Educational Development
California College of Medicine
University of California
Irvine, California 92664

UNIVERSITY OF CALIFORNIA, SAN FRANCISCO
Edward Rosinski
School of Medicine
University of California
Third and Parnassus
San Francisco, California 94122

UNIVERSITY OF CALIFORNIA, SANTA BARBARA
David Outcalt, Acting Director
Office of Instructional Development
University of California
Santa Barbara, California 92706

Stanley Nicholson, Consultant on New Ways to Teach
Office of Instructional Development
University of California
Santa Barbara, California 92706

UNIVERSITY OF THE PACIFIC
Eugene Rice, Director

Faculty Development Program
University of the Pacific
Stockton, California 95204

UNIVERSITY OF REDLANDS
Howard Hurlbut, Director
Hubert Eaton Program for Instructional Development
University of Redlands
Redlands, California 92373

UNIVERSITY OF SOUTHERN CALIFORNIA
Robert T. Filep, Director
Learning Systems Center
University of Southern California
University Park
Los Angeles, California 90007

Stephen Abrahamson, Director
Department of Research in Medical Education
School of Medicine
University of Southern California
2025 Zonal Avenue
Los Angeles, California 90033

WRIGHT INSTITUTE
Nevitt Sanford, Scientific Director
Wright Institute
2728 Durant Avenue
Berkeley, California 94704

COLORADO

COLORADO STATE UNIVERSITY
Frank J. Vattano, Assistant Academic Vice-President
Office of Instructional Development
Colorado State University
Fort Collins, Colorado 80521

UNIVERSITY OF COLORADO
Donald L. Newport, Director
Mountain-Plains Community College Leadership Program

University of Colorado
Boulder, Colorado 80302

CONNECTICUT

UNIVERSITY OF CONNECTICUT
T. Joseph Sheehan, Head
Department of Health Education
School of Medicine
University of Connecticut Health Center
Farmington, Connecticut 06032

DELAWARE

UNIVERSITY OF DELAWARE
Donald Nelson, Director
Instructional Resources Center
University of Delaware
100 East Hall
Newark, Delaware 19711

DISTRICT OF COLUMBIA

AMERICAN HISTORICAL ASSOCIATION
William R. Taylor, Project Director
Faculty Development Project
American Historical Association
400 A Street, S.E.
Washington, D.C. 20003

AMERICAN SOCIOLOGICAL ASSOCIATION
Hans Mauksch, Project Director
Project to Improve Undergraduate Teaching
American Sociological Association
1722 N Street, N.W.
Washington, D.C. 20036

ASSOCIATION OF AMERICAN MEDICAL COLLEGES
Hilliard Jason, Director
Division of Faculty Development
Association of American Medical Colleges

Suite 200
One Dupont Circle N.W.
Washington, D.C. 20036

COUNCIL FOR THE ADVANCEMENT OF
SMALL COLLEGES
Gary Quehl, President
Faculty Development Program
Council for the Advancement of Small Colleges
One Dupont Circle N.W.
Washington, D.C. 20036

GEORGETOWN UNIVERSITY
Ben A. Green, Jr.
Center for Personalized Instruction
Georgetown University
Washington, D.C. 20007

SOCIETY FOR VALUES IN HIGHER EDUCATION
Jerry G. Gaff, Director
Project on Instructional Renewal Through the
    Improvement of Teaching
Society for Values in Higher Education
1818 R Street, N.W.
Washington, D.C. 20009

FLORIDA

ECKERD COLLEGE
Mentorship Program
Eckerd College
5401 34th Street South
St. Petersburg, Florida 33733

FLORIDA STATE DEPARTMENT OF EDUCATION
Frederick W. Atherton
Program for Staff and Program Development
Florida State Department of Education
Tallahassee, Florida 32304

FLORIDA STATE UNIVERSITY
John Harris, Director

Division of Instructional Research and Service
Florida State University
Tallahassee, Florida 32306

MIAMI-DADE COMMUNITY COLLEGE
Carol Zion, Director
Office of Staff and Organizational Development
Miami-Dade Community College
Miami, Florida 33167

PENSACOLA JUNIOR COLLEGE
Edward E. Lewis, Instructional Development Specialist
Pensacola Junior College
P.O. Box 9153
Pensacola Beach, Florida 32561

SANTA FE COMMUNITY COLLEGE
Clyde C. Clements, Jr.
Santa Fe Community College
Gainesville, Florida 32601

UNIVERSITY OF FLORIDA
Jeaninne Webb, Director
Office of Instructional Resources
University of Florida
Gainesville, Florida 32601

Arthur D. King, Instructional Systems Coordinator
Office of Dental Education
College of Dentistry
University of Florida
Gainesville, Florida 32601

C. Benjamin Stevens
J. Hillis Miller Health Center
Office of Medical Education
College of Medicine
University of Florida
Gainesville, Florida 32601

GEORGIA
BERRY COLLEGE
Faculty Development Program

Berry College
Mt. Berry, Georgia 30149

MEDICAL COLLEGE OF GEORGIA
Kenneth Morse
School of Dentistry
Medical College of Georgia
1459 Gwinnett Street
Augusta, Georgia 30902

SPELMAN COLLEGE
Pauline Drake, Director
Institute for Teaching and Learning
Spelman College
350 Leonard S.W.
Atlanta, Georgia 30314

SOUTHERN REGIONAL EDUCATION BOARD
William R. O'Connell, Jr., Project Director
Undergraduate Education Reform Project
Southern Regional Education Board
130 6th Street N W.
Atlanta, Georgia 30313

IDAHO

UNIVERSITY OF IDAHO
Center for Organization and Human Development
University of Idaho
Moscow, Idaho 83843

ILLINOIS

ASSOCIATED COLLEGES OF THE MIDWEST
J. Patrick Haithcox, Vice-President, Academic Affairs
Faculty Development Program
Associated Colleges of the Midwest
60 West Walton Street
Chicago, Illinois 60610

CHICAGO MEDICAL SCHOOL
Donald F. Pochyly, Chairman

Department of Health Sciences Education
Chicago Medical School
2020 West Ogden Avenue
Chicago, Illinois 60612

EASTERN ILLINOIS UNIVERSITY
Gene W. Scholes
Audio Visual Center
Eastern Illinois University
Charleston, Illinois 61920

GOVERNORS STATE UNIVERSITY
Warland D. Wight, Director
Instructional Communications Center
Governors State University
Park Forest South, Illinois 60466

ILLINOIS STATE UNIVERSITY
Eugene H. Jabker, Director
Instructional Development
Illinois State University
Bloomington-Normal, Illinois 61761

MUNDELEIN COLLEGE
Faculty Development Program
Mundelein College
Chicago, Illinois 60626

NORTHWESTERN UNIVERSITY
B. Claude Mathis, Director
Center for the Teaching Professions
Northwestern University
2003 Sheridan Road
Evanston, Illinois 60201

PARKLAND COLLEGE
Michael Topper, Coordinator of Staff Development
Parkland College
Champaign, Illinois 61820

SOUTHERN ILLINOIS UNIVERSITY
Donald L. Winsor, Director

Learning Resources Service
Southern Illinois University
Carbondale, Illinois 62901

Maurice Levy, Director
Department of Educational Resources and Development
School of Medicine
Southern Illinois University
Carbondale, Illinois 62901

D. Dax Taylor, Associate Dean
Medical Education
School of Medicine
Southern Illinois University
P.O. Box 3926
Springfield, Illinois 62702

UNIVERSITY OF ILLINOIS
Charles J. McIntyre, Director
Office of Instructional Resources
University of Illinois
Urbana, Illinois 61801

William E. Sorlie, Assistant Dean
Curriculum and Evaluation
College of Medicine
University of Illinois
1205 West California Street
Urbana, Illinois 61801

Christine McGuire
Center for Educational Development
College of Medicine
University of Illinois
1853 West Polk Street
Chicago, Illinois 60612

WESTERN ILLINOIS UNIVERSITY
James Joyce, Executive Director
Illowa Higher Education Consortium
Western Illinois University
Macomb, Illinois 61455

WILLIAM RAINEY HARPER COLLEGE
George H. Vogel, Dean of Learning Resources
Learning Resources Center
William Rainey Harper College
Palatine, Illinois 66067

INDIANA

BALL STATE UNIVERSITY
Office of University Evaluations
Ball State University
Muncie, Indiana 47306

EARLHAM COLLEGE
Gerald Bakker, Coordinator of Faculty Development
Earlham College
Richmond, Indiana 47375

INDIANA UNIVERSITY SYSTEM
K. Gene Faris, Dean
Learning Resources
Indiana University System
Bloomington, Indiana 47401

PURDUE UNIVERSITY
Warren Seibert
Office of Instructional Services
Measurement and Research Center
Purdue University
West Lafayette, Indiana 47907

IOWA

SIMPSON COLLEGE
Hal S. Chase, Director
Faculty Development Program
Simpson College
Indianola, Iowa 50125

UNIVERSITY OF IOWA
Barry Bratton, Project Coordinator
Instructional Development Project

Learning Resources Unit
College of Medicine
University of Iowa
137 Medical Research Center
Iowa City, Iowa 52240

KANSAS

COLBY COMMUNITY COLLEGE
Terry Ludwig, Director of Human Development
Colby Community College
1255 South Range
Colby, Kansas 67701

KANSAS STATE UNIVERSITY
Richard E. Owens, Director
Office of Educational Improvement and Innovation
Kansas State University
Manhattan, Kansas 66502

OTTAWA UNIVERSITY
Thomas Maher, Director
Educational Research and Planning
Ottawa University
Ottawa, Kansas 66067

Peter Sandstrom, Director
Office of Educational Facilitation
Ottawa University
Ottawa, Kansas 66067

STERLING COLLEGE
Carol Gene Brownlee, Dean of Curricular Development
Sterling College
Sterling, Kansas 67579

UNIVERSITY OF KANSAS
Philip C. McKnight, Director
Office of Instructional Resources
University of Kansas
Lawrence, Kansas 66044

Robert G. Pierleoni, Chairman
Department of Learning Resources
School of Medicine
University of Kansas
Rainbow Boulevard at 39th Street
Kansas City, Kansas 66103

KENTUCKY

CENTRE COLLEGE OF KENTUCKY
E. C. Reckard, Vice-President and Dean of the College
Faculty Development Program
Centre College of Kentucky
Danville, Kentucky 40422

MAYSVILLE COMMUNITY COLLEGE
John H. Crockett, Assistant Director for Academic Affairs
Maysville Community College
Maysville, Kentucky 41056

UNIVERSITY OF KENTUCKY
Sam Brown, Director
Section for Educational Resources
A. B. Chandler Medical Center
College of Medicine
University of Kentucky
Lexington, Kentucky 40506

John Serkland, Chairman
Faculty Evaluation Committee
College of Allied Health Professions
University of Kentucky
Lexington, Kentucky 40506

LOUISIANA

LOUISIANA STATE UNIVERSITY
Jane K. Kuehn, Coordinator
Faculty Orientation and Development Program
Louisiana State University
Baton Rouge, Louisiana 70803

MAINE

UNIVERSITY OF MAINE
Edward P. Caffarella, Director
Instructional Systems Center
University of Maine
Orono, Maine 04473

Jon I. Young, Project Director
Improving Teaching Effectiveness Project
University of Maine
Orono, Maine 04473

MARYLAND

HOWARD COMMUNITY COLLEGE
Al P. Mizell, Director
Learning Resources
Howard Community College
Columbia, Maryland 21044

PRINCE GEORGE'S COMMUNITY COLLEGE
Peter Burnham, Coordinator for Staff Development
Prince George's Community College
Largo, Maryland 20870

Leah Nekritz
Learning Resources Center
Prince George's Community College
Largo, Maryland 20870

UNIVERSITY OF MARYLAND
Murray Kappelman
Office of Medical Education
School of Medicine
University of Maryland
660 West Redwood Street
Baltimore, Maryland 21201

MASSACHUSETTS

CHURCH SOCIETY FOR COLLEGE WORK
Joe Williamson, Director

New Faculty Program
Church Society for College Work
99 Brattle Street
Cambridge, Massachusetts 02138

GREENFIELD COMMUNITY COLLEGE
Toby B. Sutton, Assistant to Dean of Faculty
Greenfield Community College
Greenfield, Massachusetts 01301

HAMPSHIRE COLLEGE
Daniel Kegan, Director
Institutional Research and Evaluation
Hampshire College
Amherst, Massachusetts 01002

HARVARD UNIVERSITY
William G. Perry, Jr., Director
Bureau of Study Council
Harvard University
Cambridge, Massachusetts 02139

Dean K. Whitla, Director
Center for Teaching and Learning
Harvard University
Cambridge, Massachusetts 02139

MASSACHUSETTS STATE COLLEGE SYSTEM
William P. Haas, Director
Center for Educational Development
Massachusetts State College System
53 State Street
Boston, Massachusetts 02109

NORTHEASTERN UNIVERSITY
Alvin Kent, Director
Office of Educational Resources
Northeastern University
Boston, Massachusetts 02115

QUINSIGAMOND COMMUNITY COLLEGE
John Scanlon
Instructional Development Program

Quinsigamond Community College
Worcester, Massachusetts 01606

SPRINGFIELD TECHNICAL COMMUNITY COLLEGE
Edward R. Maclosky, Assistant Dean of Faculty
Springfield Technical Community College
One Armory Square
Springfield, Massachusetts 01105

TUFTS UNIVERSITY
Phyllis Schmitt, Director
Medical Education Research
School of Medicine
Tufts University
136 Harrison Avenue
Boston, Massachusetts 02111

UNIVERSITY OF MASSACHUSETTS, AMHERST
Sheryl Riechmann, Director
Center for Instructional Resources and Improvement
University of Massachusetts
Amherst, Massachusetts 01102

Michael A. Melnick, Director
Clinic to Improve University Teaching
University of Massachusetts
Amherst, Massachusetts 01102

WELLESLEY COLLEGE
Faculty Development Program
Wellesley College
Wellesley, Massachusetts 02181

MICHIGAN

ASSOCIATION OF INDEPENDENT COLLEGES AND UNIVERSITIES OF MICHIGAN
Sister Mary Martens, Coordinator
Faculty Development Program
Association of Independent Colleges and Universities of
 Michigan

Aquinas College
Grand Rapids, Michigan 49506

CENTRAL MICHIGAN UNIVERSITY
Sherwood E. Bridges, Director
Division of Instructional Resources
Central Michigan University
Mt. Pleasant, Michigan 48859

GRAND VALLEY STATE COLLEGE
Robert Toft, Dean
College IV
Grand Valley State College
Allendale, Michigan 49401

KALAMAZOO VALLEY COMMUNITY COLLEGE
Peter D. Rush
Instructional Development Program
Kalamazoo Valley Community College
6767 West O Avenue
Kalamazoo, Michigan 49009

KELLOGG COMMUNITY COLLEGE
Frank Crookes, Director of Instructional Design
Kellogg Community College
450 North Avenue
Battle Creek, Michigan 49015

MICHIGAN STATE UNIVERSITY
Ronald W. Richards, Director
Office of Medical Education Research and Development
College of Human Medicine
Michigan State University
East Lansing, Michigan 48823

Robert H. Davis, Director
Educational Development Program
Michigan State University
East Lansing, Michigan 48823

Lawrence T. Alexander, Director
The Learning Services

Michigan State University
East Lansing, Michigan 48823

OAKLAND COMMUNITY COLLEGE
Derek N. Nunney, Director and Vice President for
Academic Affairs
Personalized Educational Programs
Oakland Community College
Bloomfield Hills, Michigan 48013

UNIVERSITY OF MICHIGAN
Wilbert J. McKeachie, Director
Center for Research on Learning and Teaching
University of Michigan
Ann Arbor, Michigan 48104

David Starks, Chairman
Educational Resources Department
School of Dentistry
University of Michigan
Ann Arbor, Michigan 48104

James Griesen, Director
Office of Educational Research and Resources
School of Medicine
University of Michigan
1335 Catherine Street
Ann Arbor, Michigan 48104

WAYNE STATE UNIVERSITY
Joseph W. Hess, Jr., Director
Education Services and Research
School of Medicine
Wayne State University
1400 Chrysler Freeway
Detroit, Michigan 48207

WESTERN MICHIGAN UNIVERSITY
Howard R. Poole, Head
Office of Instructional Development
Western Michigan University
Kalamazoo, Michigan 49001

MINNESOTA

MACALESTER COLLEGE
Charles R. Green and Walter D. Mink, Program Coordinators
Faculty Renewal Program
Macalester College
St. Paul, Minnesota 55101

UNIVERSITY OF MINNESOTA
James H. Werntz, Director
Center for Educational Development
University of Minnesota
Minneapolis, Minnesota 55455

Russell W. Burris, Director
Consulting Group on Instructional Design
University of Minnesota
Minneapolis, Minnesota 55455

Judith Garrard, Curriculum Evaluator
Medical School
University of Minnesota
Minneapolis, Minnesota 55455

MISSISSIPPI

MISSISSIPPI GULF COAST JUNIOR COLLEGE
Robert L. Johnson, Executive Assistant for Education
Mississippi Gulf Coast Junior College
Perkinston, Mississippi 39573

MISSOURI

CENTRAL MISSOURI STATE UNIVERSITY
Eugene H. Aist, Director
Instructional Resources Center
Central Missouri State University
Warrensburg, Missouri 64093

FOREST PARK COMMUNITY COLLEGE
Otis L. Bolden, Assistant Dean of Instruction
Forest Park Community College

5600 Oakland
St. Louis, Missouri 63110

KANSAS CITY REGIONAL COUNCIL FOR HIGHER EDUCATION

Frederick H. Gaige, Director
Center for Professional Development
Kansas City Regional Council for Higher Education
Kansas City, Missouri 64111

MAPLEWOODS COMMUNITY COLLEGE

Arthur D. Schmidt, Assistant Dean/Instructional Services
Maplewoods Community College
2601 Northeast Barry Road
Kansas City, Missouri 64156

MERAMAC COMMUNITY COLLEGE

Walter E. Hunter, Assistant Dean for Instruction
Meramac Community College
Kirkwood, Missouri 63122

ROCKHURST COLLEGE

Faculty Development Program
Rockhurst College
Kansas City, Missouri 64110

ST. LOUIS UNIVERSITY

George Zimny, Chief
Section of Human Behavior
School of Medicine
St. Louis University
1402 S. Grand Boulevard
St. Louis, Missouri 63104

TARKIO COLLEGE

Lawrence Pattee, Director
Teaching-Learning Center
Tarkio College
Tarkio, Missouri 64491

UNIVERSITY OF MISSOURI AT COLUMBIA

Merlyn C. Herrick, Director

Educational Resources Group
School of Medicine
University of Missouri
Columbia, Missouri 65201

UNIVERSITY OF MISSOURI AT KANSAS CITY
James M. Richards, Director
Office of Medical Education
School of Medicine
University of Missouri
2220 Holmes Street
Kansas City, Missouri 64108

NEBRASKA
NEBRASKA TECHNICAL COLLEGE
Gilbert Brauer
IDL
Nebraska Technical College
Milford, Nebraska 68405

UNIVERSITY OF NEBRASKA
Gene Harding, Coordinator
Teaching and Learning Center
University of Nebraska
Lincoln, Nebraska 68508

NEVADA
UNIVERSITY OF NEVADA AT RENO
Daniel L. Oppleman, Director
Division of Educational Support and Communications
School of Medical Sciences
University of Nevada
Reno, Nevada 89507

NEW HAMPSHIRE
DARTMOUTH UNIVERSITY
William M. Smith, Dean of Instructional Services
Dartmouth University
Hanover, New Hampshire 03755

NEW HAMPSHIRE COLLEGE AND
UNIVERSITY COUNCIL
Joseph J. Durzo, Coordinator
Instructional Development Program
New Hampshire College and University Council
2321 Elm Street
Manchester, New Hampshire 03104

UNIVERSITY OF NEW HAMPSHIRE
Arthur C. Borror, Chairman
Teaching/Learning Council
University of New Hampshire
Durham, New Hampshire 03824

NEW JERSEY

BLOOMFIELD COLLEGE
John Carey, Coordinator
Faculty Development Program
Bloomfield College
Bloomfield, New Jersey 07003

BURLINGTON COMMUNITY COLLEGE
Carol Freedman
Instructional Development Center
Burlington Community College
Pemberton-Browns Mill Road
Pemberton, New Jersey 08068

OCEAN COUNTY COLLEGE
James McGinty, Education Development Specialist
Ocean County College
Hooper Avenue
Toms River, New Jersey 08753

STOCKTON STATE COLLEGE
Daniel N. Moury, Dean
Office of Academic Development
Stockton State College
Pomona, New Jersey 08240

NEW MEXICO
UNIVERSITY OF NEW MEXICO
John R. Graham, Chairman
Educational Resources Committee
School of Medicine
University of New Mexico
915 Stanford Drive N.W.
Albuquerque, New Mexico 87106

NEW YORK
ALBANY MEDICAL COLLEGE OF UNION UNIVERSITY
Paul L. Brading, Director
Medical Education
Albany Medical College of Union University
47 New Scotland Avenue
Albany, New York 12208

THE CITY COLLEGE
Gerald S. Posner, Director
Center for Educational Experiment and Development
The City College
Convent Avenue at 138th Street
New York, New York 10031

COLLEGE CENTER OF THE FINGER LAKES
Bonnie B. Larson, Director
Program of Faculty Development
Houghton House
College Center of the Finger Lakes
Corning, New York 14830

CORNELL UNIVERSITY
James B. Maas, Director
Center for Improvement of Undergraduate Education
Cornell University
Ithaca, New York 14850

CORNING COMMUNITY COLLEGE
Ann Cohen

Faculty Development Program
Corning Community College
Corning, New York 14830

JAMESTOWN COMMUNITY COLLEGE
Charles Shoup, Associate Dean of Instruction
Jamestown Community College
525 Falconer Street
Jamestown, New York 14701

STATE UNIVERSITY OF NEW YORK, ALBANY
Charles Neff, Associate Chancellor
Special Projects
State University of New York
99 Washington Street
Albany, New York 12210

William A. Robbins, Director
Two-Year College Student Development Center
State University of New York
135 Western Avenue
Albany, New York 12222

STATE UNIVERSITY OF NEW YORK, EMPIRE STATE COLLEGE
Thomas Clark, Director
Center for Individualized Education
Empire State College
Saratoga Springs, New York 12866

STATE UNIVERSITY OF NEW YORK COLLEGE, BROCKPORT
Learning Resources Center
State University of New York College
Brockport, New York 14420

STATE UNIVERSITY OF NEW YORK COLLEGE, OSWEGO
J. Richard Pfund, Director
Learning Resources

State University of New York College
Oswego, New York 13126

STRATEGIES FOR CHANGE AND KNOWLEDGE
UTILIZATION PROJECT
Jack Lindquist, Executive Director
Strategies for Change and Knowledge Utilization Project
605 North Broadway
Saratoga Springs, New York 12866

SYRACUSE UNIVERSITY
Robert M. Diamond, Director
Center for Instructional Development
Syracuse University
Syracuse, New York 13210

UNIVERSITY OF ROCHESTER
Robert H. Geertsma, Chairman
Division of Medical Education and Communication
School of Medicine and Dentistry
University of Rochester
260 Crittenden Boulevard
Rochester, New York 14642

NORTH CAROLINA

APPALACHIAN STATE UNIVERSITY
Louie A. Brown, Associate Professor of Sociology and
Anthropology
Appalachian State University
Boone, North Carolina 28608

BEAUFORT COUNTY TECHNICAL INSTITUTE
Tyrone Williams, Educational Development Officer
Beaufort County Technical Institute
P.O. Box 1069
Washington, North Carolina 27889

CENTRAL CAROLINA TECHNICAL INSTITUTE
Jimmy Foster, Educational Development Officer
Central Carolina Technical Institute
Sanford, North Carolina 27330

CENTRAL PIEDMONT COMMUNITY COLLEGE
Mimi Vollum, Director of Educational Development
Central Piedmont Community College
1141 Elizabeth Avenue
Charlotte, North Carolina 28204

COLLEGE OF THE ALBEMARLE
Thomas E. Vernon, Acting Educational Development Officer
College of the Albemarle
Elizabeth City, North Carolina 27909

DAVIDSON COUNTY COMMUNITY COLLEGE
W. G. Sink, Educational Development Officer
Davidson County Community College
P.O. Box 1287
Lexington, North Carolina 27292

DUKE UNIVERSITY
Marjorie Boeck, Assistant to the Director
Medical and Allied Health Education for Educational
    Research and Development
School of Medicine
Duke University
Durham, North Carolina 27706

JOHNSTON TECHNICAL INSTITUTE
John G. Hatch, Educational Development Officer
Johnston Technical Institute
Highway 301 North
Smithfield, North Carolina 27577

KITTRELL COLLEGE
Howard G. Herring, Educational Development Officer
Kittrell College
P.O. Box 278
Kittrell, North Carolina 27544

MARS HILL COLLEGE
David Knisley, Director of Educational Development
Mars Hill College
Mars Hill, North Carolina 28754

NATIONAL LABORATORY FOR HIGHER EDUCATION
National Laboratory for Higher Education
Mutual Plaza
Durham, North Carolina 27701

NORTH CAROLINA CENTRAL UNIVERSITY
James E. Parker, Coordinator
Learning Resources
North Carolina Central University
Durham, North Carolina 27707

NORTH CAROLINA DEPARTMENT OF
COMMUNITY COLLEGES
James H. Ellerbe, Director of Staff Development
North Carolina Department of Community Colleges
110 Education Building
Raleigh, North Carolina 27611

PITT TECHNICAL INSTITUTE
Lynda Wilms, Educational Development Officer
Pitt Technical Institute
P.O. Box 7007
Greenville, North Carolina 27834

SOUTHEASTERN COMMUNITY COLLEGE
Jack Ervin, Educational Development Officer
Southeastern Community College
P.O. Box 151
Whiteville, North Carolina 28472

UNIVERSITY OF NORTH CAROLINA
Merrel D. Flair, Director
Medical Studies
School of Medicine
University of North Carolina
Chapel Hill, North Carolina 27514

UNIVERSITY OF NORTH CAROLINA SYSTEM
J. Lem Stokes II, Associate Vice-President for Academic Affairs
Institute for Undergraduate Curriculum Reform
University of North Carolina System
P.O. Box 2688
Chapel Hill, North Carolina 27514

WARREN WILSON COLLEGE
Faculty Development Program
Warren Wilson College
Swannanoa, North Carolina 28788

WAYNE COMMUNITY COLLEGE
Jan J. Crawford, Educational Development Officer
Wayne Community College
P.O. Drawer 1878
Goldsboro, North Carolina 27530

WILSON COUNTY TECHNICAL INSTITUTE
William D. Tyndall, Project Director
Title III HEA
Wilson County Technical Institute
902 Herring Avenue
Wilson, North Carolina 27893

Adele Gray, Educational Development Officer
Wilson County Technical Institute
902 Herring Avenue
Wilson, North Carolina 27893

OHIO

CAPITAL UNIVERSITY
James L. Burke, Director
Faculty Seminar on Teaching
Capital University
Columbus, Ohio 43209

CASE WESTERN RESERVE UNIVERSITY
T. Hale Ham, Director
Division of Research in Medical Education
School of Medicine
Case Western Reserve University
2119 Abington Road
Cleveland, Ohio 44106

CLEVELAND COMMISSION ON
HIGHER EDUCATION
Lance C. Buhl

Cleveland Commission on Higher Education
Lincoln Building
1367 East 6th Street
Cleveland, Ohio 44114

CLEVELAND STATE UNIVERSITY
Feris Anthony, Director
Center for Effective Learning
Cleveland State University
Cleveland, Ohio 44115

DENNISON UNIVERSITY
Parker E. Lichtenstein, University Professor
Dennison University
Grantville, Ohio 44621

GREAT LAKES COLLEGES ASSOCIATION
Stephen Scholl, Executive Director
Faculty Development Program
Great Lakes Colleges Association
Ohio Wesleyan University
Delaware, Ohio 43015

KENT STATE UNIVERSITY
Lee J. Mullally, Director
Office of Faculty Development
Kent State University
Kent, Ohio 44240

MIAMI UNIVERSITY OF OHIO
William King
Audio Visual Service
Miami University of Ohio
Oxford, Ohio 45056

OHIO STATE UNIVERSITY
Gregory L. Trzebiatowski, Assistant Dean
Medical Education Development
College of Medicine
Ohio State University
370 West Ninth Avenue
Columbus, Ohio 43210

Delayne R. Hudspeth, Director
Educational Development
College of Pharmacy
Ohio State University
Columbus, Ohio 43210

UNIVERSITY OF CINCINNATI

Anthony Grasha, Director
Institute for Research and Training in Higher Education
University of Cincinnati
Cincinnati, Ohio 45221

OKLAHOMA

OKLAHOMA STATE UNIVERSITY

Richard M. Robl, Director
Educational Development
Oklahoma State University
Stillwater, Oklahoma 74074

ORAL ROBERTS UNIVERSITY

William W. Jernigan, Vice-President
Learning Resources and Instruction
Oral Roberts University
Tulsa, Oklahoma 74105

SOUTH OKLAHOMA CITY JUNIOR COLLEGE

Gordon Kilpatrick, Director of Educational Development
South Oklahoma City Junior College
7777 South May Avenue
Oklahoma City, Oklahoma 73195

UNIVERSITY OF OKLAHOMA

Richard R. Drisko, Director
Learning Resources Center
School of Medicine
University of Oklahoma
800 N.E. 13th Street
Oklahoma City, Oklahoma 73104

OREGON

LINN BENTON COMMUNITY COLLEGE
Dee Martin, Director of Curriculum and Development Resource
Linn Benton Community College
Albany, Oregon 97321

OREGON STATE SYSTEM OF HIGHER EDUCATION
Gaylord Thorne, Director
Higher Education Research Program
Teaching Research Division
Oregon State System of Higher Education
Monmouth, Oregon 97361

UNITED STATES INTERNATIONAL UNIVERSITY
Thomas A. Kepner, Director
Office of Instructional Development
United States International University
P.O. Box 1028
Corvallis, Oregon 97331

PENNSYLVANIA

BUCKNELL UNIVERSITY
Faculty Development Program
Bucknell University
Lewisburg, Pennsylvania 17837

COMMUNITY COLLEGE OF ALLEGHENY COUNTY
Conway A. Jeffress, Assistant Academic Dean
Division of Educational Services Allegheny Campus
Community College of Allegheny County
808 Ridge Avenue
Pittsburgh, Pennsylvania 15212

PENNSYLVANIA STATE UNIVERSITY
Melvyn J. Haber, Chairman
Campus Center for Teaching
Pennsylvania State University
Middletown, Pennsylvania 17057

Joseph Biedenbach, Director
Educational Resources

Milton S. Hershey Medical Center
College of Medicine
Pennsylvania State University
Hershey, Pennsylvania 17033

Leslie P. Greenhill, Director
University Division of Instructional Services
Pennsylvania State University
University Park, Pennsylvania 16802

TEMPLE UNIVERSITY
David Kapel, Director
Instructional Development
Temple University
Philadelphia, Pennsylvania 19122

UNIVERSITY OF PITTSBURGH
Grace French-Lazovik, Director
Center for the Improvement of Teaching
938 Cathedral of Learning
Pittsburgh, Pennsylvania 15213

Robert F. Schuck, Director
Division of Research in Medical Education
Alan Magee Scaife Hall of the Health Professions
School of Medicine
University of Pittsburgh
Pittsburgh, Pennsylvania 15213

SOUTH CAROLINA

GREENVILLE TECHNICAL EDUCATION CENTER
W. Wayne Scott, Project Director
Educational Development Team
Greenville Technical Education Center
P.O. Box 5616–Station B
Greenville, South Carolina 29606

UNIVERSITY OF SOUTH CAROLINA
Jay C. Smith, Dean
Learning Resources and Educational Development

University of South Carolina
Columbia, South Carolina 29208

TENNESSEE

MEMPHIS STATE UNIVERSITY

Douglas Mayo, Director
Center for Learning Research and Service
Memphis State University
Memphis, Tennessee 38152

MIDDLE TENNESSEE STATE UNIVERSITY

Charles W. Babb
Department of Education
Middle Tennessee State University
Box 519
Murfreesboro, Tennessee 37130

UNIVERSITY OF TENNESSEE

Earle Bowen, Coordinator
Educational Resources
College of Medicine
University of Tennessee
62 South Dunlap
Memphis, Tennessee 38103

Ohmer Milton, Director
Learning Research Center
University of Tennessee
Knoxville, Tennessee 37916

TEXAS

AUSTIN COMMUNITY COLLEGE

Barbara P. Washburn, Associate Dean of Instructional Services
Austin Community College
Austin, Texas 78702

BAYLOR COLLEGE OF MEDICINE

David Holcomb
Baylor College of Medicine

1200 Moursund Avenue
Houston, Texas 77025

BAYLOR UNIVERSITY
Raymond Biles
Faculty Development Program
Baylor University
Box 248
Waco, Texas 76703

DALLAS COUNTY COMMUNITY COLLEGES
DISTRICT
Ralph Holloway
System Office
Dallas County Community Colleges District
Dallas, Texas 75202

EL PASO COMMUNITY COLLEGE
Margaret Haddad, Education Development Officer
El Paso Community College
6601 Dyer Street
El Paso, Texas 79904

Gilberto De Los Santos, Dean of Instructional Development
Individualized Instruction and Faculty Development Program
El Paso Community College
6601 Dyer Street
El Paso, Texas 79904

MOUNTAIN VIEW COMMUNITY COLLEGE
Harryette Ehrhardt
Mountain View Community College
Dallas, Texas 75221

TARRANT COUNTY–DALLAS COUNTY
COMMUNTY COLLEGE DISTRICTS
Anita Barrett, Executive Director
Career Development Center
Tarrant County–Dallas County Community College Districts
P.O. Box 1465
Arlington, Texas 76010

TEXAS STATE TECHNICAL INSTITUTE
Clay G. Johnson, Coordinator
Curriculum Development
Texas State Technical Institute
Waco, Texas 76703

UNIVERSITY OF TEXAS, ARLINGTON
Mary Lynn Crow, Director
Faculty Development Resource Center
University of Texas
Arlington, Texas 76019

UNIVERSITY OF TEXAS, AUSTIN
James E. Stice, Director
Center for Teaching Effectiveness
University of Texas
Austin, Texas 78712

UNIVERSITY OF TEXAS, DALLAS
Fred Christen, Director
Instructional Communications
Southwestern Medical School
University of Texas
5323 Harry Hines Boulevard
Dallas, Texas 75235

UNIVERSITY OF TEXAS, GALVESTON
Harold G. Levine, Director
Research in Medical Education
Medical Branch
University of Texas
Galveston, Texas 77550

UNIVERSITY OF TEXAS HEALTH SCIENCE
CENTER
John Kleffner
Dental School
University of Texas Health Science Center
San Antonio, Texas 78285

UTAH

BRIGHAM YOUNG UNIVERSITY
R. Irwin Goodman, Director
Division of Instructional Services
Brigham Young University
Provo, Utah 84601

UNIVERSITY OF UTAH
Mitchell Schorow, Director
Medical Sciences Education
Medical Center
College of Medicine
University of Utah
50 North Medical Drive
Salt Lake City, Utah 84112

UTAH STATE UNIVERSITY
Michael DeBloois, Director
Learning Resource Center
Utah State University
Logan, Utah 84321

VIRGINIA

BLUE RIDGE COMMUNITY COLLEGE
Frank Turnage, Director of Instructional Services and
Educational Development
Blue Ridge Community College
Box 80
Weyers Cave, Virginia 24486

DABNEY S. LANCASTER COMMUNITY COLLEGE
David P. Moon, Educational Development Officer
Dabney S. Lancaster Community College
Clifton Forge, Virginia 24422

EASTERN VIRGINIA MEDICAL SCHOOL
James Scholten, Special Assistant to the Dean
Curricular and Instructional Development
Smith Rogers Hall

Eastern Virginia Medical School
358 Mowbray Arch
Norfolk, Virginia 23507

NORTHERN VIRGINIA COMMUNITY COLLEGE
Jo Anne Craig, Administrative Assistant to the Provost
Northern Virginia Community College
Annandale, Virginia 22003

J. Michael Mullen, Educational Development Officer
Northern Virginia Community College
Annandale, Virginia 22003

Jean Netherton, Dean for Instructional Services
Northern Virginia Community College
Annandale, Virginia 22003

Paul Saylor, Division Chairman, Developmental Studies
Northern Virginia Community College
Annandale, Virginia 22003

Gloria Terwilliger, Director
Learning Resource Center
Northern Virginia Community College
Annandale, Virginia 22003

SOUTHWEST VIRGINIA COMMUNITY COLLEGE
Bob Sutherland, Educational Development Officer
Southwest Virginia Community College
P.O. Box 878
Richlands, Virginia 24641

UNIVERSITY OF VIRGINIA
Ralph Ingersoll, Associate Dean, Education
School of Medicine
University of Virginia
Charlottesville, Virginia 22904

VIRGINIA COMMONWEALTH UNIVERSITY
John F. Noonan, Director
Center for Improving Teaching Effectiveness

Virginia Commonwealth University
Richmond, Virginia 23220

W. Loren Williams, Jr., Director
Educational Planning and Development Program
Medical College of Virginia
Virginia Commonwealth University
MCV Station Box 636
Richmond, Virginia 23219

VIRGINIA POLYTECHNIC INSTITUTE AND
STATE UNIVERSITY
Stanley A. Huffman, Jr., Director
Learning Resource Center
Virginia Polytechnic Institute and State University
Blacksburg, Virginia 24061

WASHINGTON

UNIVERSITY OF PUGET SOUND
Steven R. Phillips, Coordinator of Faculty Development
Faculty Development Program
University of Puget Sound
Tacoma, Washington 98416

UNIVERSITY OF WASHINGTON
Charles W. Dohner, Director
Office of Research in Medical Education
School of Medicine
University of Washington
Seattle, Washington 98105

WEST VIRGINIA

WEST VIRGINIA NORTHERN COMMUNITY
COLLEGE
Linda Smith, Assistant to the President
West Virginia Northern Community College
87 15th Street
Wheeling, West Virginia 26003

WISCONSIN

UNIVERSITY OF WISCONSIN, GREEN BAY
Eugene L. Hartley
Office for Educational Development
University of Wisconsin
Green Bay, Wisconsin 54301

UNIVERSITY OF WISCONSIN, MADISON
Howard Stone, Director
Office of Educational Planning and Development
Medical School
University of Wisconsin
610 Walnut Street
Madison, Wisconsin 53706

▼▼

Bibliography

▲▲

Even though colleges and universities have only recently established programs to provide in-service opportunities for faculty members to improve the quality of teaching and learning, the amount of literature on the topic is growing rapidly. Unfortunately, much of the experience and wisdom that could help newcomers to the field understand its scope and nature is expressed in fugitive documents, reports, memoranda, proposals, campus newsletters, and unpublished papers. Increasingly, however, materials are finding their way into general circulation, and the following references point the interested reader to some of the best of them.

The most generally useful books were described in the Preface and need only be mentioned here. They are *Faculty Development in a Time of Retrenchment* by the Group for Human Development in Higher Education, *Teachers for Tomorrow* by Terry O'Banion, *Instructional Development Agencies in Higher Education* by Lawrence Alexander and Stephen Yelon, and *A Handbook for Faculty Development* by William Bergquist and Steven Phillips.

229

Other useful works are *Professors as Teachers,* by Kenneth Eble, which provides a thoughtful overview of the professoriate with a number of specific ideas about how teaching may be improved; the special issue of the *Journal of Higher Education* on "Organizational Development in Higher Education" (May 1973, *44*), guest edited by Ronald Boyer and Campbell Crockett, which contains an excellent summary of the application of organizational-development approaches to colleges and universities; "Facilitating Faculty Development," edited by Mervin Freedman, which emphasizes the psychological development of faculty; and *Instructional Development for Individualized Learning in Higher Education,* by Robert Diamond and his colleagues, which describes their work in instructional development at Syracuse University.

The new newsletter *Faculty Development and Evaluation in Higher Education,* edited by Albert Smith, contains information about a wide range of activities in these areas on college campuses. *Renewing Higher Education from Within,* by Walter Sikes, Lawrence Schlesinger, and Charles Seashore, describes methods of working with campus teams to facilitate institutional change.

Alternative teaching styles have been discussed and described by several authors. Joseph Axelrod's *The University Teacher as Artist* describes several approaches to teaching both in and outside the classroom. *The College Classroom,* by Richard Mann and his colleagues, contains careful analyses of the dynamics of classroom teaching and learning. *Teaching Tips,* by Wilbert McKeachie, offers much advice of a practical sort to individual teachers. *The Changing College Classroom,* edited by Philip Runkel, Roger Harrison, and Margaret Runkel, has examples of various innovative teaching approaches. The importance of the student side of the teaching-learning process has been emphasized by Stanford Ericksen in his *Motivation for Learning* and by Ohmer Milton, who in *Alternatives to the Traditional* amasses evidence against many of our most cherished beliefs about what constitutes effective teaching.

Efforts to improve instruction ought to be placed in the context of what is known about the impact of colleges and universities on students. The major works in this area are *Changing Values in College* by Philip Jacob, *The Impact of College on Students* by Kenneth Feldman and Theodore Newcomb, and *Education and*

Identity by Arthur Chickering. A recent addition to this area that examines the ways faculty members affect student development is *College Professors and Their Impact on Students* by Robert Wilson, Jerry Gaff, Lynn Wood, Evelyn Dienst, and James Bavry.

ACK, M. *Is Teaching an Art or a Science or Why Wise Men Fail.* Unpublished paper delivered at Michigan State University, March 2, 1973.

ALEXANDER, L. T., AND YELON, S. L. *Instructional Development Agencies in Higher Education.* East Lansing: Michigan State University Continuing Education Service, 1972.

ARGYRIS, C. *Interpersonal Competence and Organizational Effectiveness.* Homewood, Ill.: Dorsey, 1962.

AXELROD, J. *The University Teacher as Artist: Toward an Aesthetics of Teaching with Emphasis on the Humanities.* San Francisco: Jossey-Bass, 1973.

BACK, K. *Beyond Words: The Story of Sensitivity Training and the Encounter Movement.* New York: Russell Sage, 1972.

BEAUDOIN, A. P. *A Study of a State Plan for Staff and Program Development in a System of Public Community-Junior Colleges.* Unpublished doctoral dissertation, University of Alabama, 1973.

BENNIS, W. G. *The Nature of Organization Development.* Reading, Mass.: Addison-Wesley, 1969.

BERGQUIST, W. H., PHILIPS, S. R., AND QUEHL, G. *A Handbook for Faculty Development.* Washington, D.C.: Council for the Advancement of Small Colleges, 1975.

BEVAN, J. M. *Faculty Development (A Votre Santé).* Unpublished paper prepared for Workshop for New Academic Deans, sponsored by American Conference of Academic Deans, Association of American Colleges, and Council of Colleges of Arts and Sciences, Estes Park, Colo., June 23–28, 1974.

BLOOM, R. *Stability and Change in Human Characteristics.* New York: Wiley, 1964.

BLOOM, B. S., ENGELHART, M. D., FURST, E. J., HILL, W. H., AND KRATHWOHL, D. R. *Taxonomy of Educational Objectives. Handbook I: Cognitive Domain.* New York: McKay, 1956.

BOYER, R. K. *New Applications in O.D.: The University.* Paper presented at symposium on New Applications in O.D., Organization Development Division, Academy of Management, Seattle, Aug. 1974.

BOYER, R. K., AND CROCKETT, C. (guest eds.) "Organizational Develop-
    ment in Higher Education." *Journal of Higher Education* (spe-
    cial issue), May 1973.

BRIM, O. G., JR., AND WHEELER, S. *Socialization After Childhood: Two
    Essays.* New York: Wiley, 1966.

BUTERBAUGH, J. G. *A Descriptive Analysis of Instructional Design Pro-
    grams in Selected Institutions of Higher Education.* Unpublished
    doctoral dissertation, University of Nebraska, 1971.

CHICKERING, A. W. *Education and Identity.* San Francisco: Jossey-Bass,
    1969.

CHURCHMAN, C. W. *The Systems Approach.* New York: Dell, 1968.

College Center of the Finger Lakes. *Basic Instructional Improvement
    Workshop.* Corning, N. Y., 1974

The Conference Board. *Organization Development: A Reconnaissance.*
    New York, 1973.

CROSS, K. P. *Beyond the Open Door: New Students to Higher Educa-
    tion.* San Francisco: Jossey-Bass, 1971.

Dartmouth College. *A Proposal by Dartmouth College to the Alfred P.
    Sloan Foundation for Support of Experimentation in Under-
    graduate Instruction, Including the Expansion of Technology
    in the Undergraduate Curriculum.* July 1973.

DAVIES, I. K. *The Management of Learning.* Berkshire, England: Mc-
    Graw-Hill, 1971.

DE BLOOIS, M., AND ALDER, D. D. "Stimulating Faculty Readiness for
    Instructional Development: A Conservative Approach to Im-
    proving College Teaching." *Educational Technology*, July 1973,
    16–19.

DE HART, R. *Staff Development/Program Improvement at DeAnza
    College: A Proposed Model for Staff Development.* Unpublished
    report, DeAnza College, Cupertino, Calif., 1974.

DIAMOND, R. M., EICKMAN, P. E., KELLEY, E. F., HOLLOWAY, R. E., VICK-
    ERY, T. R., AND PASCARELLA, E. T. *Instructional Development for
    Individualized Learning in Higher Education.* Englewood Cliffs,
    N. J.: Educational Technology Publications, 1975.

DRESSEL, P. L. *Evaluation in Higher Education.* Boston: Houghton
    Mifflin, 1961.

DUNHAM, R. E., WRIGHT, P. S., AND CHANDLER, M. O. *Teaching Faculty
    in Universities and Four Year Colleges.* Washington, D.C.:
    Government Printing Office, 1966.

EBLE, K. E. *Career Development of the Effective College Teacher.* Proj-
    ect to Improve College Teaching. Washington, D.C.: American

Association of University Professors and Association of American Colleges, 1971.

EBLE, K. E. *Professors as Teachers*. San Francisco: Jossey-Bass, 1972.

EISNER, E. W. "Instructional and Expressive Objectives: Their Formulation and Use in the Curriculum." In R. E. Stake (ed.), *Instructional Objectives*. Vol. 3. Monograph Series on Curriculum Evaluation of the American Educational Research Association. Chicago: Rand McNally, 1969.

ERICKSEN, S. C. *Motivation for Learning*. Ann Arbor: University of Michigan Press, 1974.

FELDMAN, K. A., AND NEWCOMB, T. M. *The Impact of College on Students*. San Francisco: Jossey-Bass, 1969.

FREEDMAN, M. (guest ed.) "Facilitating Faculty Development." *New Directions for Higher Education*, Spring 1973 (1).

FRENCH, W. L., AND BELL, C. H. *Organization Development*. Englewood Cliffs, N. J.: Prentice-Hall, 1973.

FRIESEN, P. A. *Designing Instruction*. Santa Monica, Calif.: Miller, 1973.

GAFF, J. G., AND WILSON, R. C. "Faculty Cultures and Interdisciplinary Study." *Journal of Higher Education*, Mar. 1971, 186–201.

GAFF, J. G., WILSON, R. C., WOOD, L., DIENST, E. R., AND BAVRY, J. L. "Study II. Faculty Impact on Students." In R. C. Wilson and others, *College Professors and Their Impact on Students*. New York: Wiley, 1975.

GAGNÉ, R. M. *The Conditions of Learning* (2nd ed.). New York: Holt, Rinehart and Winston, 1970.

GAGNÉ, R. M., AND BRIGGS, L. J. *Principles of Instructional Design*. New York: Holt, Rinehart and Winston, 1974.

GLASER, R. "Toward a Behavioral Science Base for Instructional Design." In R. Glaser (ed.), *Teaching Machines and Programmed Learning II: Data and Directions*. Washington, D.C.: National Education Association, 1965.

GLASMAN, N. S., KILLART, B. R., AND GMELCH, W. *Evaluation of Instructors in Higher Education*. Santa Barbara: Office of Instructional Development, University of California, 1974.

GOULD, R. "The Phases of Adult Life: A Study in Development Psychology." *American Journal of Psychology*, 1972, *129* (5).

GREEN, C. R., AND MINK, W. D. *Faculty Renewal Program: A Proposal to the Fund for the Improvement of Postsecondary Education*. St. Paul, Minn.: Macalester College, 1973.

GROSS, R. F. *Individualized Faculty Development Plans*. Unpublished

paper prepared for the Institute on Faculty Development sponsored by the Council for the Advancement of Small Colleges,
Oklahoma Christian College, Oklahoma City, Aug. 5–9, 1974.

Group for Human Development in Higher Education. *Faculty Development in a Time of Retrenchment.* New Rochelle, N.Y.:
Change Magazine, 1974.

HODGKINSON, H. L. "Adult Development: Implications for Faculty and
Administrators." *Educational Record.* Fall 1974a, 263–274.

HODGKINSON, H. L. Oral presentation at Regional Workshop, Faculty
Development Program, Council for the Advancement of Small
Colleges, Kansas City, Kansas, Nov. 22, 1974b.

HOFFMAN, R. L. *Faculty Workloads.* Memorandum prepared by the
dean of Mars Hill College. Mars Hill, N.C., n.d.

HOLSCLAW, J. E. *The Development of Procedural Guidelines for the
Systematic Design of Instruction Within Higher Education.* Los
Angeles: University of Southern California, 1974.

HOYT, D. P. "The Kansas State University Program for Assessing and
Improving Instructional Effectiveness." In A. L. Sockloff (ed.),
Proceedings: Faculty Effectiveness as Evaluated by Students.
Philadelphia: Measurement and Research Center, Temple Uni-
versity, 1973.

JACOB, P. *Changing Values in College.* New York: Harper & Row,
1957.

JENCKS, C., AND RIESMAN, D. *The Academic Revolution.* New York:
Doubleday, 1968.

KEENE, T. W. *Selected Characteristics of Faculty Workload.* Presentation at National Conference of American Association for Higher
Education, Mar. 1971.

KELLER, F. S. "Good-Bye, Teacher. . . ." *Journal of Applied Behavioral Analysis,* 1968, *1,* 79–89.

KRATHWOHL, D. R., BLOOM, B. S., AND MASIA, B. B. *Taxonomy of Educational Objectives. Handbook II: Affective Domain.* New
York: McKay, 1964.

KUHN, T. S. *The Structure of Scientific Revolutions.* Chicago: University of Chicago Press, 1962.

KULIK, J. A., KULIK, C. L., AND CARMICHAEL, K. "The Keller Plan in
Science Teaching." *Science,* 1974, *183,* 379–383.

LEE, A. M. *Instructional Development Programs in Higher Education.*
Provo, Utah: Brigham Young University, 1972.

LEVINSON, D. J., DARROW, C. M., KLEIN, E. B., LEVINSON, M. H., AND
MC KEE, D. "The Psychosocial Development of Men in Early

Adulthood and the Mid-Life Transition." In D. F. Ricks, A. Thomas, and M. Roff (eds.), *Psychopathology*. Vol. 3. Minneapolis: University of Minnesota Press, 1974.

LIEBERMAN, M. A., YALON, I. D., AND MILES, M. B. "The Group Experience Project: A Comparison of Ten Encounter Technologies." In L. Blank, G. B. Gottsegen, and M. G. Gottsegen (eds.), *Encounter: Confrontations in Self and Interpersonal Awareness*. New York: Macmillan, 1971.

LIKERT, R. *The Human Organization: Its Management and Value*. New York: McGraw-Hill, 1967.

MC GREGOR, D. *The Human Side of Enterprise*. New York: McGraw-Hill, 1960.

MC GREGOR, D. *The Professional Manager*. New York: McGraw-Hill, 1967.

MC KEACHIE, W. J. *Teaching Tips: A Guidebook for the Beginning College Teacher*. Lexington, Mass.: Heath, 1969.

MACHIAVELLI, N. *The Prince*. New York: Modern Library, 1950.

MAGER, R. F. *Preparing Instructional Objectives*. Palo Alto, Calif.: Fearon, 1962.

MANN, R. D., AND OTHERS. *The College Classroom: Conflict, Change and Learning*. New York: Wiley, 1970.

MANY, W. A., ELLIS, J. R., AND ABRAMS, P. "In-Service Education in American Senior Colleges and Universities: A Status Report." *Illinois School Research,* Spring 1969, 46–51.

MASLOW, A. H. *Motivation and Personality* (rev. ed.). New York: Harper & Row, 1970.

MATHIS, B. C. *Persuading the Institution to Experiment—Strategies for Seduction*. Paper presented at the symposium Improving Business Education Through Innovative Technology, Graduate School of Business, University of Texas at Austin, Mar. 25–29, 1974.

MEETH, L. R., HODGKINSON, H. L., AND BROWNLEE, C. G. *Sterling College: "Competency" and Change*. Evaluative report prepared for the Kellogg Foundation in connection with its grant to Sterling College, 1972–1974. Sterling, Kans.: Sterling College, 1974.

MILES, R. E. "Organization Development." In G. Strauss, R. Miles, C. Snow, and A. Tannenbaum (eds.), *Organizational Behavior: Research and Issues*. Ann Arbor: University of Michigan Press, 1974.

MILLER, W. S., AND WILSON, K. M. *Faculty Development Procedures in*

Small Colleges/A Southern Survey. Atlanta: Southern Regional Education Board, 1963.

MILTON, O. *Alternatives to the Traditional: How Professors Teach and How Students Learn.* San Francisco: Jossey-Bass, 1972.

MILTON, O., AND SHOBEN, E. J., JR. *Learning and the Professors.* Athens: Ohio University Press, 1968.

MORIMOTO, K. Personal letter to President Derek C. Bok, Harvard University, Bureau of Study Counsel, Feb. 11, 1972.

MORRIS, C. "A Call for Faculty Reform." *Change Magazine,* Winter 1973–1974.

National Advisory Council on Education Professions Development. *Staffing the Learning Society: Recommendations for Federal Legislation.* Washington, D.C., 1975.

NEIDT, C. Informal presentation at a meeting on faculty evaluation and development organized by Teaching Research, Oregon State System of Higher Education, at San Francisco, Nov. 14, 1974.

NEUGARTEN, B. L. "Adult Personality: Towards a Psychology of the Life Cycle." In B. L. Neugarten (ed.), *Middle Age and Aging.* Chicago: University of Chicago Press, 1968.

NEUGARTEN, B. L., AND OTHERS. *Personality in Middle and Late Life.* New York: Atherton, 1964.

NOONAN, J. F. "The Impact of Curricular Change on Faculty Behavior." *Liberal Education,* 1971, 57, 344–358.

NOONAN, J. F. "Curricular Change: A Strategy for Improving Teaching." In D. W. Vermilye (ed.), *The Expanded Campus: Current Issues in Higher Education 1972.* San Francisco: Jossey-Bass, 1972.

NOONAN, J. F. Case study prepared for the Faculty Development Project of the Council for the Advancement of Small Colleges, Center for Improving Teaching Effectiveness, Virginia Commonwealth University, 1974.

O'BANION, T. *Teachers for Tomorrow.* Tucson: University of Arizona Press, 1973.

Office of the Educational Development Program. *Educational Development at Michigan State University.* No. 5. East Lansing: Michigan State University, 1973.

POPHAM, W. J. "Objectives and Instruction." In R. E. Stake (ed.), *Instructional Objectives.* Vol. 3. Monograph Series on Curriculum Evaluation of the American Educational Research Association. Chicago: Rand McNally, 1969.

POPHAM, W. J., AND HUSEK, T. R. "Implications of Criterion-Referenced Measurement." *Journal of Educational Measurement*, 1969, 6 (1), 1–9.

POSTELTHWAIT, S. N., NOVAK, J., AND MURRAY, H. T. *The Audio-Tutorial Approach to Learning.* Minneapolis: Burgess, 1969.

QUEHL, G. H. Unpublished instructional development program for the member colleges of the College Center of the Finger Lakes. June 1, 1973.

QUEHL, G. H. Personal letter, May 7, 1974.

RALPH, N., AND FREEDMAN, M. "Innovative Colleges: Challenge to Faculty Development." In M. Freedman (guest ed.), "Facilitating Faculty Development." *New Directions in Higher Education,* Spring 1973 (1).

"Report of Ad Hoc Committee to Evaluate CIUE." *Cornell Chronicle,* Feb. 7, 1974, 8–9.

SANFORD, N. "Academic Culture and the Teacher's Development." *Soundings,* Winter 1971.

SANFORD, N. "Notes Toward a General Theory of Personality Development—at Eighty or Any Old Age." Unpublished paper read at the symposium Henry Murray at Eighty, at the annual convention of the American Psychological Association, Montreal, Aug. 27, 1973.

SCHMUCK, R., AND MILES, M. B. (eds.) *Organization Development in Schools.* Palo Alto, Calif.: National Press, 1971.

SIKES, W. W., SCHLESINGER, L. E., AND SEASHORE, C. N. *Renewing Higher Education from Within: A Guide for Campus Change Teams.* San Francisco: Jossey-Bass, 1974.

SKINNER, B. F. *Science and Human Behavior.* New York: Macmillan, 1953.

SKINNER, B. F. *The Technology of Teaching.* New York: Appleton-Century-Crofts, 1968.

SNOW, C. P. *The Two Cultures and the Scientific Revolution.* Cambridge, England: Cambridge University Press, 1959.

STONE, J. C., SONENBLUM, S., GREEN, J. L., HARRIS, J. C., AND SCHWARZ, W. J. *Toward Excellence in Teaching, Too.* Berkeley: University of California Press, 1974.

TAYLOR, H. "The Teacher at His Best." In R. M. Cooper (ed.), *The Two Ends of the Log.* Minneapolis: University of Minnesota Press, 1958.

Teaching Innovation and Evaluation Services. *Program Progress Report.* University of California, Berkeley, 1974.

WILLIAMS, V. Report on the Teaching and Learning Center, University of Nebraska, Lincoln, at a conference on teaching improvement sponsored by the Danforth Foundation in St. Louis, Feb. 22, 1973.

WILSON, R. C., GAFF, J. G., DIENST, E. R., WOOD, L., AND BAVRY, J. C. *College Professors and Their Impact on Students.* New York: Wiley, 1975.

Index

ABRAMS, P., 12, 235

ACK, M, 36-37, 231

Administrators: support for instructional improvement by, 105-109, 132-135; training of, for organizational development, 86-88

Adults: change in, 20, 25-27; development of, 18-27; developmental stages of, 22-24; socialization of, 20-22

Affective development, for faculty, 36-38

ALDER, D. D., 102, 128-129, 232

ALEXANDER, B., 70-71

ALEXANDER, L. T., xii, 104, 206-207, 229, 231

Alverno College, 67, 164

American Association for Higher Education, 101

American Conference of Academic Deans, 86-87

American Council on Education, 86

American Educational Research Association, 101

American Psychological Association, 101

American Sociological Association, 101, 194

ANTHONY, F., 32, 218

ARGYRIS, C., 76, 231

Associated Colleges of the Midwest, 143, 197

Association for Educational Communication and Technology, 101

Association of American Colleges, 86-87

Atlanta University, 143-144

Audio-tutorial approach, learning materials for, 61-62

BACK, K., 88, 231

BALDRIDGE, V., 92, 138

BARBER, W., 28

BEAUDOIN, A. P., 145, 231

239